ASPECTS OF DISTRIBUTED

COMPUTER SYSTEMS

ASPECTS OF DISTRIBUTED

COMPUTER SYSTEMS

HAROLD LORIN
IBM Systems Research Institute

A WILEY-INTERSCIENCE PUBLICATION

JOHN WILEY & SONS
New York • Chichester • Brisbane • Toronto • Singapore

Library of Congress Cataloging in Publication Data:

Lorin, Harold.
  Aspects of distributed computer systems.

"A Wiley-Interscience publication."
Bibliography: p.
Includes index.
1. Electronic data processing—Distributed
processing. I. Title.

QA76.9.D5L67   001.64   80-16689
ISBN 0-471-08114-0

Printed in the United States of America

10 9 8 7 6 5 4 3

PREFACE

This book undertakes to investigate distributed processing in a complete and evenhanded way. It tries to show that distributed processing is not a "thing," but a set of concepts that stem from the relaxation of a number of technological constraints on the way that information systems may be structured. It attempts to demonstrate the possibilities, explore the problems and place the phenomenon of distribution in a broad framework which transcends product biases and concepts limited by particular product offerings. Although IBM product names are sometimes used casually in examples, the reader will find that no concept used in the book is based upon the product of this, or any other, vendor. The views presented are the author's own and in no way represent attitudes, opinions or policies of the IBM Corporation.

The book brings together considerations from many subdisciplines of the computer arts and sciences in order to form a complete statement of the topic area. There is a certain risk in doing this, since many readers will find some sections of the book less accessible than others. Readers who follow the discussions of software structures may find the discussions of centralization vs. decentralization less interesting. Readers who find the economic considerations useful may find the software structure issues inaccessible. This is a problem with any complete treatment of a concept that stems from changes in perception in a number of different disciplines. Distributed processing may force us to reappraise our notions of the relationships between branches of data processing knowledge because it is a concept which depends upon the perception of a new set of relationships between systems and user components, organizations and talents.

No one can take the risk of ignorance in the area of the interaction between the new possibilities of data processing and the dynamics of enterprise. It is for this reason that both aspects of system development are brought together in this book.

By and large the book assumes very little precise product knowledge. It attempts to deal conceptually with choices and goals as much as possible. To the extent that some specific products are mentioned, an appendix provides a capsule description of the nature of these products.

Some may, in fact, be disappointed that the book does not directly describe the capabilities of specific available machine and programming products. Such a book would undoubtedly be useful, but would have a short purposeful life in

v

an area characterized by rapid change. The approach of this book is to provide an intellectual framework within which the products can be understood, their strengths recognized, their appropriateness for a given use analyzed. It will provide the reader with a view of what has been done and what may be possible to do, and it will clear much of the fog which sometimes lends an almost mythic quality to distributed processing.

The reader whose interests are primarily in management may choose to read Part Three directly after Chapter 1. He may wish to then read Chapter 2 for an appreciation of an example of the kind of system that Part Three explores the economic motivation for. Readers whose interests are primarily professional and technical can read the book sequentially.

A version of Chapter 5 has appeared in the *IBM Systems Journal*, Vol 18, No 4. The author is indebted to that publication for permitting its use in this book.

Appreciation for careful review and thoughtful comment must be extended to R. Cypser and B. Moldow, of the IBM Systems Research Institute, and to G. McQuilken, of the IBM Cambridge Scientific Center. I am also in the debt of Martin York for a continuing dialog on issues of distributed computing.

I am also particularly obliged to the students at the IBM Systems Research Institute for patiently listening as the course from which this book is derived was discovered.

HAROLD LORIN

New York, New York
July 1980

CONTENTS

ASPECTS OF DISTRIBUTED

COMPUTER SYSTEMS

PART ONE

OVERVIEW
AND EXAMPLES

Chapter 1

The Idea of Distribution

1. FUNDAMENTAL CONCEPT

One of the great dangers in discussing distributed processing is the temptation to offer a definition. The richness of variation on the general theme makes it impossible to define distributed processing without disappointing some group of interested people. Any definition so far attempted has been subject to the objections that it is too restrictive, that it is too inclusive, that it stresses the wrong attributes.

While it is impossible to rigorously define the topic area, one can offer characterization of the kinds of systems which will interest us and demonstrate some general attributes.

The general notion of a distributed system is that various elements of a data processing system can be partitioned into well defined units which may be located at various logical sites and linked by agreed upon protocols.

The concept of a logical site is important. The phrase is used to suggest that the partitions of a distributed system need not be placed at significant geographical distances in order to demonstrate important characteristics of distribution. A logical site is a conceptual place in the system structure that contains a well defined partitioning of procedure and data that interfaces with other sites in such a way that, at a systems concept level, its actual physical location need not be determined. In the computer design world phrases like "abstract machine, virtual machine" are often used to convey this notion. The basic idea put forth is that logical structures can be designed with some independence from physical structures and that the placement of physical hardware in different cities, in different buildings in the same corporate park, on different floors of the same skyscraper, in the same room in a data center represent physical choices about the placement of logical elements.

This concept allows a large number of variations which are defined by the methods used to partition a system, the distance between the sites where the partitions are placed and the protocols used for partitions to talk to each other. It is necessary that all of the important variations be understood so that we do not lose sight of the choices which must be made in a design.

The distinction between logical and physical systems leads to an observation that the needs of an enterprise for data processing services determine logical systems. The dynamics of business needs and organizational patterns define the nature of computer services which must be offered. The logical definition of a system is a response to those needs. The physical implementation of a system on computer elements and communication elements is determined by technology and the functional and cost constraints associated with technology at any period of time. Thus we define the logical systems in response to organizational need and then determine acceptable physical mappings in accordance with technology constraints.

Some characterizations of distributed systems are useful to support the general concept. In general, distributed systems:

1. Have multiple processing units.
2. Provide some level of single system image.
3. Are electronically interconnected.
4. Involve significant interaction between units.
5. Provide more design alternatives.

2. MULTIPLE PROCESSING UNITS

A fundamental characteristic of distributed systems is that there is more than one processing unit in the system. One form of this involves a complex of two or more complete computer systems. Each computer system has its own processor, its own memory and its own secondary storage devices. In addition each processing unit may have a local complement of printers, tapes and other data processing peripheral devices. The system is formed by interconnecting these complete processing units in some way so that information may flow between them.

Figure 1 shows two general purpose systems which are interconnected by the use of teleprocessing communications lines. Each of these processing units has its own operating system and a local set of programs and data. Each supports a population of terminal users of some kind. Users may have access, perhaps with some constraints, to either system.

Few would object to this hardware configuration as the basis for a distributed system. The processing units represent a natural geographic partitioning; the logical sites are two geographically distant data centers; the link is a widely accepted "TP" link supported by software which exists in all of the units. We will see later that this picture is not necessarily a distributed processing system. That depends upon how it is used.

2.1. The Idea of Significance

Figure 1 shows two total computer systems linked to each other. Consider Figure 2, which shows a general purpose processor and an attached printer. Let

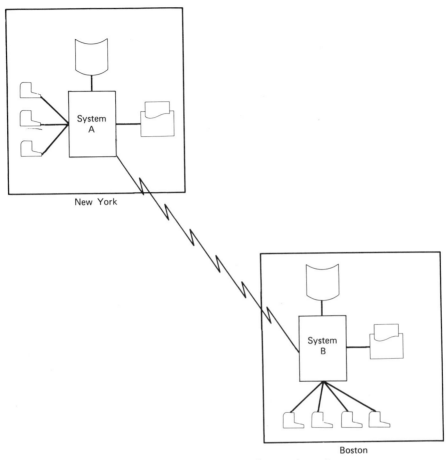

Figure 1.   Remote interconnected processing systems.

us speculate that this hypothetical printer has been built with a microprocessor inside it. All of the function of this printer is delivered by the execution of programs on the interior microprocessor. "Hard-wired" logic or "random" logic has been completely replaced by code running on the small processing unit. However, no new function is performed by the printer because it is now microprocessor driven. Although there are multiple processing units in Figure 2 as well as in Figure 1, few would characterize the second figure as a "distributed processing system."

There is an idea of "significant processing units" which separates the two systems. Various calibrations of significance may be applied. Ideas of the "visibility" of the processing unit to a user or to an installing site may distinguish Figure 1 from Figure 2. An idea of the disparity of size between the two processors may suggest "significance." Similarly the presence of auxiliary stor-

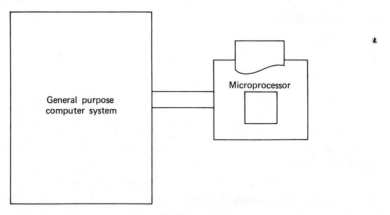

Figure 2.   Intelligent peripheral system.

age units or elements of an operating system can justify the distinction we intuitively make between the idea of interconnected computer systems and a computer and its microprocessor driven printer.

The simple idea of two or more processors in a system is not really sufficient to describe the fundamental characteristics we look for when we are trying to recognize a distributed system. We need some notions of function, interface, generality, relationships between units, secondary equipment beyond the idea of multiple processors. It is an interesting exercise to see just what would have to be done at that printer before it became "significant." Would the addition of storage to hold print files be important? Just what other kinds of changes in the interface between the general purpose processor and the printer would make the printer a significant unit?

Somewhere on a continuum of significance one encounters units of varying capacity and intelligence called "intelligent terminals." This book considers that intelligent terminals are significant processing units but that "dumb terminals" are devices.

2.2.   The Idea of Completeness

Closely related to the idea of significant processing units is the idea of completeness. Completeness concerns the extent to which basic systems components may be shared before an idea of multiple systems fades. Consider Figure 3. It represents a classical tightly coupled multiprocessor. The distinguishing characteristics of the system are a specialized I/O processing unit which all central processing units must use and common memory shared by all processors. Depending on a variety of software and application design factors, such a system may take on many of the characteristics of a distributed processing system.

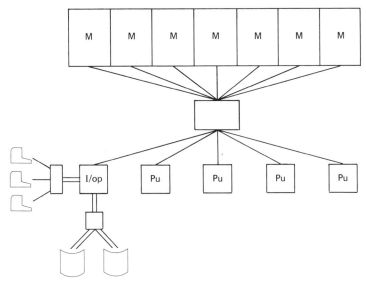

Figure 3. Multiprocessor.

Those who would exclude such a system structure from the world of distributed processing exclude it on the following grounds:

1. The processing units are not "complete." Each unit does not represent an independent node. Because of the level of sharing the system does not demonstrate reliability and availability characteristics central to the ideas of distributed processing.

2. The configuration is plausible only if all of the processors are physically proximate, in the same room, perhaps even in the same box.

Those who would include such a system in the world would do so on these bases:

1. Fault tolerance may be built into this configuration in ways which guarantee that some number of processors may run as if they shared no memory and had their own I/O.

2. A logical view of the system can be presented so that for a set of users it appears as if there was no sharing of any importance and each user subset had its own machine.

3. The idea of the degree of physical proximity of the processing units is not a central idea of distributed systems. Logical partitioning is what is at the root of systems design and not geographical dispersion.

So we see that there are very real differences in point of view surrounding the apparently simple idea that a distributed system should have multiple processing units. These differences come from different ideas about what one is trying to accomplish by distributing. We are interested in these differences because they suggest the true richness of the design possibilities which are available and the design decisions which must be made.

2.3. Logical Processing Units

An extension of the idea that multiple processing units is not sufficient to support the concept of distributed processing is that they are also not necessary. In discussing the concept of a logical site we introduced the idea that there may not be a one to one mapping between the logical concept of a system and the physical realization of a system. For example, even if there is only one shared memory and only one I/O processor it is possible, using software methods, to present an image of complete, independent units on a multiprocessor. A user may be presented with an image of a complete system with a set of I/O devices and a memory size as if each processor were a self-contained unit that shared no systems resources. It is also possible to map the idea of multiple processing units on a single processing unit, particularly in the form of virtual machines.

Those who are interested in this possibility for distribution would like the phrase "multiple processing units" to be "multiple logical processing units." They point out that the important attribute of a distributed system is the apparent control of a defined set of computing resources such as programming capability, software function, storage spaces and computational capacity.

Virtual machine definition provides the image of a dedicated machine and can provide complete control over that dedicated logical machine and its software function. Interfaces can be provided so that a user could not tell whether his logical system was mapped onto a larger, shared system, or whether there was a one to one mapping with a dedicated physical machine. In addition the virtual machines would in fact be portable, movable from one physical machine to another with mininal effort compared to other options. The logical systems of the virtual machine approach permit physical placement on dispersed local machines or on shared central machines to suit the convenience of an organization as changes occur in technology, economics and business practices.

Some designers feel that an organization interfaces only with logical information systems. The data processing needs of an enterprise are met by a set of language conventions and available function which define data processing services. The physical implementation of logical systems onto physical systems represents another, partially independent mapping. The relationship between an organization and its logical data processing power is determined by organizational need. The relationship between logical systems and physical systems is constrained by issues of technological capability and cost. A proper approach to systems design is to determine logical needs and then investigate technological potentials to determine the physical mapping across computer and communications components which are available.

In this book we will concentrate on systems that are complete processing systems, usually with a local complement of storage and peripheral devices and with a local operating system of some capacity. From time to time, where the idea may stimulate thought, we will refer to multiprocessor and virtual machine approaches to the development of distributed processing.

The various viewpoints on whether multiprocessors, virtual machines, or imbedded microprocessors are part of the concept of distributed processing give the reader a notion of the variety of approaches that are, in fact, being taken with regard to the development of systems characterized by their designers as distributed systems.

3. SINGLE SYSTEMS IMAGE

One of the characterizations of distributed systems is the degree to which they look like a single, integrated system to a population of on-line users or application programmers. Different systems which will be termed "distributed systems" will display rather different ideas about what is involved in the concept of a single system. Some say the concept involves the idea that the users or programmers are unaware of the existence of multiple processing units. Others feel that accessibility to data and function regardless of the level of awareness of different nodes is sufficient to define a system.

There seem to be two related but distinguishable elements in the concept of a single system. They are transparency and interdependency. We will discuss them in that order.

3.1. Transparency

Some designers think that an important characteristic of a distributed system is that the combined elements of that system appear to a user as a single system. In the extreme form of this idea a user of the system could approach a node and call upon all services and data anywhere in the system as if it were located at that node. The user would use exactly the same commands at any node.

For example, in a three node system, a user at System 1 would have access to System 1, System 2 and System 3 using exactly the same commands regardless of whether the data to which he referred, or the program he wished to run, was local or remote. The user would have no awareness of the existence of the physical structure of the multinode system or of the distribution of data or programs. Elements in Operating Systems 1, 2 or 3, or Data Manager Systems 1, 2 or 3, or in the application programs would determine where the data was, or where a program was, and undertake whatever actions were required to retrieve data, run programs and return results.

As an extension to the single system image for a user, many feel that it is also necessary to project this image for an application program. Thus an application program would issue requests for data or program execution using exactly the same verbs and operands whether they were in his local node or at some other node. The operating system, or subsystem, would undertake to do the necessary work to determine where objects were and to get to them.

There are many operational activities which might also be covered by a single system image. An operator wishing to start a subsystem or a user application, or to cause printing of some file, might issue a directive, and the systems software would determine exactly at what node the work was to be done. The systems software might decide on the basis of some appreciation of load across all nodes, or on information about availability and the number of operational components.

Naturally there are some constraints on how extensively the single system image may be applied. Some group of planners, systems programmers and operators charged with network control would have to be aware of the existence of individual nodes. Systems software doing analyses of where things were and what load levels existed at different places would have to know or be able to determine the node population and its characteristics.

The idea of making the existence of multiple nodes invisible to a user has many advantages and important benefits. Uniformity of interface allows users to access more than one system. Degrees of reconfigurability of data and program populations across nodes are achieved with potentially reasonable levels of effort. Load balancing, where desired, becomes more feasible if users of a multinode system do not know or care where things are happening.

3.1.1. Homogeneous Transparency

A completely transparent population of nodes is most easily achieved when each node is identical. Identical hardware, identical versions of the same operating system, identical versions of the same database managers may provide a reasonable starting point for achieving transparency. Identity of user interface falls naturally out of the fact that the population of systems software elements is identical. Identity of application interface occurs naturally for the same reason. It is more significant, actually, for software to be identical than for hardware. The conventions for use and the functions provided by software, if identical, may mask differences in underlying hardware architecture.

The interconnection of homogeneous systems does not, in itself, suggest that the most rigorous concept of a single systems image will be supported. It is possible to provide for the interconnection of homogeneous systems without providing transparency. Two nodes with identical systems software may be associated with some degree of user, application program, systems programmer or operator awareness that individual nodes exist. Concepts of "read a local record" or "read a remote record" may be distinguished to the user. It is possible to allow the capability of running a remote program or accessing a remote file without hiding the fact that the objects are, in fact, in different physical locations of the system.

3.1.2. Heterogeneous Transparency

The linking together of multiple processing units may involve different hardware architectures running different software environments. Software environments may differ in a large variety of ways. Most simple of these is the existence of different versions of the same operating system or subsystems. If the versions differ trivially, interconnection difficulties may not become intense. If, however, there are subsets of function or inconsistent local options, then a design which tries to achieve transparency must be more elaborate. The elaboration will take the form of providing, somehow, a statement within the system of what functions are available at what node. The greatest interconnection complexity is introduced when there are entirely different software environments at various nodes in the system and each node offers different functions, different structures, and different usage conventions.

A number of problems are associated with interconnecting heterogeneous nodes. Some of these problems center around how much of a single systems image should be preserved; others center around basic mechanisms which allow systems of different design, structure and interfaces to communicate in meaningful ways.

3.1.3. Transparency and Software Layers

A problem associated with a heterogeneous system is whether it is necessary that user and/or application interfaces be the same at all nodes. In order to accomplish this an entire new layer of interface would have to be developed to sit on top of the existing software systems. This layer would provide new, uniform user and application program interfaces and translate them into appropriate local interfaces for each heterogeneous node of the system. Figure 4 illustrates this concept for the relationship between an application program and system software. The uniform interface layer exists at the three nodes, Systems 1, 2, and 3. Requests for data are made by application programs in an identical manner at all nodes since the uniform interface layer provides identical conventions in all systems. A data manager subsystem A is running on System 1. This data manager system uses the local resource management functions of an operating system D. Different data manager and operating systems combinations exist at Systems 2 and 3. An application program requesting data directly communicates only with the uniform interface layer. This layer would determine where the data is. If it is not local, the layer communicates with the interface layer at the remote system where the data is located. The remote counterpart layer then translates the data request into a format meaningful to the data manager at its node which performs the data access function. Data is passed from the data manager to the local interface layer and on to the inter-

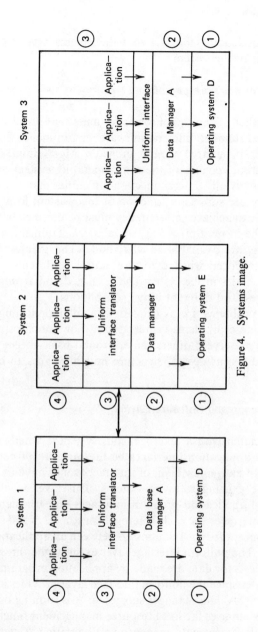

Figure 4. Systems image.

12

face layer at the node where the application program made the original request. The uniform interface layer provides both locus transparency and apparent homogeneity by hiding the conventions of the data managers. When perfectly achieved an application program which has used only the conventions of the interface layer might be moved from one system to another without change. Data might similarly be freely moved. By extension such a layer might be defined for end users as well as for applications programs.

There are various techniques for achieving a similar effect that result in a variety of systems software structures. More about software structures is said in later chapters.

3.1.4. Relaxed Transparency

A somewhat different view of single systems image would allow each heterogeneous node to display its unique interfaces to a user or application program at that node. Thus, for example, a user of a small departmental system would use the languages and conventions appropriate to that system without regard to an interconnection which existed between it and a large system at a data center. Systems software would provide for translations of system requests when those requests involved access to the remote data center system. The differences in the software environments between the local and data center machine is handled in such a way that the software conventions of the remote system do not intrude into the operating habits of a local user. Similarly a user of the data center machine could access the remote local machine using only conventions associated with the large system. Single system image is achieved in that the existence of multiple nodes is hidden. However, each node displays its own unique characteristics to programmers and users at that node. The advantages of such an approach lie in the fact that a community of people used to the languages and conventions of a system need not change their patterns of use and interaction in order to achieve coherent systems usage.

The impact on the system structures is shown on Figure 5. Essentially the translation mechanisms are moved deeper into the system.

3.1.5. Nontransparency

It is such a massive effort to modify and extend software systems or subsystems to form transparent systems that it cannot be expected that all of the systems marketed by a set of vendors, or even by a single vendor, will provide transparency. In order to get on with interconnecting heterogeneous nodes it may be necessary to allow the exposure of their existence. It may even be desirable to do so. It is possible to find demonstrations of successful systems where nodes of different types are closely related to each other and where a user is aware of multiple nodes.

Some systems allow a user to invoke services from one system and then invoke services from another at will. The difficulty in doing this in some sys-

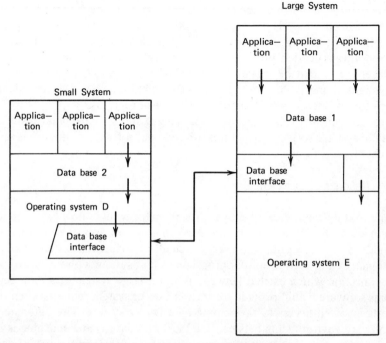

Figure 5.   Relaxed single systems image.

tems is no more than the difficulty involved in invoking a program and then another program in the same node. The cost may be the necessity of doing two LOGONs, but very little more. In some cases certain users will find it to their advantage to know about multiple nodes. They may desire to specifically choose a node as a place to hold back-up files or as a place to send particular types of programs for execution. They may desire for performance reasons to define the set of nodes they wish to participate in their problem solution. The essential requirement for a nontransparent system is that the burden of use, in terms of procedure and knowledge imposed on a user, is reasonable and that the view that a user has of a network of nodes is a useful view. He must see what is useful for him to see and have hidden what is complex and burdensome.

Philosophically, those who do not hold that transparency is a necessary attribute of a distributed system point out that the universe is commonly perceived as a coherent system despite the fact that we are aware of the existence of individual galaxies, stars and planets.

3.2.   Dependency

The concept of a collection of nodes as a single system depends on more than access conventions and interfaces. There are questions of the degree to which the nodes are really used as a single system within the context of the work they are performing. The degree to which they rely upon each other, the degree to which they constrain each other, the intensity of the rate at which they must respond to each other are dimensions of the degree to which a collection of processing units are truly organized into a single system. Here again we have divergent design and conceptual positions. Some feel that distributed systems design encourages and facilitates high degrees of dependency and interaction. Others feel that distributed designs are feasible only when one can define partitions that interact relatively infrequently.

Sometimes the words network and distributed systems are used as synonyms to describe any collection of nodes that can communicate with each other. In the set of communicating systems there is a very broad range of reliance and intensity of use. There are networks, sometimes called "anarchic" networks, in which there are minimal degrees of interaction. It is possible, for example, for users to send each other messages or programs to send each other files. However, these capabilities are peripheral to the main thrust of work. Sometimes members of a network may at their own discretion disconnect from that network. Such arrangements are very difficult to conceive of as a single system, regardless of language conventions.

It is true, however, that subsets of the nodes of a casual network may form, at various times, closely cooperating relations and that certain nodes may have homogeneous interface characteristics because they are running identical software. Thus a network of any kind of interconnection may serve as the basis for the definition, dynamic or static, of a distributed system.

At another end of the spectrum there are collections of processing units that absolutely depend on each other, that communicate with each other intensively, perhaps on a transaction basis, and that wait for each others' responses. The population of programs for a single application is spread across these nodes and the performance of the application requires that the nodes be operational and interact at fast rates.

Somewhere on a continuum from casual, intermittent interaction to required, intensive interaction a collection of nodes becomes a system. Since the very definition of words like system and application and coordination are vague it is very difficult to precisely describe the point at which a collection is a distributed system. The author likes the concept, shown in Figure 6, that a network is the larger idea and that distributed systems is the contained concept. Thus all distributed systems are networks but not all networks are distributed systems.

Another notion of the relationship between ideas of distributed processing and ideas of networking views a system as a collection of networks. There is a basic interconnection network which can be used in order to support the establishment of various systems and application networks. Thus one can characterize a system in terms of the layers of networks which may exist and the combinations which may be statically or dynamically formed to support logical software networks on top of a basic physical network.

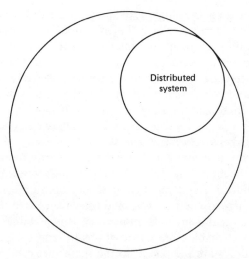

Figure 6.   Networks and distributed systems.

4. ELECTRONIC INTERCONNECTION

Another characteristic of distributed systems that is useful is that the processing units must be electronically interconnected. It is not necessary that this
interconnection be a teleprocessing facility. Nodes in the same building, connected by limited distance facilities, or nodes in the same room, connected by
channels (traditional computer to device pathways), may show more points of
similarity than dissimilarity with teleprocessing systems. Thus this book will
consider all such interconnected systems to be distributed systems. To do otherwise would be to ignore many important designs.

However, because we expect the nodes of a distributed system to have the
potential for intensive interaction, we will exclude nodes that talk to each other
only across dismountable media as members of the class of distributed systems.

The practice of shipping data on portable media in vans and station wagons
is both widespread and cost effective. However, such "interconnection" avoids
many interesting design issues. So in our examples and discussion we will re-
strict the population of distributed systems to those that use some form of
electronic interconnection mechanism. This is a middle position between those
who would include all systems that are in any way related to each other by
virtue of any rate of data flow and those who would include only teleprocessing
interconnected systems.

5. FREEDOM OF DESIGN CHOICE

The design of a system involving multiple logical processing units involves a
number of unique design decisions and an elaboration of other decisions com-

mon to all system design. Distributed processing systems may be developed using a top-down approach. Alternatively they may be developed by using a bottom-up approach. There is serious discussion about the benefits of these alternatives and the situations in which they are most properly applied.

There are considerations of management structure, application ownership and corporate data flow that are at the intersection of management and system designs concepts.

5.1. Top-Down

The top-down approach undertakes to design the system as a unit. It is most clearly applicable when a system will be dedicated to a single application or set of related applications so that each node cooperates on the performance of parts of what is clearly a single problem solution. Each node in the system is assigned a set of tasks, a data flow and control flow is designed and the general planning and development of the application proceeds in a manner similar to nondistributed applications. The difference is that the system components will be dispersed across multiple nodes, perhaps at multiple geographical locations. The single systems image, in its aspect of interdependency, is probably high and success depends upon serious systems planning.

5.2. Bottom-Up

A pure example of the bottom-up approach is when a system is developed by interconnecting nodes that are previously stand alone nodes. It is most applicable when there is a set of independent applications under the control of independent departments. Data sharing or functional service relationships may be developed between initially autonomous systems at the convenience of the owners or at the insistence of some higher management level. Improved data flow, increased interdepartmental cooperation and minimization of software purchase costs are among the motives for interconnecting systems. Distributed systems formed this way may still be able to achieve high levels of single systems image if the interconnected nodes are homogeneous or if there are extended interfaces that make them appear so. Sometimes such bottom-up systems are called "cooperative computing."

The advantages to such a development approach lie in the ability to move applications development forward within departments without the need for a major strategic design that is often difficult to achieve. Further, greater degrees of local control are implicit in the approach.

The danger of the approach is that the later interconnection may be very difficult to achieve. Care must be taken that the individual systems have software mechanisms to allow interconnection and that the possibility of such interconnection is provided for to some extent in the design of the applications for the independent processing unit.

When applications or sets of applications cross organizational lines, combinations of top-down and bottom-up approaches will be necessary and will be applied at different stages of the design and development process.

5.3. Choices and Constraints

The design of a distributed system necessarily expands the choices available to a designer. He has a greater range of choices about the placement of programs, data and elements of systems control. But before one makes decisions about where to put elements the elements must be discovered. From within the structure of an old application, or from within the concept of a new one, the separable parts must be recognized. These separable parts must not only be logically separable but must be defined in such a way that they map with reasonable efficiency onto a set of available hardware offerings and a set of available software capabilities for interaction.

Sometimes design choices are constrained by work in place. If an older form of an application exists on a centralized system, perhaps in a batch form, designers may be unwilling to disturb the running application system. They will prefer to leave the old application in place and build interfaces to it. Figure 7 shows an older batch system surrounded by a population of small nodes that have an on-line user interface. Copies of necessary data are maintained for transaction support at the small systems. From time to time batched records representing the activity at the small nodes are transmitted to the older programs, which then process the records as part of a batch operation. When it is desirable to continue the life of an existing system a number of possible system designs fall out of consideration.

Another constraint in design is the availability of hardware that matches the load that a particular partition will place upon it. The split of function between nodes is necessarily constrained by the capacity of available nodes. A design would not distribute data and programs the same way for a system using an intelligent terminal interconnected to a large system as it would for a family of intermediate sized computers connected to each other.

Theoretically one discovers the logical partitions by doing analyses of data reference patterns and program usage patterns. Only after meaningful partitions are discovered in the logic should hardware choices be made. Realistically, however, this is at least an iterative and most likely a joint process of discovery.

An additional consideration in the design of logical partitions and their allocation to physical components is that provision must be made for change. Changes occur due to the evolution of business and organizational practices and any satisfactory design must attend to methodologies which will enable the system to evolve. This evolution may involve changes in data reference patterns and program usage leading to necessary repartitioning, reallocation or replacement of physical components. It is important not to design systems which lock an organization into practices which have become obsolete.

It is usual for designers to complain about constraints but one should be

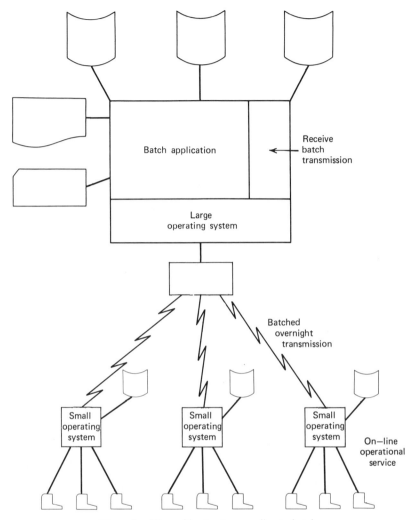

Figure 7.   Hierarchic structure: on-line to batch.

thankful for them in the design of distributed processing systems. Given the plethora of possible logical partitions that can be found in an application structure, and given the richness of hardware offerings in the marketplace, unconstrained design is just too expensive to undertake. Usually a designer has a small set of possible machine bases in mind when he undertakes the design of an application system.

5.4.   Systems Design Levels

In addition to determining program, data and control partitions and then deciding where these partitions should be placed, the designer also faces a "level of integration" decision. In the very early days of distributed processing the software offerings of many vendors supported only a very limited set of interconnection possibilities. In selecting the specific processing nodes that would be used, consideration of how much "systems type" software must be created was important.

At one time the issue of centralized vs. distributed system configuration was closely related to the degree to which an organization was willing to write systems level software not available on small systems. The inhouse development nature of distributed solutions has been considerably reduced by the announcement of standard vendor packages that support many more possible system interconnection and interaction structures.

It is still true, however, that additional effort in programming of the systems type must be undertaken to support certain kinds of relationships. As an example this is true for operating systems of vendors that do not talk to each other or on hardware units of limited software support. Some organizations prefer to work with a "clean box" or a minimally supported box; others prefer higher degrees of programmed support leading to minimization of implementation effort.

Unique applications with limited functional goals at each node and with rigorous performance requirements might lead to a greater interest in "roll your own" system solutions. The choice between an IBM Series/1, for example, and an IBM 4300 might be affected by the perception of how much general purpose, standard software support was necessary or desirable for an application.

At an even more basic level, there are those who are interested in building systems out of processing units or logical elements where they have choices about packaging, wiring, microcode, software tradeoffs. Systems appropriate for implementation of families of cooperating microprocessors provide an opportunity for designers to make fundamental choices about systems structure and behavior. Such developments are more commonly found in industrial and military applications than in the mainstream of management, scientific or commercial data processing.

The freedom of design choice may excite some and dismay others. It is going to be unavoidable that distributed systems will involve a set of partitioning and location decisions. In addition there will be some new kinds of software problems that will either augment or replace those associated with centralized systems. The selection of hardware will become more difficult just because there are more kinds of units available.

On the other hand the trend by vendors to supply additional functions to support various concepts of distribution will certainly continue and the level of effort associated with the installation, operation and development of such systems will be at some future time similar to efforts associated with the design and development of very large, shared centralized systems.

Chapter 2

Examples Based
On Banking Industry

1. BACKGROUND OF EXAMPLES

The examples and considerations used in this chapter are based upon, but not limited by, actual or proposed systems.

It is the author's intention, however, not only to describe systems but to explore motives, alternatives, concepts which are not known to be part of the actual systems. It is important not only to present a system but to understand why the system was conceived and even, for the purpose of rational narrative, to fill in some holes left in the available descriptions.

The desire to extend the discussion of the examples into philosophical and conjectural areas comes from the author's dismay at the volume of examples and case studies which are not really instructive in any way because they do not go beyond the "what they did." The resulting examples, therefore, cannot be represented as accurate accounts of real systems. They are examples of approaches and concepts which the author feels to be useful and instructive.

Two things must be kept in mind while reading these examples. First, they are in a sense "naive" because they concentrate on positive aspects of distribution. Problems may be referenced in passing but the intent of the material is to provide a basically encouraging description of the systems being discussed. Problems and potential difficulties are given sufficient space in later parts of the book. Second, and closely related to the first, much of the philosophical material represents the alleged viewpoints of the advocates of the systems design rather than a viewpoint of the author.

2. A PEER LOCALLY INTERCONNECTED SYSTEM

The characterization of this system derives from the fact that the processing nodes are not geographically dispersed and that the relationship between them is essentially one of cooperating equals.

We will postulate a banking organization which is interested in bringing a set of retail banking services "on-line" to its customer population. The bank offers credit services, demand deposit services and mortgage services on a state-wide basis. They wish the computer system to allow customers to receive credit or cash checks from any branch in the system, to transfer funds from credit to checking accounts, to pay mortgages with transfers from accounts. They wish this system to be:

1. Highly reliable and available.
2. Quickly installed.
3. Cost effective.
4. Predictable in response times.
5. Able to grow with minimum disruption.

A partitioned or distributed solution seemed attractive because it was not clear to those responsible that contemporary large uniprocessors could provide orderly growth or predictable response times. In addition the price/performance characteristics of small systems used in aggregation seemed sufficiently attractive to make a multinode design seem economically feasible for this application.

The system will be described in an evolutionary manner. We will move from stage to stage of distributed processing notions as if the system structure emerged from a first idea of partitioning followed by insights into how the partitioning process could be moved forward in response to observed needs at each stage.

2.1. First Possible Partitioning Notion — By Application

The organization of the bank is such that management responsibility for mortgage, credit services and demand deposits was dispersed into different units. The first apparent method for partitioning work, therefore, was across the three "businesses" suggested by the company's organization.

Figure 8 shows three dedicated processing units, one for each business, with data representing accounts dispersed across the three systems. Figure 8 also suggests that each system could stand alone and support a private network of terminals interconnected by teleprocessing lines to branch offices. The diagram does not show any of the network management units which might lie on the path from a terminal to the dedicated application system. Certainly some number of concentrators, multiplexors, demultiplexors and so on, would exist.

The concentrators, multiplexors and similiar units represent network control functions for message routing, circuit selection and other activities necessary for efficient use of long distance communications facilities. We will assume their existence but discuss only the application and system control aspects of this design.

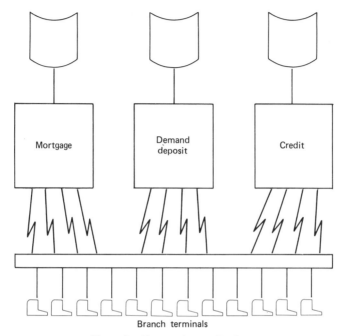

Figure 8. Cooperating applications.

The three dedicated units of Figure 8 do not really constitute a system but merely an old technique of dedicating processing units to the function of a department and giving the machine to the department. This first level of partitioning is well understood and often adequate. In this example, however, we will undertake alternate forms of distribution because:

1. A sufficiently large processing unit to handle the volume for each function state-wide could not be found.
2. The interconnection of terminals from the entire state was not economic. Since the state contains two primary centers of activity it looked preferable to have machines at both centers.
3. The physical separation of credit and demand deposit functions was not necessary to support their logical separation across business units.

2.2. First Geographic Partitioning

The bank does business in a state which has two major centers of population and banking activity. The centers are hundreds of miles from each other. Each supports a region of economic activity which is largely operationally autonomous.

In order to reduce communications expenses a processing node for each application was put in each of the major centers. Thus there is a credit system at point A and a credit system at point B. Similarly there is a demand deposit system and a mortgage system at points A and B. Terminals from branch banks talk to the systems in their regional centers.

To facilitate state-wide credit and account manipulation for transient customers the credit and demand deposit machines talk to each other over a fast teleprocessing interconnection. Fast in this context means 9600 bits per second. Figure 9 shows one possible configuration with a line connecting the credit systems and a separate line connecting the demand accounting systems. These interconnections allow customers with accounts at point A to have their balances checked by tellers at point B when they are in the service area of point B.

The relatively modest capacity of the connection between cities is a result of an assessment of the intensity with which people will move from A to B and require banking services.

2.2.1. The Interconnection

The teleprocessing interconnection shown on Figure 9 suggests the technological possibility of interconnecting these systems. There are many variations in the design and selection of an interconnection facility between remote cities.

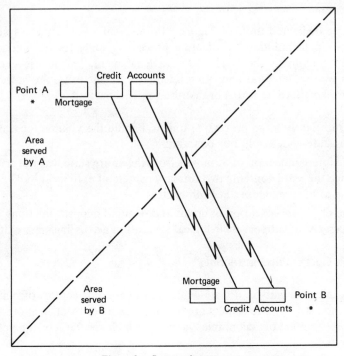

Figure 9. Systems interconnect.

This book contains little discussion of communications technology and offerings. The bibliography contains references which will help provide important details of that area.

Among the choices available to a designer are:

1. Whether to obtain the connection from a common carrier as part of tariffed services as one acquires telephone services.
2. The specific offering which is best for this connection. Dial up, dedicated lines, other specialized tariffed offerings which may be available.
3. The speed of the line and the manner in which that speed will be obtained. The degree of multiplexing and demultiplexing, the degree of sharing which will be employed across various options to deliver a nominal rate of a certain speed.
4. The necessity for providing alternate routes from place to place.
5. The desirability of installing a "private network" of some kind provided by a specialized network vendor or the desirability of joining a public network offered by a specialized network vendor in the area of operations.

These decisions are by no means unimportant, nor is the above list exhaustive. The cost of interconnection between geographically distant sites may be as much as or more than the cost of processing nodes in the future. No one should proceed with a distributed processing design without communications expertise available. Unfortunately a full discussion of these considerations merits a text in itself. We excuse ourselves from addressing them here on the basis that the issues we do address will, ideally, determine the network requirements and not the other way around.

Naturally communications issues will seriously affect systems configuration decisions since communications costs and capability play such a central role. However, it is important to understand that issues of logical partitioning and applications concept must drive system design.

2.2.2. Decentralization and Distribution

We have before mentioned that this system is to be addressed to retail services. The importance of this lies in the homogeneity of service to be offered at each regional center. Customers doing business out of any branch in the state are offered the same services.

As a result of this homogeneity of service the systems at points A and B will be functionally identical. If they differ at all they may differ in details of available mass storage or processor speeds which may reflect local loading levels. The programs to be run at each point should be identical. The services offered at each point are not only identical but they are not determined by the management at each point.

The above strongly suggests the following:

1. The design of the system will be dominated by policy made at a manage-
    ment level above the management at points A and B. It is also probable
    that the system will be entirely conceived at this higher level and passed
    down to points A and B.
2. The implementation of the system therefore will be done by one group.
    A single team of programmers will code and install an essentially equiv-
    alent set of programs in both locations.

The system, although beginning to take on attributes of distributedness because
there are interconnected nodes at two sites, in no way suggests decentralization
of data processing management. A clear distinction must be made between the
dispersion of hardware and software systems elements and the dispersion of
data processing design, implementation and management skills. This system is
highly centralized in that both function and implementation transcend points A
and B.

2.3. Second Geographical Partitioning

Let us now speculate that rather significant processing nodes are still required
for demand deposits at both points A and B. Let us further speculate that the
power required is significant enough to suggest reason for designer concern
about whether a single uniprocessor can support the load over a period when
volumes will be increasing.

In addition to the growth problem there are concerns about the reliability of
the system. The bank wishes the system to display three important
characteristics:

1. A malfunction of a processing unit will not bring the system down.
    There will be a standby processor ready to assume the work.
2. In the event of a malfunction that renders the system partially inoper-
    ative, the scope of impact of this malfunction can be contained to affect
    a minimum number of customer transactions.
3. The response time at a branch is stable and predictable.

These requirements suggest some form of further partitioning. Let us address
requirement 3 first. If all of the branches for a region are to run on one processor the achievement of stable response times suggests that the processor will
have to run characteristically underutilized during nonpeak periods. However,
a large processor running at low utilization levels may not be economical. In
addition some nontrivial expenses in tuning and adjusting complex software
structures may be necessary to achieve stable, acceptable response times.

Given the availability of medium capacity small processing units with acceptable price/performance, a design using a collection of these units might be able to achieve stable performance with a reduced investment in performance tuning and adjusting. If a set of geographical zones could be defined where each zone was a collection of branches, then a processing unit of appropriate size could be dedicated to that zone. The constraint here is that it would be necessary for those units to talk to each other very reliably and very quickly.

The finer partitioning of the workload also addresses requirement 2. By assigning a processing unit to a zone a malfunctioning unit would affect only the customers of that zone.

These considerations lead to an analysis of banking loads coming from various branches and a definition of a number of zones of equal load. It would, of course, be impossible to determine what a proper zone load was without some notion of the class of machine which would be applied to a zone. Even at this stage the designers require some idea of whether they are talking about large, medium or small processing units. The class of processing unit desirable in this situation is determined by a number of considerations. Among them:

1. It must be sufficiently inexpensive to allow characteristic underutilization

2. It must be sufficiently powerful so as not to overburden any processing unit to processing unit interconnection mechanism. Given a load from a zone and some expectation of transients which will require cross-zone communication, the cross-zone load must be small enough so the intercommunication does not become a bottleneck.

3. The processing unit must have large enough memory to support nontrivial message analysis and file management software.

4. The processing units must have operational and development software which makes undertaking a major application on the architecture a reasonable risk given the capability of the design and development organization.

Given these constraints the appropriate processing unit for this application appeared to be a mid-sized system in the 300,000 to 500,000 instruction per second range with memories in the 1/4 to 1/2 megabyte range.

2.3.1. Why This Configuration?

Figure 10 shows a system of 10 medium-scale systems, each with its own random storage and communications capability, interconnected to each other over a mechanism called an interprocesser bus. This bus has a speed in the area of 2 to 3 megabits per second, considerably faster than any possible teleprocessing lines. It is the availability of this bus that has attracted the zone nodes from some site in each zone to the regional centers. An additional consideration in placing nodes in a regional center is the potential avoidance of increased oper-

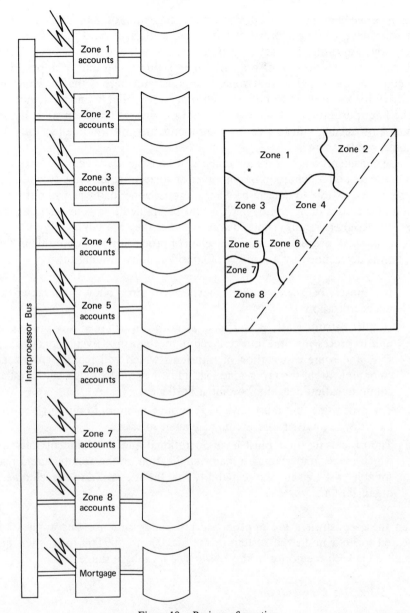

Figure 10. Basic configuration.

ational costs which might be incurred if an operational staff was required at each site.

There are actually two configurations of this type which talk to each other over teleprocessing lines. One system is at point A and the other is at point B.

The configuration shown involves a zone system for the demand deposit and credit activities of each zone. Although a business unit distinction may be maintained, the functions share machines.

The indicated configuration allows fast zone to zone intercommunication. A transient asking for funds from a Zone 1 terminal may have his account at Zone 9. The Zone 1 processor will use the fast interprocessor connection to talk to the Zone 9 processor and ask it to access Zone 9 data and return a result. The fast interconnection between machines in a region is necessary on the assumption that there is greater interzone traffic than interregional traffic. The stability of the system depends upon properly chosen nodes which will absorb local peaks and upon an assessment of zone to zone cross-talk which will prevent the interprocessor bus from becoming a bottleneck.

2.4. First Functional Partitioning

The system of Figure 10 shows each processing unit in an interconnected configuration undertaking its own communications responsibility. There are certainly application scenarios in which such a design is desirable. However, there is an alternative set of designs that lead to a concept of partitioning by function. Figure 11 shows the system with the addition of a gateway machine. This processing unit provides an interface between the terminals which are connected to the system and the sibling system at the other regional center. The figure does not show the network of concentrators and other units that may lie on the path between terminals and the gateway machine.

The term "gateway machine" is used in the communications world to represent a place where two networks, each with different protocols and conventions, intersect with each other. The gateway translates, as a kind of adapter, the conventions of one network to the conventions of the other. Gateway is used specifically to refer to a point of interface between an external network, coming into a building, and an internal network. In this example, the gateway interfaces the remote terminal network with the network formed by the interprocessor bus.

A gateway machine centralizes the basic functions required to interface the system at a point with the outside world. Those activities related to basic line control and detailed interaction with the telecommunications lines are performed by the gateway. Each zone node is relieved of attention to such details.

We said above that there were a number of alternative designs which would relieve node processors from communications problems. The set of alternatives is defined by various options relating to how much function is to be placed in the centralized gateway processor. It is possible to place path control and routing functions in the gateway so that alternate paths to terminals can be attempted and defined by the gateway. Placing both link and path level functions in the gateway still requires a modest machine that might do its function without any knowledge of the application and without associated storage units.

How much more function might be taken from the zone processors and placed in the gateway machine involves details of the application logic. For example, transaction message validation might be put into the gateway. Routing of a message from a terminal directly to the proper zone processor might also be put into the gateway. If this is done, then the gateway begins to participate in application logic and might grow in its required resources.

In the system of Figure 11 the function of the gateway processing unit will be to transmit a message to the zone node which is associated with the originating terminal and to pass responses back to terminals.

Exactly how much function is placed in a gateway machine is also partially determined by the intelligence which may be placed close to remote terminals

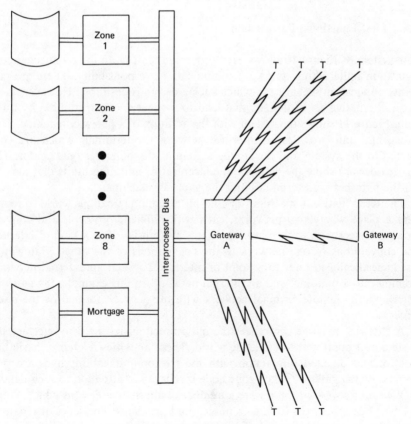

Figure 11.   The gateway.

in cluster controllers or in intelligent terminals, as well as by the relationship between the gateway and those processors containing application logic.

The partitioning of communications interface services onto the gateway machine leads to the concept of partitioning by function. The word function will be used in this book to represent operations of a computing system which are not usually thought of as being the responsibility of an application program.

Systems software differs widely in what is considered to be application program responsibilities and what is considered to be systems software responsibilities. Interfaces between applications programs, subsystems, operating systems, access methods are not standard. Therefore there is a kind of fuzzy set of activities which in some systems are application responsibility and in other systems are system software responsibility. Despite this there is some residue of activity which is universally felt to be system software activity.

For example, the lowest levels of communications interface, called the link and path control level, are truly generalizable and independent of application logic. The idea of partitioning by function is the idea of taking code which supports this set of activities out of application processors to some single place or set of places in a configuration.

2.5. Application Partitioning

The very first partitioning idea was a form of application partitioning in that we separated three major applications. Such a partitioning might be thought of as "vertical partitioning," separating partially independent applications. The decomposition of data into zones was an example of a second common application separation technique.

There is yet another form of application partitioning which can be applied within the structure of a single application. It is a form of "horizontal partitioning." The flow of data through an application can be analyzed so that separate stages can be defined. The actions required to accept and validate a message may be grouped together into a program module. The actions required to access a data file to retrieve data, to format data on the way from the storage device and to operate on data may be grouped into another program module. The first module might be called a message handler, the second module a file handler. Database management systems are often structured into tranaction manager and data manager elements. An interface between the two modules may be defined so that data can be passed from one to the other. Frequently the interface is a queue which receives data from one module and from which a second module takes data.

The compartmentalization of programs into modules is generally considered good programming practice. It leads to easier debugging and greater programmer productivity. Naturally the specific clustering of activity to be placed in each module must be the result of careful analysis. There are various texts in the area of structured programming, composite design and related topics which describe methodologies for module definition.

The definition of a message handler module and a file handler module is possible for the application evolving here. An extension of the idea of defining the two modules is the idea of having each module running in its own processor. That is exactly the configuration shown in Figure 12. Each processing unit contains two closely interconnected processors, one running the message handler and one running the file handler. The function of the message handler is to analyze each message and then pass it on to its associated file handler or place it on the interprocessor bus to be received by the zone processing unit which has the referenced account.

2.6. Replication

In order to increase the reliability of the system it is possible to add processors to serve as back-up units. One of the attractions of constructing systems out of accumulations of small processing units is the ability to select points of granu-

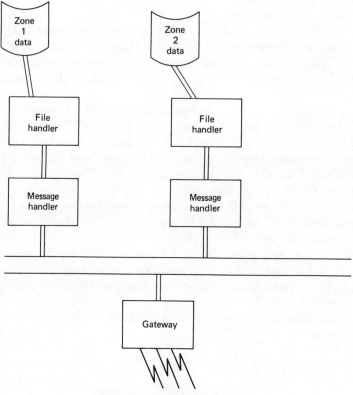

Figure 12.   Application structuring.

lar replication. Since each processor is small and relatively inexpensive it is possible to increase reliability by adding additional processors at selected points in the system structure.

Such replication has been undertaken for the configuration in Figure 13. Each zone processing unit now contains two file handlers and two message handlers. Interconnecting switches can route messages and data to whichever of the duplexed units is operational. Thus the failure of a zone requires the failure of two message handlers or two file handlers. It is possible to design the software so that all four processors may be operational in parallel when all four are operative. If one unit fails, all work is routed to the remaining processor of its designated activity.

Beyond the reliability achieved by replication in a zone processor, the impact of a total zone failure is limited to transactions which involve that zone. Thus the probability of the entire system being down or more than a fraction of customers experiencing inconvenience is minimized by this design.

Of course the extent to which replication of processors increases reliability is also a function of how reliable the disk units are and how reliable the software is. No amount of processor replication will keep a zone operational if the software at that zone has failed.

2.7. Summary Remarks

The system described has a large number of processing elements and random storage units organized into two major configurations. The feasibility of such a system depends upon the availability of processors powerful and economic

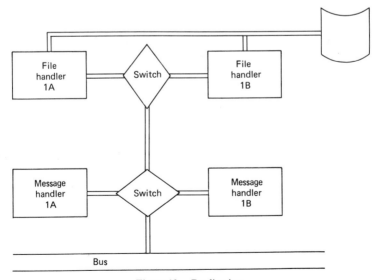

Figure 13.   Replication.

enough to support the necessary loads. It further depends upon the availability of a local interconnection mechanism which is fast, reliable and inexpensive enough to provide processor to processor interaction for transient transactions. It further depends upon the availability of adequate systems software support to limit the risk of implementation.

The entire systems concept depends upon the ability to recognize the partitions which were described. The system will be a success if:

1. The processors have sufficient power to handle the workload assigned to them and deliver stable response times at peak load. A condition for success, therefore, is the success of the zone analysis and an understanding of the power of each processor.

2. The cross-zone load has been well understood and the interprocessor bus can handle the load without becoming a bottleneck. A condition of success is a correct understanding of the level of cross-zone action.

3. Available system software is reliable enough so that processing unit failure is not a result of software malfunction.

4. Sufficient support function is available from the system software so that application programming costs are not dramatically higher than what is expected on a large system.

5. The application is designed so that the system can grow easily by the addition of more zone nodes as volume increases and zone redefinition is required. In addition there must be some planning for the addition of as yet unforeseen enhancements of function.

6. Methodology for system-wide problem determination is adequate to identify malfunctions and efficiently respond to them.

If all of these conditions are achievable, the system will meet its goals. If misappreciations are made about the capacity or workload, reliability or sufficiency of software, then the system will be a disappointment.

3. ALTERNATIVES NOT TAKEN

The narrative which described the evolution of the first example did not dwell on the alternatives which were available at points along the trek. One of the impressive facts about designing distributed processing systems is the richness of alternative and decision. An almost overwhelming set of alternatives is available once the idea of distributing a system is put in place.

The following is just a partial list of things which might have been considered:

1. A complete processing unit for each zone might have been physically put in each zone. Zone interaction would then be handled by teleprocessing

communication. The desirability or undesirability of this depends upon the intensity of cross-zone communication and the rigidity of the requirement that a transaction be processed in the same time whether it is local or remote. By extension it would be possible to put a processing unit in each branch if appropriate processing nodes could be identified.

2. The message handlers might have been put in branches or zones. Terminals would communicate to local or zone message handlers which would in turn talk to the gateway machine for file handler routing.

3. It might have been desirable to share larger and more price effective disk units between zone processors. This would reduce the price of bytes stored but it would have introduced contention and enlarged the scope of impact of a disk failure. Still, it is a tradeoff to be considered.

4. Each zone processor might have also contained a replicated storage unit with replicated data. This would have introduced a requirement for updating two units per transaction but it would have introduced higher reliability. In the same spirit each transaction might be given to both message handlers and passed up to both file handlers with response to a terminal dependent upon successful and coordinated completion by both parallel paths.

4. A VARIATION

Figure 14 shows a very similar system which might be appropriate if the area in which service is given is geographically smaller. The system consists of two centers which are duplicates of each other. At each center there is a multinode interconnected system with a processing unit dedicated to savings accounts, credit and checking account services. In addition there is a gateway processor at each site. The gateway processor in this variation contains enough application logic to route a particular transaction to the appropriate dedicated processing unit. It is not a "pure" gateway, but a unit commonly called a "front end" processor.

The network in front of the front end processor is shown with this system because it has the important attribute that terminals at any branch can reach either central system. Any particular branch has a primary system to which it normally goes but if this system is not operational, the branch can connect to the secondary processor.

To support this notion of back-up all accounts are represented at both points. In order to synchronize the replicated data, each processing unit talks to its remote alternate whenever a transaction occurs in order to inform it of the changes it has made in the account files. Thus each system is data current and can be used if the sister system is not available. When a system recovers changes which have occurred during its period of inactivity and recovery are sent to it by its alternate.

The essential differences between this design and the earlier are:

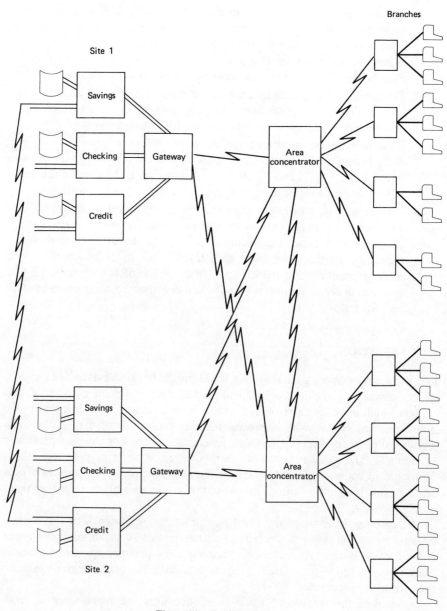

Figure 14.   Replicated sites.

1. The idea of replication is across systems and not within a system. This might be motivated by a desire to have independent power sources for each system.

2. Any branch can get to either system. This is feasible because the geographical area served is smaller than in the first system.

3. Data replication and synchronization is inherent in the design.

4. The "gateway" has application logic which makes it a front end processor rather than only a network interface communications controller.

5. A SUBSTANTIALLY DIFFERENT APPROACH

Two important strategic assumptions made by the systems we have described are that there will be a uniformity of service at each branch and that the services offered will be determined by higher levels of management. These assumptions are reasonable for retail operations where large numbers of customers may be serviced in a standardized way.

It is possible, however, to postulate another kind of environment for banking operations. If a bank wishes to service a small set of very large corporate accounts, it might be desirable to offer rather specialized services to each large account. In order to do this an account manager might be designated to handle an individual client or a group of individual clients. This account manager would be responsible for developing a service program for his account or set of accounts. The challenge to data processing design is how to apply technology to the desire to give individualized service to very significant clients.

Inherent in the strategy must be an ability that permits account managers maximum discretion and a method for supplying data processing support to a diverse set of account strategies. One approach to this is to make the account manager ultimately responsible for his data processing support but with sufficient technological guidance to enable him to expect success.

The technology support might come from an information technology service which keeps abreast of technological developments, tracks products and performs acceptance tests for equipment which might be useful to account managers. Further, the support group can offer training, contract negotiation assistance, standards and systems design reviews.

The account manager is empowered to acquire, install, operate and implement useful applications on whatever basis he chooses in line with his perception of his needs. There is a considerably higher level of decentralization in data processing decision making in this situation than in those previously described. The goal is to enable the account manager to do what is necessary quickly without reliance on bureaucratic structures not under his control.

Each account manager is free to choose from any number of hardware and software systems which have been qualified by the technology support service. He may, at his risk, perhaps be empowered to ignore the technology service,

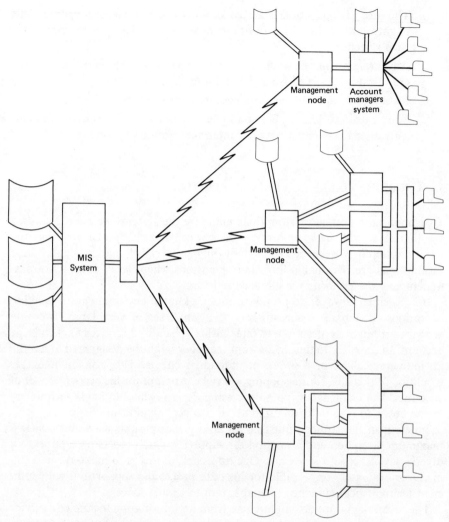

Figure 15.   A management/operational interface.

but there would be rather little motive for him to do so.

Figure 15 shows operational nodes for three account managers. Account manager one has acquired a large version of a medium-sized uniprocessor. He has three major applications which he runs for all of his accounts which time-share this processing unit. He has designed and implemented these applications himself, perhaps under contract with a software development company. Account manager two has a family of interconnected small machines, each of which is dedicated to a particular application. Account manager three has a processing unit dedicated to each account which runs all services for that account.

The hardware and software for each account manager is unique and the services offered by any account manager may differ from customer to customer. It is necessary, despite the degrees of independence offered account managers, to interface these operational systems to higher level management. We must introduce the concept of the bank.

It is possible for the technology services group to define a set of data flow standards between the account manager systems and the management information system existing at a corporate center. In developing the account level applications the account manager would be responsible for sending designated data in designated formats. To support the interconnection between the MIS and the account manager systems the technology services people might provide communications oriented software modules to run on the account manager systems.

Some problems develop when the account manager systems are asked to talk directly to the MIS. One is that the burden on his system to sustain the interaction may force him into systems larger than he requires or eliminate some system structures. A second problem is that the MIS interface may not be stable. Higher levels of management may be changing the data transfer requirements, each time impacting the programming in the account manager's operational system.

In order to avoid additional burden in hardware capacity and programming modification, the corporation may take the view that the definition of data flow between MIS and account manager systems is a higher level responsibility. To support this notion the technology services group will supply its own interfacing processing node. This node will be on the account manager's site and interconnected to the account manager's collections of hardware. On the other side it will talk, probably with telecommunication links, to the MIS system.

The function of this new node is to provide a stable interface for the local systems. Local systems pour all raw data into the local "management node" which is then responsible for formatting, extracting and organizing data for transmission to the MIS level system. All modifications which are necessary to satisfy new reporting requirements are undertaken by staff personnel and the account manager is shielded from interface perturbation.

The connection between the management node and the operational node is local because data must flow between them very quickly and because less data will flow from the remote management node to the MIS system than between the two remote nodes.

Such a system is motivated by a desire to permit maximum local discretion and to provide stable interfaces to locally designed systems. It is feasible to the extent that account managers become capable of bringing systems up quickly and effectively and to the extent economical configurations can be identified. As regards the last point, the proliferation of offerings of various types of hardware and software capability is such that the problem is not how to find a potentially suitable system but how to choose between many.

Chapter 3

A Service Industry Example

1. NATURE OF THE EXAMPLE

This example has been chosen because of the light that it sheds on what the author calls the "sociology of distributed processing." As with the examples of the last chapter, we will take an evolutionary approach, trying to identify the stages which led to the final design. As with the previous examples, we are basically talking from a supposed interior monologue ascribed to the designers.

2. A HIERARCHIC APPLICATION DEDICATED SYSTEM

The system is fundamentally a service order system. The developer has a large customer base who are users of his manufactured equipment and wishes to be able to dispatch servicemen as quickly as possible when the equipment malfunctions. The intent of the system is to minimize the time between the receipt of a telephoned complaint and the time of service.

Service personnel who receive complaints will be associated with a terminal upon which they may display characteristics of the calling customer and through which they may cause work orders to be dispatched to service personnel. An associated goal is to be able to predict with accuracy when service will be done. A customer, after a call, should have a very good idea of when he will be visited.

The designers of the system are particularly interested in reliability since relations with customers are going to be influenced by how efficiently the company responds to complaints. They are also interested in good human factors because it is necessary that the personnel who receive complaints are comfortable with the displays they are using. Finally, design is concerned with the ability of the system to absorb considerable growth over a long lifetime.

3. INITIAL SYSTEMS CONCEPT

The initial systems concept involved the use of a very large uniprocessor with teleprocessing connections to unintelligent terminals at a complaint center. The large uniprocessor would run a highly reliable operating system and database manager available from the vendor. The data for each customer would include a service record, purchase data, terms of servicing agreement, type of installed equipment and other data necessary to support an intelligent dialogue between a complainant and personnel of the company.

The use of a large uniprocessor introduced some concerns about capacity growth and reliability. Although the intended processing system had been rigorously qualified, its hardware as well as its software, it was not clear that the node and the associated teleprocessing network could offer no-fail service. It was also not clear that uniprocessor designs could match the rate of application growth.

3.1. Considered Centralized Solutions

Figure 16 shows the company's anticipated volume growth over a five year period. It also indicates that the current largest available uniprocessor will not be able to sustain the load beyond three years. Projections of the rate of performance improvement in large scale machines over the history of the industry, however, suggest that the "top of the line" machine available in three years might well have sufficient capacity, and at a reduced price, to handle projected growth in capacity requirements.

The company is reasonably assured that a faster system might be available but it remains concerned about two issues. One is the deliverability of that system. The other is the financing basis for the acquisition of equipment. It is the policy of the company to purchase equipment which it writes off over a five year time period. The dislocation of a piece of equipment before its writeoff involves procedures to find a home for the equipment and a justification for its replacement. This leads the developers to prefer a system structure which can grow by module addition rather than by module replacement. Additionally it is preferable that the modules are small and not subject to the usual stringent financing considerations.

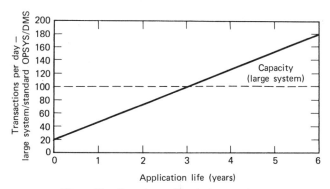

Figure 16.   Capacity and load—large system.

The large uniprocessor configuration problem appears in this scenario as presenting a problem for future growth. In other scenarios the problem may appear in its opposite form. If the largest available processor can fulfill the growth requirements, then for some interval it will be too large for the application. The importance of this point depends somewhat on there being economy of scale, an issue which we will address in Part Three. If there is economy of scale, then excess capacity may be relatively cheap for the uniprocessor solution. If there are no economies of scale, then early installation of a machine which will fulfill eventual capacity requirements may be economically unacceptable. The obvious solution, to acquire a smaller machine of the same architecture and then replace it, encounters the difficulty that the smaller version may not be able to host the systems software which is desired to create an operational environment for the application. This suggests possible nontrivial migration problems in the future and possibly reduced function or increased application development cost in the present.

The example of this chapter is concerned with outgrowing the largest available system, but the constraints on system design are similar in both situations. The constraints on design are to avoid migration problems and achieve nondisruptive growth whether the problem is outgrowing the largest machine available or the largest machine affordable.

A possible physical configuration addressing the desire for incremental growth would be a multiprocessor configuration. The addition of a second processor will allow the application to grow and might, theoretically, provide an acceptable back-up capability. There are, however, some concerns about the multiprocessor approach. It is not clear that the tightly coupled configuration, with multiple instances of shared resources and a single operating system can achieve sufficient partition isolation to provide the availability desired for this application. In addition, structuring an application to take full advantage of increased performance on a multiprocessor may degrade its performance on a uniprocessor.

A possible solution to the configuration problem is to use loosely interconnected uniprocessors. Loosely connected systems are systems that do not share memory but which may share random storage devices and which may have some direct communication path for processor to processor interaction. With this solution a smaller uniprocessor capable of running the same software as the "top of the line" machine might be acquired initially. When volume grows a second system might be acquired and the two systems interconnected through a channel. Subsets of the application could then be defined by a regional data partitioning similar to that of the first banking example. For the low level of complaints which might involve reference to both machines, cross-systems reference could be undertaken.

This solution is not at all unnatractive; it is essentially a distributed solution where the nodes are kept in the same room. However, because of the desire to define an isolated set of constantly available, "failsoft" functions which would be available at the same speeds regardless of instances of system outage, a more distributed approach was undertaken.

3.2. First Look at Hierarchy

In order to economically fill the capacity and reliability requirements for the application, in view of configurational problems with variations of large systems, the designers began to consider a technique which would offload some work from the large processor and which would provide an important failsoft capability when the large processor or the lines to it were down.

Figure 17 shows a configuration of a hierarchic system which would be appropriate for this application. The large system is surrounded by a set of medium-sized processors. Personnel at complaint centers work at the medium-sized systems. Here they record complaints and undertake whatever dialogue with the system is necessary to complete a complaint transaction. When a

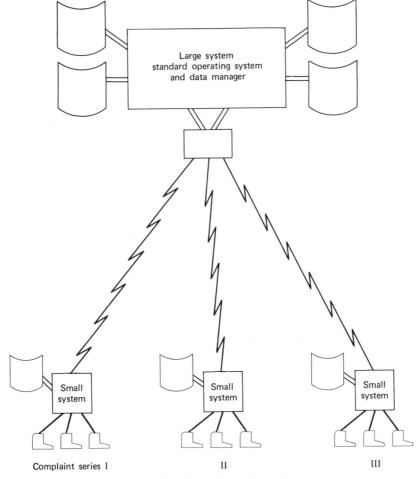

Figure 17. Hierarchic configuration.

complaint dialogue is finished information about the complaint is forwarded to the central system where repair work orders are created. Service personnel are located at the site of the central system. If the central system is not up or if links to it are not up, the complaint information is retained at the small system until the large system is available.

The intent of the design is to provide a failsoft interface to complainants when access to the central system is not possible. In order to do this the specific definition of a minimum level of meaningful service is required. Associated with the definitions of meaningful level of failsoft service is a set of data entry and data inspection functions which must be available at each smaller processing unit. The screens must be controlled by the smaller unit, data entry formats and checking functions must be provided and some local data must be available.

The support of terminal interaction at the smaller processing unit is consistent with the desire to offload the larger unit in order to extend its productive life. Moving support of the user interface to the smaller machines will reduce the load on the large machine for interrupt handling, message formatting and data entry checking and analysis. In this design there is the possibility of achieving increased availability and increased capacity at the large node by moving basic functions necessary for failsoft operations out of the large processing node. An additional advantage of the configuration is that high level systems software providing functional support appropriate for a large system may be maintained in the system structure because a large system is included in the configuration.

The full definition of failsoft level of service in this application also involves the movement of some data to the smaller nodes. This data design discloses some of the data partitioning techniques and also suggests some vendor relation problems in designing distributed systems.

3.3. Data Partitioning

A first approach to the application is to partition the data geographically and put at each smaller processor only that data which is relevant to a defined customer subset. This partitioning provides smaller collections of data at a smaller node. Smaller nodes have more limited and more expensive data storage capacity than the large processing node. With data so partitioned and distributed it is possible for an employee to support a dialogue with a complainant when the large node is not operational or inaccessible.

It may be desirable to further constrain the amount of data at a smaller node. The minimization of local data may be made consistent with the definition of failsoft levels of service. The complete record of a customer may contain, for example, 100,000 bytes. The 100,000 byte record may be analyzed to determine which fields in it are necessary to support the failsoft level of service defined as acceptable. The analysis may be done on the basis of some percentage of the fields being adequate to support 80% of the complaint situations, or on the basis of some percentage of the fields being necessary to do 80% of the work on all complaints, or some combination.

The attempt to find significant subsets of record structures is sometimes called extraction. By virtue of this analysis a smaller, subset local record may be defined. It is this local record which is placed at the smaller machines.

The data at the smaller nodes has now been geographically partitioned and logically extracted. If the large node is not available, an employee uses the local extract data to support a failsoft dialogue and enter the complaint. The local system generates a complaint transaction which is sent to the large node when it becomes available.

3.4. Data Reference Pattern

This application uses the local record only in failsoft situations when the large node is not available.

When the large node is accessible it is desirable to use all of its data to support a dialogue with a complainant. Background data, service history data, repair workload and schedule may be available only from the large node. Therefore it is desirable to get additional data when the system is available.

This means that each dialogue will result in an interaction between the local and large node. The total number of interactions with the large node is decreased from the level associated with terminal to large node interaction. This decrease will occur because dialogue support is isolated on the smaller node and because it is possible to gather all of the data required for a dialogue with one request. A transaction may consist of many messages and interactions. Except for the initial data request the larger node need not be involved.

3.5. Synchronization

In defining the data elements to be brought to the small nodes we extracted from records existing at the large node. These fields were retained at the large node. There is now replicated data in the system. In general replication of data leads to a set of synchronization problems in order to achieve some form of consistency between values at one site and values at another site. Later in the book we will discuss problems of replicated data in a more general way. The replicated data problem is not severe in this design.

Some level of synchronization is necessary between the large node and a smaller node which has an extracted copy of the customer record as well as a temporary large record. The large node is not interested in the full customer records while they are at the small node. It is sufficient that the small node send the necessary modifications up to the large node at the end of a complaint dialogue. This is done by the small node generating a change record which the large node uses to update its local copy of the customer record. When a complaint dialogue completes, the large node uses its received change notice to update its records and develop service orders.

When the large node is unavailable, the small node works with its extract data. It creates a local file of complaints which it transmits to the large node when it becomes available. This simple mechanism works because the small node is designated to be the only possible point of change of data and the only required synchronization mechanism is to eventually conform the data at some later time. If changes could come from either node, or if multiple copies might be sent to different small nodes, then a more elaborate synchronization scheme would be required.

4.   HARDWARE AND SOFTWARE FOR THE APPLICATION

The concept of this system requires a large uniprocessor configuration at a central site and a number of smaller medium-sized processors with teleprocessing interconnection at some number of complaint reception centers. The number of centers and/or the number of small processors at a center will be discovered in a manner similar to the way the zones were discovered in the first example. There is no particular attraction to having the smaller nodes together in this particular system since there is no small system to small system interaction.

4.1.   Interfaces

In almost all regards the interface presented by the computer system to the user is defined by the software of the small system. The presence of the larger system is suggested only when the smaller system informs the user that the large record is not available.

At the application programmer level it would be convenient if the interfaces to large and small node software were identical. It would also be nice if large and small nodes were compatible machines. There is a certain amount of function which might go on at either place and if the system and machine interfaces were identical, then the siting of various functions could be determined during performance testing of the system. In addition there may be multiple regional centers with different performance and load requirements suitable for different permutations of function.

In order to come close to this ideal the designers chose a small node which presented a set of almost compatible data manager interfaces. Using these data manager interfaces a program could be written which would run on either the large or the small nodes. In addition the two types of nodes were instruction set compatible.

The desire to use a data manager system at both small and large nodes was also based upon the desire to minimize programming expense for the small nodes. However, a problem occurred in the software licensing policies of the vendor of the large node. The policy of the vendor is to price each copy of a software product without giving preferential pricing based on multiple copies.

The company computed the total price of all necessary licenses across the population of small nodes over a five year projected application life. The total bill was sufficiently large that a nonstandard software solution looked economic under certain circumstances. The nonstandard software solution was the creation of a local data manager on an inhouse development basis as part of implementation of the application. Since the notification of activity to the large node was on a change notice basis the data manager at the large node and the small node need only agree on some standard notice protocol. Each was free to use whatever local data structures were convenient. If a homegrown local data manager were undertaken, its cost would be distributable across all of the multiple small nodes in the system. In order to be feasible, however, an analysis is necessary to determine how sophisticated the local manager must be.

The analysis must determine whether functions associated with a rich and extensive database manager were necessary at the small machine. If such advanced function was required, then the undertaking of a homegrown product would be highly undesirable. If only basic data management functions were necessary, then it would be reasonable to undertake a private product. The analysis must involve the nature of data access at a local node and some reasonable prediction of what processing activities might, in future, come to a local node which might complicate its local data manipulation requirements. The analysis determined that very simple data reference functions were needed and speculated that the total cost of an inhouse developed package would be less than the licensing costs of the vendor package. In addition the homegrown package might provide performance advantages over the vendor supplied product.

The decision not to use vendor provided data manager software suggested that a vendor other than the vendor of the large system might supply the small nodes. Although this would seriously limit some future growth options and eliminate shifts of function from large to small node without reprogramming, a possible advantage was that a second vendor offered some machine sizes very appropriate to the kind of load which would be placed at a smaller node.

The company had developed an expertise on a small system produced by a second vendor of known credibility. It was also determined that the software existed for processing units of the two vendors to talk to each other and that it would present no particular increase in development costs to build the system out of units from multiple vendors. Finally it was discovered that the deliverability of small systems from the second vendor was acceptable. As a consequence the determination was made to undertake a mixed vendor system to support the hierarchic concept.

4.2. Review of Basis of Decision

The decision was based on the points mentioned above which are summarized below with some relevant additions.

1. The development of a local data manager was feasible because its functions were simple.

2. Sufficient expertise in the software of the second vendor constrained the risk of developing a simple data manager on the operating system of that vendor.

3. Interconnection software between the systems was known to exist and was known to be reliable. Numerous instances of successful interconnection between the selected large and small nodes existed.

4. Both vendors were highly reliable, stable companies with proven ability to support contractual obligations.

5. Both systems were well understood in terms of performance characteristics so that a reasonable split of work could be discovered.

It is probably profitable to state the negative versions of these considerations explicitly:

1. The requirements of data management at the small node might be complex or might, over time, become complex and more sophisticated as the application evolved. Considerable effort might have to be undertaken to constantly evolve the small system software or move the application to larger nodes as it functionally matured.

2. One vendor's software, which looks attractive at an analysis level, proves to be disappointing in performance or in operational stability. There was insufficient knowledge of the system to anticipate its problems.

3. Interconnection between the vendor's system is not supported and involves considerable effort to bring about by creating communications conventions and software.

4. A vendor proves unable to deliver operational equipment on schedule.

The reason for listing both positive and negative aspects of a multivendor solution is to suggest that there are factors which lead to some amount of increased risk inherent in coupling "alien" machine/software systems in the current state of the art. There is also potential risk in undertaking an inhouse development solution to the local data manager problem. A designer must be very sure that all of the positive aspects of the above scenario apply before making decisions of this kind. This is not an area for the uninitiated.

5. THE GOALS AND THE PROBLEMS

This system is another example of a system which has been designed top-down. There is no suggestion that the sites at which the small nodes are placed participated in the design or the implementation, test and installation of these nodes. Thus we see again that the dispersion of hardware and software need not imply the dispersion of data processing skills or data processing decision making.

The advantages which are expected of this design are fundamentally step growth and failsoft operability. We shall investigate the degrees to which these goals might be achieved with this design.

5.1. Failsoft

Failsoft is achieved if the large system is not available and the small systems are. However, the design as described makes no provision for the opposite situation. If a small node is inoperable, the system is down for those at a particular complaint center. In order to increase the probability that a small node will be operable, duplexing of both processors and storage units is undertaken. Despite the hardware replication at each node the small nodes may go down as a result of software errors. Software errors are a major problem because there is no provision in the system for the remote analysis and correction of software errors at local nodes. Thus it is necessary to provide some kind of on-site service to software at a local node. This leads to the desire to bring the complaint center to the same site as the large system. Unfortunately this moves complaint centers from locations convenient for customer distribution to places convenient for the large system and systems support. In any case the problem of down small nodes is not really addressed by moving them. On the other hand, the failure of a small node affects only a subset of the system so that the effect of a failure is contained.

To succeed the design of this system must assure that the recoverability features of the operating system and the homegrown data manager are fully designed so that quick recovery can be accomplished at a small node. The mere presence of replicated hardware does not address the failsoft problem. Very splendid small operating systems which deliver clean interfaces and good performance may lack recoverability features desirable in a failsoft environment. Similarly the homegrown data manager may be underdesigned with regards to its recovery features.

5.2. Step Growth

Step growth is obviously achievable by adding additional small nodes for so long as the large processing node can accommodate them. The constraints here are the physical ports which the large node has and the incremental load placed on the large system as it services more and more small nodes. The physical constraints may be overcome by various concentrator techniques. The incremental load problem is real and presents a true constraint on systems growth.

Another constraint on systems growth relates to the ease with which work can be redistributed among additional small nodes. One scenario for growth is that the areas serviced by each node are redefined as volume grows. This redefinition implies a redistribution of data between the nodes on a geographical basis. Care must be taken in initial design that this redistribution can be painlessly accomplished and that its expenses do not preclude adding additional nodes. As an alternative, of course, larger but compatible systems might replace small nodes as required. Naturally it is necessary that larger versions of the small nodes are acquirable at convenient times.

Another scenario for growth is the redistribution of function between the large and small nodes or the addition of function to the small nodes as the application matures. To achieve this kind of step growth it is necessary that sufficient latent capacity in the small nodes be assured.

Chapter 4

A Joint Operational/ Management System

1. NATURE OF THE EXAMPLE

This example is based upon a proposed system for a retail store enterprise. It is interesting for a rather rich set of hardware, software and organizational reasons. It is rather an edge of the art design which was not actually installed but which demonstrates so many potentially attractive features and raises so many interesting questions that it deserves space in any treatment of distributed processing. We will treat the example as if it were operational and discuss its motivations and the standard objections to it as a design concept. In addition we will impute certain operational characteristics which are potential and impute certain viewpoints to the designers.

The system must be characterized as:

1. Structurally compound. It contains elements that are related hierarchically and elements that are related as peers. In addition it contains both geographically distant and geographically proximate elements.
2. Multiapplication. It contains functions for a number of applications from different business units in the enterprise.
3. Joint operational/management. It contains functions which serve both on-line retail operations and management analysis.

Despite this apparent complexity the system is built of components from a single vendor with close to standardized software across many of its nodes.

2. FUNDAMENTAL STRUCTURE

The system consists of a set of small nodes which are located in retail outlets in the region serviced by this enterprise. Each retail outlet contains a small processor with very limited storage capacity, in the order of 5,000,000 bytes, a terminal for use by the store manager and a set of on-line point of sale devices, such as sales ticket printers, which are controlled by the local small processor.

Order entry is done from stations in the store into the local processing unit. In addition there is local credit authorization capability, an invoice preparation facility and local inventory status at the local processing node in each store. The application programming at the stores is accomplished by a data processing department and is identical in all stores.

The store nodes talk to a central site through a dedicated gateway machine of the same architecture as, but of greater processing capacity than, the store nodes. The gateway machine exists at a corporate headquarters site. It provides access to a multinode system consisting of a set of departmentally dedicated intermediate sized nodes and a system control point node interconnected on a high speed "ring." The characteristics of this ring will be discussed shortly.

The application dedicated nodes exist physically in departments which are in the same building but not in the same room. Each node runs a packaged data manager which provides simple inquiry and report preparation ability. This software package is part of the offering of the vendor. Each application node supports a set of terminals and a population of data processing peripherals with significant amounts of storage capacity. Any application node may be configured in accordance with departmental requirements for memory size, processor capacity and storage. Although the configurability options are not vast in terms of what might be available with large systems, they cover the range of requirements anticipated by each using department. The systems control processor is a node which is programmed to make a set of global systems decisions.

Figure 18 shows the central and store configurations. On a daily basis the store sales data is sent from the stores to the central configuration. Also on a daily basis the central system transmits pricing information and some inventory data to the stores. The interaction between store and central system, in this regard, is essentially a batch interaction. Throughout the day the store systems operate autonomously to record sales, print invoices and adjust local inventory records. Throughout the day the central system permits query and report preparation based upon day old data.

Let us characterize the nodes of the central system as an inventory node, an accounting node and a market analysis node. Each of these nodes services a corresponding departmental function. The inventory department is responsible for controlling inventory and purchase orders. The accounting node is responsible for general ledger, accounts payable and other accounting functions. The market analysis node determines prices, sets commission policy for various items and tracks sales experience with offered items.

Each of these departments has a set of programs which they have developed themselves using the program preparation facilities and the data manager of their system. The vendor offers COBOL and other high level languages for program preparation. At each node there are a number of small applications programs which can time-share the departmental system.

Because the systems are low in price little attention is given to their effective

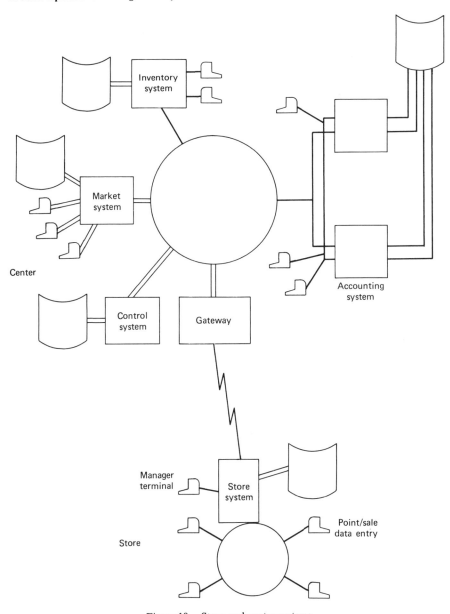

Figure 18. Store and center systems.

utilization. Of course it is necessary to determine the general capacity of the system. Help in determining this and in choosing a required configuration is provided by the data processing department. There is a degree of central control in that the data processing department has chosen the vendor and provides education in programming and systems use. In addition the data processing department provides systems programming support, when required, for the vendor provided operating system, data manager and programming language compilers. Physical maintenance of the hardware is also provided by the data processing department.

The using department has large degrees of freedom in selecting and developing the applications which are to go onto the departmental systems. Perhaps even more significant, the departments have complete control over their own data. The design of file and record structures is the prerogative of each department and data for each department is located completely at its physical site. There is no notion of a company-wide database design function, although, as we shall see, there is a very strong interest in being able to determine corporate-wide status as regards inventory, on order, and to ship positions.

The services offered by the data manager provide basic file creation, insertion, deletion, correction capability. Records in a file are referenceable by key and simple inquiry capacity is available from a terminal. Files may be referenced in either batch or on-line mode. The system encourages "flat file" structures that are considerably simpler than the structures which are describable in more sophisticated hierarchic data management structures. Departments and the data processing staff agree that the simplicity of the system is attractive and that it offers sufficient function to using departments.

The description of the nodes so far suggests a collection of independent and completely autonomous units and a strong bias toward bottom-up design. However, there is an overriding systems concept which links the departmental nodes. This systems concept is suggested by the presence of the interconnecting ring and the control processor.

3. THE CONCEPT OF THE SYSTEM

The ring which interconnects the departmental nodes is a high speed serial device which has two important properties. One is that data that passes on the ring can bypass an inoperative node. For example, a message sent from the marketing processor to the accounts processor will reach its destination even if the intervening inventory processor is inoperative. Such a ring is called a T ring, suggesting that data flows by a node without the intervention of forwarding activity on the part of a node. The second important characteristic of the ring is that it is a serial device. Data flows on a time multiplexed basis from node to node. Thus if the marketing processor sent a message at Time 0 it would reach the inventory processor at Time 1. At Time 1 it would not be available to the accounting processor. Thus the essential structure of the system is that of a pipeline with a single, timed flow of information in one direction.

In this detail a ring differs from a bus. When data is put on a bus by one system it is effectively instantaneously available to all systems which can talk to that bus. The structures which most naturally emerge from a bus are concurrent synchronized structures. The differences may be reflected in the programming stylistics of an application or an operating system. The essential difference is whether or not a program can rely on the occurrence of a previous event in the system. Because data flows serially from node to node in a pipeline fashion in the ring structure there is the concept of a left and a right neighbor. A node can anticipate what its neighbors are doing and in the simplest design neighbors only talk to their rightmost neighbor and listen to their leftmost neighbor. This kind of logical pipeline can be simulated by buffering and queue logic even if a bus interconnection is used.

Pipeline logic is often used within the design of a single large uniprocessor. The execution of an instruction may be decomposed into various stages. An instruction preparation stage, an instruction decode stage and multiple execution stages may be defined. A special purpose instruction fetcher gets all instructions from memory. While this is being done the decoder decodes a previous instruction; while this is being done an executor can be performing various functions on a more previous instruction. Thus all units work in parallel on different instructions at different stages and then pass an instruction to a next stage. Figure 19 illustrates this concept.

A concurrent parallel structure is illustrated in Figure 20. Here an instruction fetch unit passes an instruction onto one of a set of specialized execution units. The units work in parallel on all stages of a completely different instruction.

The pipeline concept applies equally well to units of work other than instructions. One can conceive of a transaction which occurred at a store and which has been transmitted onto the ring through the gateway. This transaction will flow, let us say, to the marketing processor. The marketing processor will ac-

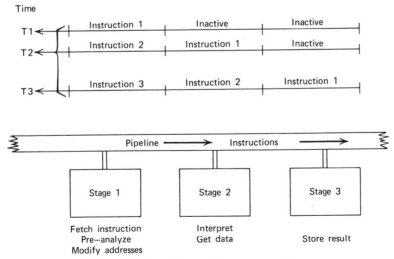

Figure 19.   Pipeline concept in processor design.

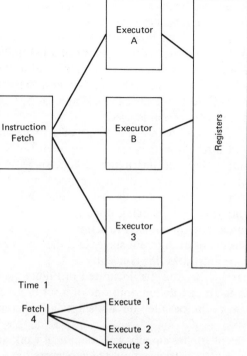

Figure 20.   Simple parallel structure.

cept it and process it according to its local needs. It will then create an addendum to the transaction which indicates it has processed the transaction. This
addendum may be forwarded to the inventory processor with the original
transaction. When it arrives the inventory processor will know that the marketing processor is operational and that it has accepted this transaction. The inventory processor will, in turn, process the transaction, add an addendum and
forward it to the accounting processor. The accounting processor knows its two
left partners have processed the transaction and it may now undertake to process it. In this way a transaction which affects all departments may flow on the
ring from department to department. When the transaction has visited all
nodes then all of the departments are in agreement about the status of the
company-wide effect of this transaction. The system, although departmentally
partitioned, operates to give the same effect as an integrated hierarchic database system.

In order to accomplish this systems level interrelationship between the nodes
it is necessary to have software which receives messages and transmits messages. It is also necessary for application development to be aware of the need
to analyze messages from a leftmost processor and create and forward addenda
and transactions to a rightmost processor. In order to accomplish this a set of

systems conventions and standards must be established not only at the link level but in application logic. The intrusion into application logic is necessary because an addendum may represent application oriented information. A processor may tell its neighbor more than "I am alive and I have seen this message." It may tell it that it found the transaction invalid and unacceptable and is sending a veto message out to the gateway for transmission to the store.

The system needs one additional feature to be a system. It requires logic which determines which nodes must react to a particular transaction and logic to provide for reactions for inoperative nodes. In addition the system must provide for rejection of a transaction by rightmost nodes to cause leftmost nodes to back out of the transaction.

It is possible to put such logic at all departmental nodes to form a truly distributed control system. This design, however, felt that it would burden those nodes to contain such logic and consequently created the control processor node to impose a coordinated system image across the nodes. It is largely the responsibility of the control node to synchronize the departmental nodes and route multinode transactions to interested nodes on the ring. It is the presence of the control processor which gives the system its management information level characteristics.

4. DATA FLOW CHARACTERISTICS

In the above section we used the word transaction to describe the passage of a record which represented an event at a store to all interested departments. Since the sale of an item at a store will change the data for the inventory, marketing and accounting nodes it is necessary that this transaction be reported to all nodes.

There may be, however, some transactions which do not need processing by all nodes. There may be transmissions from one departmental node to stores which do not need processing by other departmental nodes. The transmission of price data from the marketing node is an example of this.

The control processor determines proper routing for any received message. A processing node receiving a message from a leftmost node can inspect the routing codes established by the control processor and determine if the message requires processing by itself. It can also determine if the message has received processing by a leftmost processor whose attention is required.

When a message passes the rightmost processor it may be in a complete or an incomplete state. If it is in a complete state, then every processor that is required to accept this message and confirm its validity will have recorded its acceptance. The control processor will receive the addenda placed by all processors. It will inspect for complete state. At this time it may destroy the history of that transaction or it may confirm the transaction as part of what is called a two-stage commit.

When a node receives a transaction it makes a tentative update to its files. For some interval of time it retains enough information so that it can restore the original value of records if the transaction is later discovered to be invalid. A commit point is a point at which a node loses its ability to restore itself and commits itself to a transaction. When the control processor determines a transaction has reached a complete state it issues a commit message to the ring with a transaction identifier and the routing. On receipt of the commit message the nodes delete recovery information.

If a transaction reaches the control processor in an incomplete state it is because not all processors are operational or because some processors have rejected the transaction. In either case the control processor must inform nodes which have posted the transaction to back away from it and restore their initial conditions. It does this by issuing a routed recovery or restoration message.

Notice that the logic of node to node data flow is independent of whether data from store nodes is transmitted in a batched or transaction by transaction basis. However, the interface between the central system and the store nodes is necessarily sensitive to this. The control point acts as a staging area for batched transmission from the store nodes. A transaction file is streamed to the control point through the gateway and then distributed on a message basis to the departmental nodes. Massive transmission from a node to a store is managed by the control node to the extent that a sending departmental node must inform the control processor it wishes to do a transmission of a file. The control processor then informs the departmental node whether it can undertake such transmission. When it receives permission data flows on the ring from the processor to the gateway. Such batched transmission is done at specified times so as not to interfere with departmental node support of its local terminals or message flow between nodes.

The full data flow between the central system and the stores involves:

1. Some transactions which are batched at the store and transmitted in batches to the central system for distribution to interested processors.
2. Some summary data prepared on behalf of particular departmental nodes which is transmitted in batch.
3. Some pricing and inventory information sent batched to the stores from a particular departmental processor.
4. Some transactions which are immediately transmitted from the store because they require confirmation or additional analysis and information available at a departmental processor or a set of departmental processors.

The specifics of the business will determine what transactions are immediately reported and what transactions are batched. The system has the potential capability of keeping the departmental nodes up to the minute if each transaction is immediately reported. The realization of this capability depends upon the performance capacity of the processing nodes and the interconnecting ring.

5. DISCUSSION OF THE SYSTEM

The system is interesting for a number of reasons. From a design viewpoint it violates a basic ground rule which is widely accepted by most designers. This rule is that multinode processing should be discouraged. In investigating an application for implementation on a distributed basis many designers feel that high "local hit ratios" are a requirement. If more than 10% (some say 5%) of transactions cannot be handled by the local node, then the system is not safely distributable. The hierarchic system previously described also violated this rule but the small processors were not primary processing nodes. Here every action must potentially visit all nodes. The performance of the system is very vulnerable to this and coordination and recovery problems can be severe. In the presence of internode dependency of the type illustrated by this design, system availability may well decrease.

In order for this system to be a success the reliability and performance of the ring must be very good. The 10% rule may be violated because of the characteristics of the ring and the short distances between the nodes. It would be a greater risk to design such a system across long distance communications lines. It would not be clear what economic advantages would motivate the structure of this system across long distance interconnections. The pipeline characteristics would cause considerable delay and impose serious additional store and forward function on the departmental nodes. The excellent performance and reliability of the ring, however, does not decrease systems vulnerability due to node processing interdependencies.

The central concept at the heart of the design is an inexpensive, reliable, fast ring which can reach the distances between departments. Such rings or buses which can be used as rings seem likely to be available in reasonable time. There is talk of 40 megabit multikilometer mechanisms of very low cost. At the present time there is limited availability of such equipment. Anywhere near similar speeds for long distance interconnection seems further away. The difficulty is that the promising technologies, particularly communication satellites, impose a long entry time and seem more suitable for bulk data transmission than for transaction based, interactive sessions.

The other interesting aspect of the system is that its most important partitioning occurs at the management level. It is common to see partitioning of function in hierarchic systems between operational and management environments. Since operational functions can be split from management functions and operational points isolated from each other, such partitioning is natural. The management function tends to be viewed as more natural for a large single processor than for a set of aggregated processors. The reasons for this are:

1. Management functions tend to be more throughput oriented and more complex and require large processors for effective performance.
2. Managing the corporation naturally seems to involve a high level of administration of company level data bases. Departments may interact

and share data; data is an important resource which deserves specialized management.

3. Applications development is considerably improved by the support of very sophisticated database managers which provide data independent application implementation. Large systems are required to support these data managers. This may be particularly important if changes in methods, procedures and business style suggest constant functional modifications.

These reasons suggest the adventurousness of this approach. The approach is defended, by advocates of this kind of design, for the following reasons.

In situations where the full function of a very sophisticated, large database manager are not required these products are expensive because they run on large machines and may need large staffs to support them. When the application environment is well partitioned and reasonably stable, and when some sufficient level of programming development support is available without a large data manager, the argument is made that it may be possible to provide many of the benefits of the database concept without a large database product. This might be particularly true, the designers of this system seem to argue, if there is an alternative less ambitious system in an interconnect environment.

The benefits of corporate-wide coordinated data may be achieved without a central data management function actually doing data design. Function management, given reasonable support, can define their own data structures in ways convenient to them without compromising corporate data management concepts. In addition, departments should be able to determine the rate and pattern of application development in their own areas. Using local database management can provide enough support for departmental application programming. The environment of this system is an interesting mixture of top-down and bottom-up. It is top-down in its systems aspects but bottom-up in its application aspects with the constraints mentioned before.

The conceivers of such a system would argue that while it is useful and necessary to coordinate the data of related departments it is not necessary to do this on a single processor. They suggest that it is an obsolete notion that the goals of an integrated data collection implies a single site for data. When very fast interconnections are available a new set of systems structures can deliver the effect of one system across multiple systems. The argument is made that advances in interconnect methodology and technology lead to a rethinking of database assumptions. These assumptions have always been based on the idea that it is more efficient for a fast processor to talk to a data collection multiple times than it is for processors to talk to each other.

This concept, it might be mentioned in passing, need not be limited to environments where small systems intercommunicate. There are scenarios in which large systems, running large data base managers, also require cross-system data manager communication to service user needs. We may reasonably expect vendors to provide multisystem communications between large database managers in the reasonably near future. Some announcements of this type have already been made for some large database products.

Finally, a point is made about the efficiency of large versus small machines. Given that small systems of adequate capacity are available, and given the current pricing structure of the industry, it is no longer clear that one large system is more price effective than a set of small systems. This suggests that large systems may be built from aggregates of small systems.

This discussion throws a good deal of light on an interesting aspect of distributed systems design. That is that it is highly motivated by judgmental and philosophical considerations as well as by perceptions of technology and economics.

There is a fascinating interplay of management and technological issues surrounding this sytem. The management issues address the relationship between operational departments and a data processing organization, particularly as regards who should be responsible for justifying, controlling and undertaking applications development. The view is that a proper design requires a system definition activity which is highly professional. This activity defines the systems basis for computer power and guarantees that the collection of computers will actually be a system. Entrepreneurial interests are seen to be best served when each department has control over its own application of data processing equipment. Undesirable responsibilities for data processing service are maintained by the professional staff.

From a technological point of view the major premises are that simpler software elements may provide enough support for effective business unit programming, that it is economically reasonable to use collections of small machines which deny economy of scale, that the existence of powerful and reliable interconnect structures will fundamentally change the way systems may be designed.

Chapter 5

An Assessment

1. PRELIMINARY REMARKS

The general notion of a distributed system is that various elements of a data processing system can be partitioned into well defined units that may be located at various logical dates and linked by agreed upon protocols. The examples we have seen of systems which meet that characterization have as many points of dissimilarity as similarity and reflect a diversity of system solutions to system problems. Distributed systems take different views of the distributable system components, of the essential shape of the system and of the geographical proximity of the nodes. Various choices are made concerning placement of data and programs, and the form and location of systems control.

The diversity of system details suggests that distributed processing systems are not a new class of system. Definitions fail to distinguish precisely among different levels of cooperation, interaction and extent of appearance as a single system (single systems image). There are too many variations of too subtle a nature to achieve a comprehensive definition.

Figure 21 suggests an aspect of distribution as a feature of all systems, wherein each circle represents a layer of system function. The inner layer is that of hardware and represents a physical processing node. This layer supports a layer of software that is the fundamental operating system, which is often characterized as the kernel and is made part of a single structural element of programming. Above the layer of the kernel is a set of extended services that an operating system undertakes in support of a program running in its environment. Such services might be to acquire and release memory space, get and place records in files, and so on. Above this layer, the figure shows a "monitor" which is a layer of a software structure, such as a database manager. Above the database manager there is an application layer.

Figure 21 suggests that a system is a number of software layers resting on a hardware layer. Each software layer depends upon a lower software layer for the delivery of certain services and cedes certain aspects of control to a lower layer. The figure is an attempt to unify some thinking about distributed systems. One can think of various kinds of systems as a result of configuration and

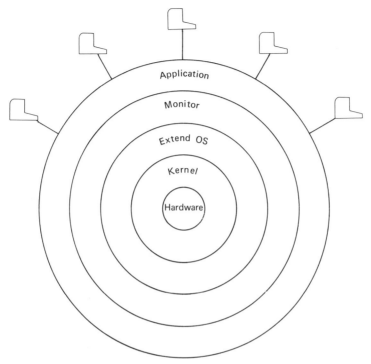

Figure 21. System layers.

sharing decisions applied to the layers. Figure 21 suggests a dedicated application system. Any transaction entering the system from any terminal talks to the same application, sharing application code and application logic.

In Figure 22a, lines have been drawn through the application layer suggesting that more than one application is sharing this node. A terminal population may talk to different applications that share no application code.

The multiple applications of Figure 22a suggest a uniprocessor that has been multiprogrammed to support independent applications. It is possible that the uniprocessor is a multiprocessor that is running under the control of the same operating system and appears to all applications to be a uniprocessor because of the image presented by the monitor and operating system levels. This system suggests a lower level of sharing in that a specific application partitioning has been undertaken.

Figure 22b shows a line extended through the monitor level, suggesting that terminals have access to different monitor level software as well as to different applications. The system of Figure 22b has multiple subsystems that share an underlying operating system. Each subsystem presents a unique interface and a unique set of services to an upper layer of application and an upper layer of terminal users.

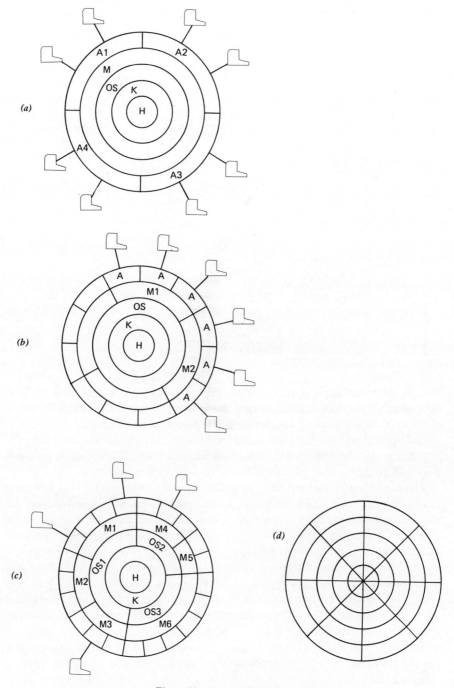

Figure 22.   Partitioning levels.

Figure 22c shows an extension of the partitioning line through the extended operating system layer, which suggests virtual machines. Not only do application programs interface with unique subsystem layers, but also the subsystem layers interface with a set of unique extended operating systems. The monitor levels might be a database manager, a time sharing monitor or a transaction manager/file manager. The extended operating systems might be any standard operating system; the underlying kernel would be a virtual machine operating system. In actual implementations, the virtual machine level is not a well defined base for an operating system, but a complete operating system upon which other systems may reside. In Figure 22c a decision has been made to partition work so that multiple operating systems can be run on the same hardware.

Figure 22d shows a final level of partitioning. The partitioning line extends through the hardware circle and gives a family of dedicated nodes. The decision has been made to dedicate hardware to an operating system kernel.

The circle is complete, having started with an application dedicated system followed by a series of partitioning decisions through multiple applications, multiple monitors and multiple operating systems to a family of dedicated hardware nodes. The sequence of Figure 22 shows a relationship among systems of various types along a continuum of sharing and partitioning choices. It implies that it might be possible, in the future, to configure large systems that are software partitioned and systems which are hardware partitioned at various levels in a manner not too unlike the way we currently choose the number of channels or storage devices we want for a configuration. In future systems, it might also be possible to move a set of applications from systems of the type shown in Figure 22b to those like Figure 22d with ease, or at least with acceptable levels of effort.

A great deal of software and hardware packaging thought must be undertaken before Figure 22 is a real picture. However, the view of distributed processing as a point in a set of alternative configurations is useful as an aid to understanding the relationships among distribution, virtual machines, multi-subsystem nodes and multiprogrammed nodes.

There is no conceptual limit to the process of partitioning. Starting with any of the slices of Figure 22d more partitions can be undertaken so that each slice decomposes into a number of smaller slices, and so on. The real limit to the process is the available hardware, interconnection mechanisms and understanding of the way application and system software structures can be layered and decomposed.

2. THE NATURE OF THE DISTRIBUTION PROCESS

Distribution as discussed in this section has strong top-down overtones. Although much applies to interconnecting autonomous systems, the major thrust is toward concepts and activities used to design an application across multiple nodes, where the single system image is high.

Distribution is a result of a system design process in which it is necessary to:

- Define partitions of work. Systems and application activities should be discovered that cluster together into well defined, separate units of program.

- Define partitions of data. One should seek to discover natural segments or extractions, and determine where these partitions are used, where they are changed and to whom they must be made available. One should also determine what access paths to data must be defined, where partitioning is useful, where replication is useful, and identify synchronization requirements.

- Identify relationships between data and work. This is truly a reflection of the need to define work and data partitions somewhat iteratively and jointly. Data reference patterns are part of recognizing separable programs. Program reference patterns are part of recognizing separable data.

- Recognize relationships among partitions. Determine the degrees of autonomy among programs and the intensity of their interaction and interdependency. This will partially indicate how geographically distant the partitions may be. In addition, the method of interaction must be defined. This involves determination of whether the partitions will be synchronous or asynchronous, talk to each other on a message basis or on a batched queue basis.

- Determine a set of possible work structures. Given degrees of freedom for the previous determinations, the work structure variations are expected to differ in the specific clusters, execution speeds, access times, and interaction characteristics at a program level.

- Define a set of potential hardware bases. For the possible logical work structures, a choice must be made between large systems surrounded by trivial work stations, large virtual networks, geographically distributed small systems, multiprocessers, and so on.

- Choose hardware. This choice requires estimates of the ability of the nodes to meet capacity requirements for each partition, and the ability of the system to meet interaction requirements across interconnect facilities. Also required is the ability to meet reliability goals. Software available with hardware must be sufficient to minimize the risk and cost of applications development. The hardware and software must be available in reasonable time from a reliable source or set of sources. Finally, there must be an acceptable cost balance involving cost tradeoffs with respect to processor/memory, storage, device population, communications, operations, programming, installation, maintenance and end user convenience.

If the above sequence of activities seems to suggest that undertaking a definition of a distributed system may not be less work than undertaking the design of a centralized system, the point is well taken. The design of multinode systems is not simpler than the design of complex single node systems. Certain aspects of systems use may certainly be better with a distributed system, and certain kinds of complexity may well disappear. But the image of simple distributed systems as an antidote for the complexity of large single node systems cannot be expected to hold up in general. As we discuss further in this paper, it is not usually clear under exactly what circumstances the design and operation of distributed systems is simpler, more stable and more attractive than centralized alternatives. This is an arena of equally astonishing counterexample.

3. MOTIVES FOR DISTRIBUTION

This section will discuss some reasons commonly given as motivations for distribution. Each motivation is discussed from the point of view of whether the goal desired is a natural attribute of any distributed system or whether it can be achieved only in certain design contexts.

3.1. Maintain Advantages of Centralized Management

Centralized management is cited first to emphasize the distinction between distribution and decentralization. The position taken by many enterprises is that they wish to maintain an enterprise level of control over the development and operation of data processing applications and equipment. Although computing power is becoming rapidly less expensive and, in some versions, need no longer be thought of as a capital investment subject to classical return on investment justification, it is still true that a company benefits from enterprise-wide direction and planning.

There are situations in which it is not necessary to apply enterprise-level direction and standards. Computing devices that affect only the work of a small unit of the business, that require no professional systems support, that involve no expensive programming effort or operational staff, that operate as a departmental tool may be allowed with a minimum of higher level control. It is important, however, to define the situation in which the installation of such equipment is permitted in order to avoid unforeseen complications. Even where independent installation of computing equipment is feasible, it is useful to provide some central technological guidance as to qualified vendors, contract negotiation and application feasibility. The intent is not to discourage or constrain the installation of equipment but to ensure that the degree of the autonomy of the unit is well specified, and to limit the risk of failure.

Centralized services may assume various forms. These services range from a computer in the data processing department (in support of remote operation, maintenance and software service) to on-site personnel employed by the data processing department rather than the using organization. Once again the intent is not to limit or constrain the use of local computer units but to provide various services that ease the burden on the using business unit or location.

The maintenance of a centralized systems management function is essential when the distributed computer structure supports cross-departmental functions that are planned as a single system although they are applied to multiple computer nodes. In this situation there is need for professional systems planning and high levels of systems assurance.

The desire to maintain centralized management even for dispersed computer nodes is based upon three underlying needs: better control, personnel and avoiding the costs of incoherence.

Better control implies a site for the generation of standards for programming, equipment, operation and interconnection. The function is to set a policy to ensure the orderly acquisition and use of computing and avoid bad surprises in vendor selection, equipment quality and availability, programming difficulty, and so on. The actual amount of decision making power possessed by a central policy and competence organization may vary widely from that of adviser to that of enforcer, depending upon the particular style of policy enforcement.

As for personnel, a data processing staff provides the ability to attract good professional data processing management and operational skills. No matter how hardware is dispersed and interconnected, a minimum set of skills is required to define and ensure systems and to avoid expensive mistakes. In order to maintain these skills, there must be a company-wide career path. Technology change and the importance of data processing equipment to the competitive and profit position of the whole enterprise suggest the continuing need for skilled computer planning and analysis.

An incoherent system is one that springs up and develops as an afterthought. Such an unplanned system may be costly. Nodes that start autonomously may grow toward each other as profitable instances of intercommunication are discovered. A framework must be provided for achieving postinstallation communication at reasonable cost and effort. Otherwise, the organization that has allowed uncontrolled growth of computer nodes may find major problems in causing these nodes to communicate with one another.

3.2.   Association of On-Line Operations with Small Systems

In the early 1970s, on-line systems were sometimes associated with small systems. Figure 23 presents some background for this association. It depicts a large-system problem at a time of transition when interest in on-line systems was becoming widespread.

Consider first a large system of 1968 as represented by point A on Figure 23. This system had an associated price/performance ratio determined by its hardware architecture and the software that it supported. The Y axis of Figure 23 shows some notion of price per transaction for on-line use of this large system. The achievement of a particular price/performance ratio was determined in

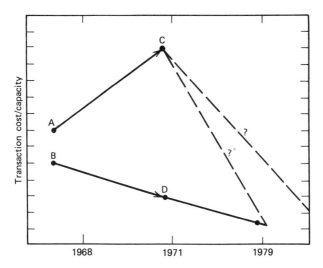

Figure 23.   On-line and small systems.

part by the interrupt structure of the hardware and by the software structure of the operating system and data manager system. The structure of both hardware and software was heavily influenced by its orientation toward a batch environment. On-line use of large systems was just beginning to receive serious attention in the late sixties, and very few hardware or software designs were oriented toward on-line commercial use.

At the same time, as represented by point B on Figure 23, there already existed a class of small machines of important computational power and attractive prices. These small machines were frequently generalizations of architectures aimed at good performance in process control applications. They had interrupt structures that were characteristically more sophisticated than large batch commercial processors and they had other architectural features that suggested good performance in on-line environments similar in requirement to process control. At one time in their early history, however, they lacked mature or complete operating and programming development systems.

Figure 23 represents, at point C, the evolution of a late 1960s large system to an early 1970s large system. The astonishing slope of the line suggests that the price/performance ratio of the 1970s large system, in terms of cost per transaction, was seen in some cases to have degraded when compared to the 1968 system. This degradation occurred in selected software environments despite an increase in raw system capacity and a general lowering of prices across components of the system. The phenomenon may be explained by the fact that the functional richness of new software placed a disproportionately heavy load on the system in an on-line transaction processing situation. The batchlike hardware and software architectural features remained in place and new software function reduced the ability of the system to process transactions at an acceptable rate. Very large systems had very disappointing rates in transactions per second when running standard operating systems and data managers. There was an unacceptable burden of systems software on the large system and a number of basic activities associated with terminal support that a large system did not do well.

Point D represents the maturity of small systems in the early 1970s. Small systems had continued to demonstrate very good price/performance ratios, had improved in raw capacity, and had acquired a reasonable set of software for node control and programming. The operating systems tended to be event driven in structure and to demonstrate some properties that made them attractive for on-line applications.

The effect of software burden and complexity of use of large systems in on-line environments, coupled with maturing capacity and software support for small and intermediate systems, led a number of designers to the inspection of single or interconnected small systems as possible alternatives to single node large systems.

Two basic alternatives emerged. The possibility of augmenting a configuration by adding small processors to undertake on-line application functions led to systems shaped as hierarchic trees. The possibility of building a system completely out of aggregated small processing nodes led to cooperating peer structures.

The trend toward on-line applications has had an effect on software for large systems. In the interval between the early 1970s and the present time, important results have been achieved in reducing burden on a large processor and significant improvements in large-system efficiency have been achieved.

As a result of hardware and software trends it is no longer clear whether small machines have a natural advantage over large machines for on-line operation. Setting aside considerations of reliability and availability, which will be discusssed later, large systems may now be effective in more instances than a decade ago because they have experienced impressive capacity increases in the mid-1970s as a result of technology and software improvements.

One very important aspect when considering large versus small systems, or a large system versus a small system aggregate, is the nature of the load to be placed on small systems. Small processors of a given capacity may be very effective for simple transactions that require low levels of computational service and have simple data reference patterns. Thus sets of simple inquiries or basic data entry activities may be very effective on small nodes. Transactions requiring massive computation or involving complex patterns of data reference may exceed the capacity of a small node or perform poorly on a small node and be better supported by a large system of greater computational power and more flexible data subsystem interconnections.

It is important, of course, to understand that the concept of a small system and a large system is a very relative concept. Technological advance is increasing the capacity of small systems very rapidly and improving their ability to support uses previously reasonable only on large systems.

3.3. Communications Costs

A frequently stated motivation for distributed processing is the desire to reduce the cost of a set of unintelligent terminals communicating at geographically significant distances with a data center.

Although it is possible to achieve a reduction in communications cost, it is by no means clear under what circumstances this reduction will occur. Communications costs may be a function of the specific offerings of communications carriers, sensitivity or insensitivity to geographical distances between points of data or query entry and data manipulation, required speeds, applied loads, complexities of network definition, and so on. Experience has shown that distribution of data processing capability has caused communications costs to rise or fall, depending on many factors related to each particular system. Instances where these costs rise are by no means failures if other costs are reduced or if some value is added to offset the rise in communications costs.

Typically a system in which communications costs are lowered is one that has intelligent terminal processors at a using location. Traffic on communications lines is reduced because the local processor reduces the volume of traffic to the data center. It does this by sending summary data rather than raw transactions, by eliminating the need for reference to the data center for a class of transactions or by batching and timing transmissions to take advantage of special features of certain tariffs or economies of scale in transmission bandwidths being offered. If a set of processing nodes is geographically dispersed to sites where there was no previous computational power and if high speed, point to point interaction between nodes is required, it is clear that communication costs may rise.

3.4. Reliability and Failsoft

The view that distributed processing can provide greater reliability or availability is based upon the economics of replication and the granularity of configurability that interconnected smaller systems may provide. The duplexing or triplexing of small processors into multiple processor logical nodes is quite common. The practice is attractive because small processor/memory units are inexpensive and additional units give disproportionate reliability increments while adding modestly to the total system cost. Thus various partitioning and replication designs can provide scope of error containment, equivalent performance back-up and failsoft levels when multiple machines are used. The same approach is not equally well applied to large processing nodes because of the larger prices and the incremental jump in total system cost when a large unit is replicated in a system.

This approach, however, is constrained by a number of considerations. The processing/memory units are the most reliable components of a data processing system, and it is not clear, in general, how replication of the most reliable units addresses system wide issues of reliability. The replication of data storage devices is limited by their relative costliness, in terms of cost per byte stored, when compared to larger units and by the logic of an application. The replication of storage units implies design conventions about how data are to be spread across units, transferred, synchronized and accessed. Problems of data integrity emerge in systems that can be partially operational which do not occur in systems that are either up or down. Increased reliability comes not from the replication per se of hardware units but from systems designs that provide quick recovery while guaranteeing integrity.

If failsoft levels and scope of error containment points can be defined, it is probably cheaper to replicate critical points than to replicate larger, more monolithic systems. It is important, however, that the replication be selective. If it is necessary to replicate the entire system of collected small nodes to achieve a desired reliability, it is not clear that the replication of a single large node may not be equally effective.

The operability of the system is the joint probability of the operability of all nodes. The probability that some part of a system will be down is very high. On the other hand, the probability of all nodes being down is equally small. Thus if a system depends upon all nodes being up, it is not a reliable system. If proper back-up and failsoft levels can be defined so that the system is meaningfully operational with inoperative nodes, a reliable system may be designed from collections of smaller units. In the end, reliability expectation is an expression of the definition of failsoft and back-up levels.

In order to achieve better availability for an application by removing it from a system where it coexists with other applications it is necessary to determine that a significant number of application outages are caused by hardware or software malfunctions which are caused by other applications or by system software which provides resource sharing. If a small number of outages are a result of hardware or software failures related to a particular application, the availability of that application may well be increased by isolating it in hardware/software units which are not serving other applications.

3.5. Better User Interfaces

Better user interfaces are frequently cited as an advantage of distributed processing. The nature of such interfaces is not well understood in the data processing industry at this time. Nevertheless, there seems to be converging opinion that a good interface has some of the following characteristics:

- It provides system response times appropriate to the activity; it does not introduce a perception of instability, unpredictability or lengthiness that disturbs a user so as to make him less effective.
- The semantics of a good interface are consistent with the semantics of the work being done.
- The syntax of the interface is as natural as possible and appears intuitively obvious to a user.

- The syntax is uniform and consistent within the context of the work. Accomplishing the same function by multiple variant forms is minimized and the use of variant forms for similar functions is eliminated.

- The system allows selectable levels of aid and guidance for users of different degrees of expertise. Friendly software need not be chatty software, and experts should not be burdened with conventions for aiding trainees.

Clearly, the placing of a processing unit at a geographical site does not in itself provide good end user interfaces. It may be true, however, that good end user interfaces are more affordable in the context of some distributed designs. Elements of good user interface relating to systems response times may be achieved by the dedication of processing units to application activities so as to reduce instances of resource contention which occur on intensively shared systems.

If the load on a node is more predictable because the workload is more homogeneous and the system is simpler to analyze, responsiveness may increase. Similarly, if end user actions are completely contained within the node they may be faster than if they must be serviced by a remote node running a complex workload. The requirement for fast or consistent responsiveness cannot be met, of course, if the local system is overloaded. It is also true that small systems have tended to become unresponsive at lower workload levels than large systems. Consequently, better responsiveness is achieved at the cost of maintaining consistently lower loads on the smaller local nodes in a hierarchic system. In a peer system, stable responsiveness may imply increased partitioning across a set of nodes and very careful attention to cross-node referencing. The responsiveness of a node should not be perturbed because it is waiting for interaction with other nodes or because other nodes are inflating its local workload.

Those aspects of end user interface that are concerned with the quality of dialogue may be improved by distribution because distribution may make good dialogue more affordable. Good dialogue characteristics involve increased potential interaction with a processing node and potentially more significant displays of data and format. A user operating in tutorial mode, for example, may require many more transmissions between his terminal and a processor than an expert. Similarly the replacement of terse codes by descriptive phrases increases data flow from system to tube.

Large computationally effective processing units may have a disproportionate burden placed upon them when they do formatting and display organization. This increase in load discourages designers of interfaces from rich support of dialogue and encourages cryptic and sometimes artificially terse message formats. This tendency is enhanced by a desire to minimize data flow into and out of the system. In view of this, it is reasonable to provide for a node in the system that can effectively improve dialogue without a serious increase in load on the computational engine. Very terse and compressed messages may flow between the dialogue support node and the computationally oriented processor. The dialogue support node expands the messages into a form convenient for users, supports tutorial phases and compresses user entered syntactical structures without burdening the computational or data manipulating element of the system.

The partitioning of dialogue support function suggests both that the dialogue processor is very good at these functions and that its load is sufficiently low so as to maintain good responsiveness. It is not clear, except for some improvement in interrupt logic, that smaller processors are more efficient format and character handlers than large processors; thus very careful definition of load and activity on the dialogue processor must be undertaken. If major application logic is also resident in the dialogue support processor, response characteristics may become undesirable.

Once the dialogue support function has been isolated, a decision must yet be made about where it is to be placed relative to using terminals and the computational node. It is probably true that the dialogue support processor is best placed local to using terminals to achieve lower transmission volumes across teleprocessing lines.

Although it seems natural for screen quality and message control to be local, it is not always true that the data managers or operating systems of a vendor are able to permit such partitioning, so that some degree of duplication of function may be necessary to achieve the result.

The point is sometimes made that cost to a business unit to use data processing power is reduced with distributed processing. The argument shows confusion between the issue of distributed versus centralized processing and that of batch versus on-line processing. In discussing the advantages gained by going to a distributed system, much of the literature points out how much less expensive and how much more convenient computer use has become because of the availability of on-line terminals that replace awkward batch submission interfaces. It is clear that the increase in convenience and reduction in costs come from changing the mode of access and not from the dispersion of processing nodes. Most users agree that terminals are an effective input/output medium for computers, but whether the presence of local processing and storage contributes more than the presence of a terminal is not generally clear. The confusion comes about because many batch systems that were centralized have been replaced by some form of on-line distributed system. The virtues of going on-line are mistaken for the virtues of going distributed.

In a similar but complementary vein, distributed systems are sometimes said to be more complex than centralized systems. Frequently this point of view arises out of a movement from a batch to an on-line environment. Many aspects of design and planning for on-line use are more complex than designing and planning for batch use. The complexity is a function of being on-line, not of being distributed. The real issue is whether the relative increase in complexity by being on-line over being batch is less or greater when one goes on-line with a centralized or a distributed system.

3.6. Security and Privacy

The use of separate hardware nodes is justified by a desire for increased security of data and for increased privacy. This is also an area of astonishing counterexample and differing judgments for a number of reasons.

Many users of large systems are disturbed by the fact that they have no control over access to their data. Because of various back-up and archiving procedures used at a data center and because of data center operational prerogatives, it is virtually impossible for a user to control access to his files.

Similarly, there are varying degrees of confidence in both the center and software procedures for ensuring against intrusion by other users. Although the subversion of software structures is not a general skill, it causes concern in many places, particularly where sensitive information is involved. The concern is sufficiently great that the government agencies, vendors and universities are undertaking studies to determine exactly what the structural and functional characteristics of a secure software system really are.

With this as a background the idea of private data on physically inaccessible data media in rooms where access can be controlled by the owning business unit or mission unit becomes very attractive. Whether increased security and privacy are achieved by using central professional security staffs or by using private safes is largely a judgmental issue. But the increase of these characteristics in a centralized or distributed system must follow the same lines of argument.

An important aspect of the discussion is the source of potential violation. If there is reason to suspect that the source of violation lies in persons or agencies unknown, one may prefer privately imposed security. If there is reason to suspect that the source of violations is from within the mission or department, there is reason to prefer professional security at a central place.

Professional security at a central place occurs in the form of large software packages that impose security within a well disciplined set of staff members following well planned security procedures. Private security must rely more on physical control of media and access, since smaller systems may not be able to sustain the software loads of high level access control software packages.

Another dimension to this issue is that distributed systems are distinct from stand alone systems and by their nature imply some amount of physical access from one node to the data of another. A secure system must provide software that protects against remote violations of privacy. It is not absolutely clear just what software designs will ensure privacy and security in multinode systems and be less subject to subversion than software in large systems. The problem is compounded, of course, in systems consisting of heterogeneous nodes.

3.7. Economics of Dedication

The fundamental assumption of the idea that it is better to distribute activity across a family of processing nodes is that economy of scale in systems pricing is no longer an important aspect of the computer marketplace. Small processing units may display price/performance ratios equal to or even better than those of large scale processors. To illuminate the issues surrounding this point, consider an example involving a review of current prices for different processor classes and a division of these numbers by a rated processor speed. (Very strong arguments against this kind of exercise can be mustered, but it does provide some instructive results.)

The total hardware cost of a system is determined less and less by the price of processors and more and more by communications, storage and peripheral equipment. Therefore, despite the loss of economy of scale across processors, a collection of small systems with power equivalent to a large system may cost more in hardware than the large system with more price effective random storage units. In addition, there is evidence from queueing theory in support of the idea that a single system of a given power can deliver more service than a system composed of a set of smaller units of equivalent nominal power. Even considering our confidence in queueing theory, it is, nonetheless, by no means clear how much more power is required for small systems to match a large system, nor under what exact conditions of workload and software load characteristics the superiority of the large single system obtains.

In any event, the economic feasibility, if not the preferability, of building large systems from interconnected processing nodes is a reality. There seems to be a potential economics of dedication that is replacing the economics of sharing based upon economy of scale. Thus it is at least doubtful whether a consolidated workload machine that attempts to support a large number of unrelated and disparate users is in general a more efficient instrument than a machine dedicated to the work of each using business unit or location.

There are degrees in the notions of dedication. Some distributed architectures built from single board computers dedicate very specific and small units of work to each processor to form a system of highly specialized activity nodes. Such designs may be found in aircraft or submarine monitoring systems. At the other extreme, the entire set of applications relevant to an entire department or business unit may be put on a single system node. The departmental application set may contain a number of unrelated applications sharing the machine on a multiprogrammed or time-shared basis. Between these extremes there are many points on a continuum of sharing of equipment between units of work.

There are a number of factors that determine the perfection of the activity equipment mapping. One is the extent to which units of work are decomposable and isolatable. Work units that tend to access the same data or talk to each other intensively should be left on the same system. Another factor is the availability of various kinds of interconnection. It may be possible, for example, to decompose work into thirty-four areas of major activity and dedicate a processing unit to each area. It may not, however, be possible to achieve an interconnection between them that displays desirable characteristics of speed and performance. Another detail is that traces of economy of scale may remain, in that very small versions of an architecture may be less attractively priced than somewhat larger versions. Although price/performance ratio advantages may, for practical purposes, disappear in comparing machines from the middle performance range to the upper performance range, it is possible to rediscover them in comparing machines at the low performance range to those tending toward the middle.

The rapid performance improvements in the middle range processors have shifted the balance somewhat toward the use of multifunction rather than single function small systems. Nevertheless, the heterogeneity of work and extensiveness of sharing across a population of such systems is certainly less than with a large single processing node.

Associated with the idea that collections of small systems may be economically feasible is the idea that they may be less expensive to operate. A number of very important systems expenses are associated with trying to share a large machine at significant levels of utilization. There is a constant tuning and performance effort to achieve acceptable response times and maintain required utilization levels. This contrasts with populations of small machines that can be run at lower utilization levels and provide good performance at much lower systems tuning costs.

There is an argument that money invested in performance tuning might be better spent on more hardware. Here we immediately run into a problem with the idea that, in general, families of small machines generate fewer operational expenses than a single large consolidated workload system. Depending upon the software interface characteristics of a system, the cost to operate and adjust tends to vary. Thus a number of geographically distributed units may require local systems programmer or operator staffs at each site. Although the effort of tuning and adjustment may go down at each site, the total cost may go up. The total cost of operating the equipment becomes the sum for all sites and may exceed the cost of operators on a large system at a single center. The additional dimension here is that different systems generate different operational and software support expenses.

There is widespread interest among vendors of computing products in reducing the operational costs of remote processing nodes. This reduction is brought about by providing a facility whereby certain operational activities can be provided from a processing node in one place. Thus a collection of remote nodes can be serviced by a single operator. Similarly, mechanisms for remote software support and remote performance analysis are beginning to receive attention. It may be some time, however, before heterogeneous systems can profit from remote operator support.

An alternative approach to reducing operator expenses in geographically remote systems is to improve the operational interfaces presented by those systems. Thus, instead of remote operator services there would be programmed operator services whereby each node would sufficiently automate its operational interfaces that only a very reduced operational staff of very reduced skill levels would be locally required.

In general, from both an equipment and operational point of view, it is no longer absurd to consider various levels of dedication that would have been prima facie infeasible in an industry with the pricing structure of the 1960s.

3.8. Incremental Growth and Flexibility

Since distributed processing systems contain a number of nodes, it should be easy to achieve growth by adding additional nodes to the system as load increases or as new function is added. So goes an argument that finds support in the hardware base for distributed systems. The major hardware limitation seems to lie in the limits of interconnect mechanisms. Although incremental node addition allows an orderly increase in power with small granules of system cost, it is not clear that this can be achieved across all interconnect designs. A single bus interconnect design is limited by the load it can carry. Considerable reanalysis of load patterns and cross-node loads may be necessary to successfully repartition work. Another limitation in some connection schemes is the capacity of the system to add more members because of physical constraints. In general, it is preferred to have an idea of how the system is expected to grow in order to ensure that growth steps are nondisruptive.

A further aspect of modular growth is the rate at which the total cost of the system will increase as a result of adding an additional node. Ideally the cost increase will be linear, each new node adding a fixed incremental cost to the system. Not all interconnect designs provide linear cost increments, or provide them only within a narrow growth range.

The addition of more nodes to support new independent applications may be a simpler task than adding new nodes to support increased load or increased function within a single application. Unless care is taken in structuring program modules and attention paid to defining the mechanisms that repartition data, the hardware potential for growth may be denied because of expenses associated with software and data restructuring.

3.9. Capacity Limitation

Closely connected with the idea of incremental growth is the idea of overcoming the capacity limitations of a system by putting new functions on additional nodes. The classic scenario lies in the idea of extending the life of a central large system by offloading function onto associated peripheral processing nodes. In general this is probably a workable notion. It is not clear, however, exactly how effective an offloading strategy may be. The support of a set of small nodes may create a new kind of load for the large system. Many installation managers believe that distributed systems should be controlled from a single point. Software and operator functions to establish systems control, recovery and remote operation, and to permit remote program development and testing, also add to the load at the central site. Whether this load trivially, importantly or unacceptably counterbalances the offloaded activities is an assessment that must be made for each system. It depends in part on the activity that can be moved out into the smaller nodes and the degrees of control and central function that are vested in the large system.

3.10. Increased Installation Simplicity

The idea that distributed systems allow applications to be developed and made operational more quickly is often heard expressed, but it is flawed for a number of reasons. It is essentially a carryover from an image of the use of stand alone autonomous processors surrounded by business unit programming staff. An image of quick installability of applications accrues to small systems because no negotiations with a large data processing organization are necessary to get programming staff and computer resource, because the systems are easy to use and because the applications are often small.

It is not demonstrable that the planning and design of multinode systems represents more or less effort than the planning and design of single large systems, and it is not clear that the stylistics of the autonomous use of small business systems applies to the definition and implementation of distributed processing.

It is not yet known to what degree the aspects of simplicity which associate with small machines will associate with distributed systems.

3.11. More Stable Software Environment

The idea that operating systems and subsystems environments are more stable for small systems than for large systems is founded on the current methods of announcing evolutionary software offerings in the marketplace. Large-systems vendors have tended to announce software products on an evolutionary cycle, making improvements and enhancements from version to version. Thus a user of a large system who depends on an operating system and a collection of access methods and subsystems experiences a constant churning. Each major software component has an independent version release cycle that keeps an installation in perturbation to stay in the mainstream.

By contrast, software for small systems has tended to be offered on a purchase basis at different levels of function and to remain stable through the lifetime of the hardware it supports. There may be multiple software systems offered for a single hardware system, but each system tends not to be modified during its lifetime.

While this has been the historical perception a clear picture has yet to emerge about the preferability of the two approaches. There seems to be a trend toward new features of large software packages announced as optional purchase units for the more stable underlying program. (An example is the MVS operating system and its optional features.) It may be preferable for some users to pace an evolutionary cycle rather than commit to stable software environments that must be radically revised or replaced at certain intervals of time. If the large-systems software evolution can be made to be somewhat less disruptive, draw off less resource for installation and intervene less in application development cycles, the perception of churning can be ameliorated. Large-system software suppliers seem to be sensitive to the need for less installation effort and more mature software systems. It seems today that many of the stylistics of large-system software marketing that have been previously unattractive are being addressed.

3.12. Fit System to Organization

The granular structure of distributed systems suggests the possibility of mapping the system onto the organizational structure. Regardless of the amount of control exercised over each node, the structure of computing fits the structure of the company. Two caveats apply. Company organizations are not always stable, and organizational reforms must not be hampered by computer structures. Although there are many businesses that have achieved a mature organizational structure, there are those that are continuing to discover their proper organizational attitudes, and many that find it useful to change for the sake of change. Experience of successful organizations shows that the computer structure should fit the organization and not that the organization structure fit the computer structure.

It is also probably true that it is less burdensome to modify a centralized database system to represent new business units than it is to move data and computer hardware from one business location to another. It is critical, therefore, when mapping systems to organizational charts, that this be done only when there is confidence that the chart will at least endure for the payback period of the system, or that provision for reasonable variations be included in initial design.

An additional problem with fitting a system to the organization is that organizations are rarely the neat hierarchic trees drawn on the organization charts. The true organization is a network of which only some of the connections are known. Thus, unless it is very clear who needs specific data, who needs various reports, who needs various system activities, it is risky to undertake hardware partitioning along formal organizational lines. As regards distribution for organizational reasons, the message must be to undertake distribution for this motive only if the organization is stable and really understood.

4. CONCLUDING REMARKS

The intent of this chapter has been to introduce even handed critical thought to distributed processing, which is surrounded by so much mythic and legendary material.

In the face of the many unclears, caveats, cautions and counterexamples, when is it reasonable to undertake the effort of distributed systems? Insofar as there is an answer to this, it seems to be when the following are clear and well understood:

- Relationships among business organizations and data.
- Relationships among organizations and applications.
- Relationships among applications and data.
- Loads placed upon the system at various points as well as the capacity of nodes present at those points.
- Cross-node loads coming from planned internode interactions.

If these are the elements of a desirable environment for distribution it is necessary to determine whether the organization is willing to undertake necessary action to clarify its own shape and form.

Certainly all systems design depends upon stability and clarity. However, distributed designs may be more sensitive and require better definitions of applications characteristics. This may be a strength of the distributed approach.

From the above list of desirables one can infer a list of uncertainties, according to which distribution should be looked at very cautiously.

- Communications skills in an enterprise.
- Interconnectability of various nodes because of hardware and software capabilities at each node.
- Data reference patterns and sources of load combined with uncertainty about node performance.
- The direction of evolution of applications.

We do not know, in general, whether complexity will increase or decrease in distributed processing systems, nor how operational costs will evolve. We are just discovering an art.

Despite these factors, distributed processing is a data processing design alternative that is real for any set of applications. We have tried here to highlight the considerations necessary to make considered decisions in order to achieve the potential advantages and avoid the potential disappointments.

UNDERLYING CONCEPTS

Chapter 6

Distributable Elements of a System

1. SYSTEMS ELEMENTS

The characterization of distributed processing offered in Part One begins with the idea that the elements of a data processing system may be distributed. Throughout Part One we discussed some ideas of partitioning and interconnecting partitions. We attempted to make some distinction between distributed systems and networks and between distributed and decentralized systems. Part Two will address itself to systems aspects of data processing systems and to the considerations which are appropriate in conceiving of distributed designs.

Because there is so much general discussion about decentralized and distributed systems we will undertake to start this section about the systems aspects of distribution by yet another attempt to distinguish between decentralization and distribution.

Since the characterization of distribution involves a dispersion of the elements of a data processing system, it is helpful to look at what these elements are.

At a very high level of abstraction a data processing system consists of:

1. *Hardware Components.* Processing units, memories, channels, control units, communication media, and so on. This collection of hardware is configurable and dispersible to form physical systems of different structure.

2. *Data.* Collections of records, files, data sets which form the collection of objects of information which the operators of the system will modify and maintain. Data structures can be defined, interrelated and dispersed in almost limitless combination, theoretically. There are real practical constraints in the context of systems design.

3. *Application Operators.* The set of programs which represent the logic of

applications. Programs, modules within programs, sets of programs may be related in a very large number of ways as a result of data reference patterns, interprogram communication patterns, programming design principles.

4. *System Operators.* The set of programmed activities which are performed by operating systems, utilities, subsystems, access methods and other software elements commonly provided by a software vendor and not developed by an installation. The specific structure, interfaces and function of this "systems programming" will present constraints and possibilities for distributing a system.

The elements listed above are what the author calls "systems elements." They are the nonhuman components of an operational computer system. A complete computer system also contains a number of human or "staff" elements and a set of data processing skills. Some of these skills will tend to naturally disperse as the systems components disperse. Others, however, need not. Thus operator skills may or may not move with boxes which must be operated. However, they may have a greater tendency to disperse with boxes than systems analysis skills, application development skills and enterprise level planning and decision making skills.

A distributed processing system which disperses only the systems elements has no overtone of decentralization whatsoever. As the staff elements are dispersed, then elements of decentralization are introduced. Distribution is largely a hardware/software design concept. Decentralization is a management and staffing concept.

Figure 24 attempts to illustrate the separability of various aspects of systems dispersion. It is borrowed, conceptually, from John Rockart of M.I.T. Consider the origin of the three axes to represent maximum centralization of all elements of data processing. The systems components are together in a single room; application development is done only by programmers employed by the data processing department, and all planning and operational decisions are made by the data processing staff. This is a pure centralized environment.

Since there are three axes it is conceptually possible to locate points on each axis arbitrarily. The end points of each axis represent some idea of maximal dispersion. It is possible to locate a point on the systems components axis midway between the origin and the end point. It is not clear what effect any chosen point on the systems elements axis will have on the application development and systems management axes. It is possible to conceive of a scenario where hardware and software are extremely dispersed, located at remote geographical regions, but where all applications development is done at a development center and where systems management is strongly vested in a high level planning staff. Similarly it is possible to visualize an environment where application development skills have been dispersed to operational business units or locations. This dispersal may or may not be accompanied by dispersal of systems elements or system management function.

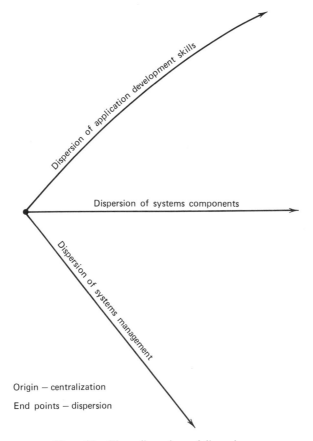

Dispersion of application development skills

Dispersion of systems components

Dispersion of systems management

Origin — centralization

End points — dispersion

Figure 24.   Three dimensions of dispersion.

The ultimate decentralized environment occurs when all systems elements, application skills and data processing decision making have become part of operational units. This represents points at the end points of the three axes.

The degree of dispersion across the three axes is not independent. But there are considerable degrees of freedom which lead to diverse sets of systems images and requirements. In an environment where systems elements are centralized but applications development skills are dispersed we expect certain kinds of function from supporting software. We are, perhaps, thinking about virtual machine support for groups of working programmers. In an environment where applications skills are left at a central point and systems elements are dispersed we are concerned with remote test and debugging facilities, program distribution techniques, remote program modification and maintenance techniques. Similarly, concepts of the degrees of central operational control or the universality of data processing standards varies as we move systems management function from the origin to the end point of Figure 24.

If Figure 24 could be accurately calibrated then it would be very valuable indeed. One could infer from it all of the desirable systems features for different scenarios evolving from different dispersion decisions across the three axes.

As a matter of fact the phenomenon suggested by Figure 24 is a very real one. In various organizations there are very different combinations of dispersion:

1. Systems elements are physically dispersed but system definition and application development is centralized. Many organizations doing "top-down" systems design find it is convenient to centrally develop applications for dispersion to remote nodes. The dispersion of nodes leads to a centralization of programming activity either because all nodes will run the same programs or because program elements are closely related and should be designed and implemented by closely knit groups. Thus the dispersion of hardware serves as a force leading to the centralization of planning and development.

2. Systems elements are centralized but application development is dispersed. In this situation each using department has development skills and development rights. The data processing department acts as a service to provide systems resource in an efficient manner. Decisions about what kind of resource is to be made available may be the choice of the data processing staff, a negotiation between using units, or at the discretion of using units. All in place systems, however, are centrally located and managed.

The factors which influence decisions to disperse the application development and management skills are interesting in their own right. They are discussed in Part Three of the book. However, there is a very rich set of considerations even when only the dimension of the dispersion of systems elements is addressed. Issues in software and hardware structure, interconnection mechanisms, applications structure, data partitioning, control definition and distribution reveal the range of choice available to a designer without the further complication of management issues. It is this set of problems and opportunities which we will immediately address.

2. THE DECISION SPACE

The initial approach to distributed processing involves three major aspects:

1. Why distribute? What benefits will accrue from the distribution of elements of a system in terms of cost, reliability, availability, convenience of use, and so on?

2. What distribution methodologies should be used? Given some idea that distribution can contribute to the effectiveness of data processing in an

organization, what different kinds of distribution can be undertaken? What are the constraints, design problems, opportunities across a full range of distribution choices?

3. What products are available to support the distribution techniques which seem most appropriate? What selection from the offered set of software and hardware components will allow most effective implementation of the distribution which seems most desirable?

The last chapter of Part One tried to provide a critical perception of the reasons for distributing. Unhappily, when considering distribution possibilities, it is common to begin with a product analysis and only then to explore what distribution possibilities are offered by a product set or by competing product sets. Frequently product comparisons and product commitments are made before a clear understanding of goals or general techniques has been achieved. It is surely better to define goals rigorously, select the distribution techniques which will achieve these goals and then inspect the marketplace for appropriate hardware and software products. Otherwise an organization will not ever achieve a mature understanding of what the possibilities for distribution may truly be. The proper sequence goes from goals, through possible techniques, to most feasible technical product to support techniques. Using this sequence it is possible that the most desirable distribution technique will not be supported by any available product, but at least the enterprise will have seen what it wants and understood its direction.

In this spirit this section will introduce the aspects of the decisions which must be made in considering what kinds of distribution should be undertaken. The decisions to be made may be broken into three major areas:

1. System structure.
2. Distance.
3. Allocation of activity and data.

Systems structure relates to the basic flow of data and control throughout the system. It has two major components, degree and shape. Degree addresses the notion "How distributed is the system to be?" Degree addresses the extent to which a large measure of "centralness" should remain in the system and the extent to which a set of nodes share various activities in common. Shape addresses the fundamental tendency of nodes to control other nodes or to participate as peers in the various activities of the system.

Distance involves the decisions which determine how physically proximate nodes in the system will be to each other. A full range of distance choices involves placing machines in the same cabinet, the same room, the same building, the same industrial park or at significant geographical distances from each other. Various organizational and responsiveness factors will influence the distance decisions.

Allocation involves the set of choices which must be made across various options for partitioning and locating software, data and control elements.

The various combinations of decisions about system structure, distance and allocation intertwine with each other to form the essential character of a distributed system.

The result of a survey of techniques will probably reveal a set of feasible or profitable designs. The application of product knowledge will reduce the set by demonstrating which of the possible solutions is "safest" in terms of cost and risk within available or reasonably available product. If available product constraints do not allow safe implementation of a desired distribution, it may be judicious to either abandon the techniques or postpone the plan for distribution until required products become available. In some cases the benefits to be achieved by a particular form of distribution may be so large that it is worth the risk of proceeding with less available software support than would be desired. If it is desirable to distribute data in a certain way but no available data manager will support that kind of distribution, it is conceivable that it is worthwhile to undertake to create a data manager which will support the concept. An organization must be very sure of its benefits and skills before undertaking to provide major systems elements to support a particular concept of distribution.

Chapter 7

Systems Structure

1. ELEMENTS OF SYSTEMS STRUCTURE

Systems structure emerges from a set of decisions about where to place elements of application, systems software and data. The structure of a system derives from the flow of data and control across the nodes of a system. Decisions in this area are primarily driven by enterprise organization, application structure and systems programming structures associated with available systems offerings. This chapter will discuss the influence of systems software structures as embodied in operating systems, subsystems and access methods. Two aspects of structure, degree and shape, involve a set of choices about how the functions of software are to be dispersed across a population of hardware nodes.

2. THE IDEA OF DEGREE

The idea of degree quite simply involves an answer to the question "How distributed do I wish to be?" Many of us in data processing like single valued answers to as many questions as possible. We would like to be able to define a Level One distributed system, a Level Two distributed system, a Level Three, and so on, and weigh the merits and demerits of each level to determine whether we are to be "one distributed,", "two distributed," in response to the question of degree.

Unfortunately it is very difficult to do this without oversimplifying many important elements of choice. We will discuss degree in terms of three factors:

1. System software layers.
2. Node autonomy.
3. Node generality.

3. SYSTEM SOFTWARE LAYERS

Figure 25 shows another simple view of a single node as a collection of operational layers. There is a bottom layer which intends to represent hardware which is involved in support of communications with terminals or with other nodes.

Above the hardware layer Figure 25 shows a layer of software which is called the operating system. This layer intends to represent those activities of an operating system which provide services to an application program which wishes to interact with a terminal or with another processing node. The layer is a simplification for a number of reasons but it is useful in this introductory stage.

The next layer of Figure 25 represents an application program. This applica-

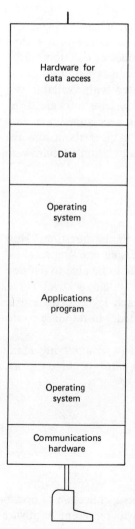

Figure 25.   System as a collection of layers.

tion program has a set of interfaces which it uses to call upon the services of the operating system layers for access to communications services on one side and data management services on the other. The interface consists of a number of service request directives which enable the application program to send and receive messages on one side and to get and put data on the other side. The specific split of responsibility for function between the application and the operating system varies widely from system to system. Some operating systems relieve an application program of more functions than others.

Figure 25 shows another operating system layer on the other side of the application program. This part of the operating system is responsible for providing data storage and retrieval services to the application program. At its interface there is a set of commands for referencing files and records which relieves the application program of much of the work involved in interacting with disk or tape devices. As with the communications interface, the data management interface varies widely in system to system, providing more or less support for various mappings of logical concepts of data and physical structure of data.

Behind the operating system data layer there are data and the hardware on which the data resides. This hardware is a combination of the storage devices, the architected paths to the storage devices and those general functions of the processor involved in interacting with storage devices.

3.1.   Layers and Degree

Each horizontal line representing an interface between programs on Figure 25 represents a possible "distribution level." If each horizontal line represents a well architected, truly layered interface such that data and directives flow only across that interface and no knowledge of internal details of a layer is known beyond that layer, then it is possible to take a layer "away" from its neighboring layers. By taking away we mean to move a functional layer out of a physical node where a neighboring and interacting layer resides. The extent to which this is done and the manner in which it is done determine degree of distribution.

Figure 26 shows three systems. The first, called "nondistributed," shows all of the layers together in a single node with a connection to a terminal. This configuration is sometimes called "distributed access," but it is truly a nondistributed layering because all functions are supported from within a single node.

The next drawing of Figure 26 shows a "distributed function" system. Here the communications access (in computerese, CAM) part of operating the operating system has been taken out of the single node and placed in another node. Whenever the application program issues a request for communications service, or data is to be passed to it from communications service, the connection between two processing units must be traversed. To accomplish this the coding generated to support application to communications services interaction must

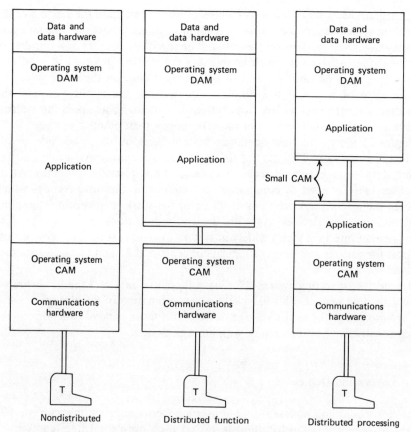

Figure 26.   Degrees of distribution.

invoke instructions which will cross the interconnection. Some thin, residual layer of the operating system to support physical unit interaction will reside in the physical unit with the application.

The possibility naturally exists for accomplishing the same dispersion of function on the other side of the application program. The operating system functions supported by data management (DAM) of the operating system could be moved onto a processing unit which is dedicated to DAM-like functions and a mechanism for supporting a cross-node interface between the application processor and the DAM processor could be developed.

If CAM- and DAM-like functions are moved into dedicated processing nodes, it will be necessary to provide independent node resource management functions in each node. Allocation of memory, buffer spaces, and local procedure scheduling would have to be undertaken at each node in addition to support of the interface between the nodes. Since the requirements for CAM,

DAM and the application program might not be the same, and since it is known that CAM and DAM are the only users of local resource management, both the structure and function of each local small operating system may be quite different. In the CAM and DAM boxes these functions could be tightly integrated into CAM and DAM programming structures.

The last drawing of Figure 26 shows a system characterized as a distributed processing system. The essential characteristic of this system is that the application layer has itself been split across two nodes. The processing of application logic will involve interaction between user written programs which must communicate with each other. This implies that each node which hosts an application must have a CAM-like function in its general operating systems services.

There is a continuum presented by the three figures of Figure 26 that suggests three degrees of distribution: nondistributed, in which all software activities are in the same node; functionally distributed, in which the structure of systems software allows communications and data services to be placed in separate nodes; application distributed, in which application functions are dispersed to multiple nodes.

Another way of looking at degree of distribution is to look at a population of software layers in a spirit not unlike that of Figure 21. Consider a system of one large processing node which is running a number of applications dispersed among major subsystems. The major subsystems may be, for example, a time-shared program development subsystem, and an on-line data management subsystem. In addition there are application programs running directly on the underlying operating system.

Figure 27 shows a large node running multiple major subsystems as described in the preceding paragraph. A number of degrees of distribution are suggested by the figure. A first level of distribution would be to remove major subsystems and dedicate a node to each subsystem. Thus there would be a

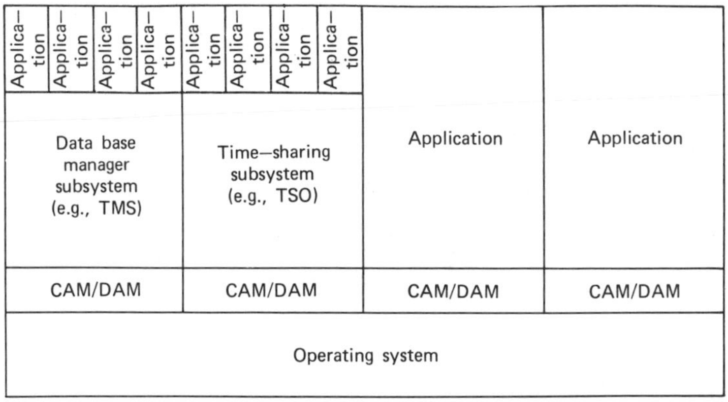

Figure 27. Multiple subsystem consolidated workload node.

time-sharing machine and a database machine. A second level of distribution would be to separate the applications in each subsystem and develop multiple nodes for each subsystem. Interconnections between the subsystems could be available over channels or teleprocessing lines. Such structures could be currently built using existing database management systems which allow multiple copies to communicate with each other.

Even further levels of distribution could be achieved by replicating on the basis of virtual memories within the structure of a single application. Thus a continuum of degree of distribution is defined by the ideas of dedicating a processing node to each major subsystem, dedicating nodes to subsets of applications within multiple subsystem nodes, dedicating nodes to structures within the application.

3.2.   A Finer Look at Layers and Degree

Figure 28 shows something which is closer to the potential conceptual structure of a complete systems software package.

Figure 28 shows three distinct layers in CAM. There is a link control layer responsible for the management of the physical lines between nodes or between nodes and terminals. There is a path control layer which is responsible for routing and choosing alternate paths between elements of the system. There is a communications interface layer which is responsible for auditing and translating the various types of requests which an application program makes.

On the DAM side there is a layer which is responsible for translating the image of logical data which the data manager knows into an image defined by the program. A programmer, using a programming language like COBOL or PL/1, can issue data descriptive declarations which describe the structure and format of records which his program wishes to receive or send to the data management software. A transformation must be made between this logical structure and the logical structures which have been described to the data manager by use of a data description language. In addition to this transformation it is necessary to map the physical structure of data, the way it is laid out on disks, onto the system logical structure. Thus there is a layer on Figure 28 which maps from physical structures into data management logical structures. Beneath this layer there is a layer which maps physical structures across populations of devices, and finally there is a layer which is responsible for the physical control of devices and response to device specific peculiarities.

Each of the horizontal lines of Figure 28 is intended to represent a clean interface between each layer. As such there is the suggestion that any population of nodes may be placed underneath the software layers. Thus it is possible to envision a one to one mapping between physical nodes and logical software layers. If this mapping exists there is a maximal degree of distribution of function in the system.

Decisions about the dispersal of layers may bring about two fundamental forms of distributed system. If layers are dispersed so that a layer exists alone in

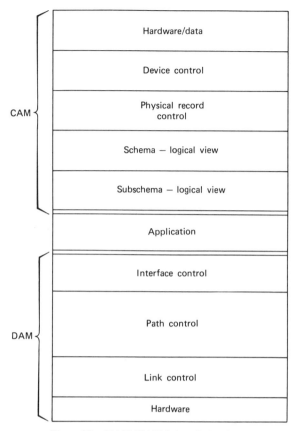

Figure 28. DAM/CAM internal structure.

a physical node, then each node is a highly specialized node capable of only one function. If layers are dispersed such that multiple nodes may have replicated layers, then the nodes of the system become more general purpose. The nature of system is determined by a set of layer dispersion decisions across a population of physical nodes. Technology currently permits both functionally specialized distributions and general distributions of functions in multiple nodes. As logic and memory costs decrease it becomes feasible to isolate function in small, special-purpose units or to increase the functional capability of units of modest size.

3.3. Populations of Fully Capable Nodes

A node which has all of the software layers suggested by Figure 28 is sometimes called a fully capable node. A full range of distribution choices may be addressed in a system built from fully capable nodes. In such systems there are full operating systems, CAM and DAM services and applications modules at every node. The programs at various nodes have generalized intercommunication requirements of three types:

1. Send a data element or receive a data element as requested by a program running at another node.
2. Request the operation of a program at another node.
3. Request the operation of some system service at a remote node. Such services may be the enqueueing of a message, the allocation of a buffer space, some remote operational procedure or some system status data available from the systems software at a node.

Different systems designs provide different specific services for each type of interaction and package these services at different places in the software structure. In analyzing the suitability of a software package to support a particular distribution it is necessary to understand the constraints that structure and function impose upon design.

3.4.   Software Structures and Distribution Constraints

Underlying software design constrains distribution choices in a number of ways.

First, it determines how much effort must be put into an application program to achieve certain kinds of distribution. This is a characteristic of the amount of service which the package of system software offers. The system software may not allow certain kinds of internode references unless the application group adds the functions or restructures the software. The systems software may provide certain functions at so primitive a level that some specialized code must be developed to create conceptually simpler and safer interfaces to the programmers writing pure application code. On the obverse, the performance burden of the provided code may be so heavy because of richness of function that a particular distribution technique cannot be afforded unless a specialized functional code is developed by the using organization.

Moreover, the granularity of structural definition in a software package implies the granularity of distribution. Consider Figure 29. This software package has no regular internal structure beneath the concept of data manager or communications manager. It would be very risky or infeasible for a user to attempt a distribution of the various levels suggested by Figure 28. The software package just does not support partitioning and dispersion at that level of granularity. If distribution of function at a finer granularity is desired, the using organization must provide its own software with the desired structure.

Software granularity does not necessarily imply that different layers will be placed at different nodes. It is possible to replicate all layers but provide a granularity of choice involving where specific activities will be performed. Consider Figure 30. This represents a well structured system which has the capabil-

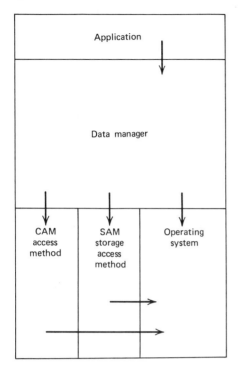

Figure 29. Gross structure.

ity for any layer to ask for a service at a local layer beneath it or at a remote layer. This is accomplished by use of a routing block which is set to call for local or remote layer service. When an application program establishes a connection with a file it can specify, or the system can determine, whether that file is local or remote to the application. It might be possible for the application program to specify, or for the system to determine, a pattern of layer connections depending on whether it was convenient for record formatting, blocking and buffering services and device control to be done locally or remotely. A system control element would be created such that each layer contained a pointer to either the local layer at the next level or a remote layer at the next level. The CAM function of the system could be invoked to provide communication between a layer and a remote layer at any interface point. If all services were to be performed locally, then layer by layer descent could occur on the local machine. If the device was remote but blocking and record services were to be local, then CAM would be invoked coming out of the blocking layer. Whenever the remote device was to be read or written, the CAM program would communicate with a CAM program at the remote location of the data in order to cause the execution of device handling programs at that node. The data read would then be passed back to the requesting node to appear at the interface to deblocking layers as if the data had been read from a local device.

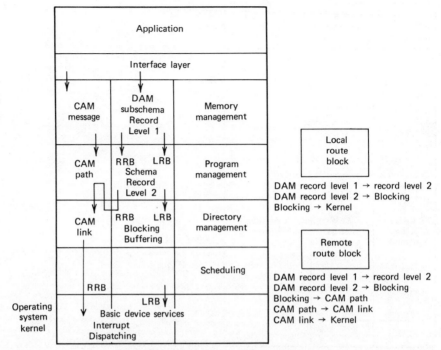

Figure 30.   Fine structure with flexible routes.

Such a system structure could be configured so that a design might be able to put particular layers at particular nodes or put all layers at all nodes.

If a software system is not layered and separable in the spirit described above, then it is necessary to replicate all functions at all nodes in order to achieve a system where local or remote data references may be made. It is possible to have a data manager which is not structured into layers. The entire unstructured program could exist at each node and achieve equivalent function. An ability for the data manager to communicate with other data managers to acquire remote data can be designed. The disadvantage of this is that each node in the system must contain the entire data manager program even when it is not intended to exercise all functions at all nodes. The size of the smallest node in the system becomes enlarged because it is necessary to replicate large amounts of systems software at all nodes. Small, functionally specific nodes are difficult to place in the system structure.

The functional definition of each layer in a software structure determines what layers are necessary to perform certain functions. In a system with no structure beyond the concept of an operating system, a data manager and an access method it is possible to place new functions to support off-node references in the operating system, the data managers or the access method. The specific allocation of function made by a provider of software product will determine what layers of software must exist at a node for it to be a fully capable node. If application program to application program off-node communication services are placed in the lowest layer, the operating system layer, then it is possible to write application programs which can talk to each other with only the operating system layer present. If data reference and application to application message interfaces are supported by the data manager, it is necessary to have that layer present before off-node interaction can be supported. Since software elements may be priced more aggressively in the future the complement of layers which are necessary to perform certain functions represents a real dollar outlay to a using organization.

The relationship between software elements may determine the portability of programs and the modifications necessary to move programs from one node to another. Much of this consideration has been addressed in earlier comments about transparency. It is thought to be desirable that references to data or programs be made in the same manner regardless of whether local or remote interaction is involved. Many software packages are tending to support this concept.

There is, however, a lingering problem in that not all the interactive or synchronizing functions of software are being taken into the transparency mode. This is because in older systems the new functions tend to be provided by new modules rather than a generalization of old modules. An older application program running on an operating system and using directives to synchronize data references in a multiprogram environment may find that the form of the directive it issues to gain exclusive use of data is not the same as a directive newly introduced to gain use of a remote data record. It may also be that local data may be referenced through the operating system, but that the data manager must be present to gain control of remote data. Thus dispersing the application logic may involve changing the synchronizing directives or rewriting the application to conform to the interface of the data management system.

One of the more attractive structural designs of a software system comes from IBM's DPPX operating system for the 8100 information system. DPPX provides granular structure with transparent interfaces for local or remote reference. In addition it provides for the interspersion of subsystem functional layers within the layered structure of the basic operating system. Finally it provides for layer replacement and addition as users need or desire in developing software for various distribution designs.

4. SUMMARY OBSERVATION

We have seen that there are important issues in underlying systems software structure which will influence how much of what kind of software is necessary to achieve various kinds of distribution. Structure will determine how much programming cost is involved in achieving various kinds of distribution. An important part of distributed processing design is the inspection of the suitability of software from various vendors to support the distribution techniques which a using organization wishes to undertake.

The question of "how distributed" a system may become is a partial function of the nature of software interfaces, the separability of software functions and the dispersion of specific functions within layers.

5. NODE AUTONOMY

A measure of the distributedness of a system may be sensed by the degree to which individual nodes are allowed to pursue their own destinies. One of the design decisions which must be made is the extent to which local control functions will be available at each node so that each node may undertake some degree of local scheduling, prioritizing and resource control. To achieve this it is necessary for each node to have resident operating system functions which go beyond the ability to send and receive data elements and messages.

In a pure master/slave relationship there is a strong sense of centralized system-wide control vested in a central node which controls the behavior of associated nodes. The local resource management functions may be trivial or nonexistent.

As additional activity is brought to a node it may begin to assume control over itself to some degree. It may choose on what basis to service requests from another node when they contend with local service requests; it may make itself unavailable to other nodes. As more local control is put at a node the intensity of interaction and dependency upon other nodes may decrease.

Nodes which have local operating system resource control functions are generally more "intelligent" than nodes which do not. The sense of increased distribution comes from the increase in the distribution of intelligence and computational power throughout the system.

There is a point at which a node may become so independent that it violates our notions of a distributed system because there is not sufficient interaction and dependency. Figure 31 suggests that as local autonomy increases our sense of increased distribution increases until a point is reached where the concept of a single system is violated.

The dispersion of local control functions is distinguishable from the concept of distributing global control. Later in the text we will discuss various control structures in more detail. Figure 32 suggests the complexity of this issue.

The simple matrix suggests that there is a distinction to be made between global control functions and local control functions. For example, the decision to process a transaction from a local terminal before processing a transaction sent from another node is a local control function. However, the decision to select a particular node to perform a particular program is a global control function.

Global and local control may be either distributed or centralized. The global decision about which node is to perform a particular unit of work may be

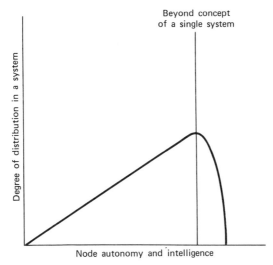

Figure 31.   Increased distribution as function of autonomy and intelligence.

centralized so that a work control processor makes all decisions for the system. The decision may also be made by a system of cooperative bidding and negotiation between nodes. Such a mechanism provides distributed global control.

Local control may also be centralized. In a system consisting of rather unintelligent units a central point may keep the work list for each unit and dispatch units of work in an order determined centrally for each unit.

What makes the issue more complex is that it is not absolutely clear what the bounds of the concept of control really are and that across a set of resources to be controlled each resource may be controlled differently in a single system.

The control of access to data sets may be placed centrally in the same system which allows multiple nodes to negotiate who will perform a particular transaction. The routing of messages may be distributed among nodes in a system which permits only one designated node to perform system-wide scheduling, and so on.

6.   GENERALITY OF NODE

The design of a distributed system must also address the issue of the degree to which various nodes may share different workloads, may substitute for each other, may be selected as sites for different types of processing. A system of highly intelligent nodes may be used as a general functional pool, almost like a multiprocessor, providing high degrees of work balancing and functional generalization.

Alternatively, a system may consist of sets of highly specialized nodes dedicated to single functions. If the decision to functionally specialize is based upon

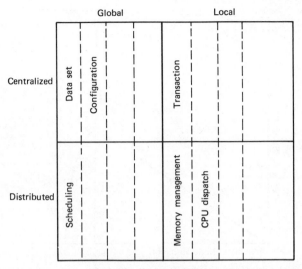

Figure 32.   Control matrix.

a limitation of the capacity of each node, the system will have different characteristics from a system of general-purpose nodes.

7.   RATIO OF LOCAL FUNCTION/TOTAL FUNCTION

One measure of the degree of distribution is the extent to which nodes participate in the burden of the workload which is undertaken by the system.

A highly centralized system may have a single node which does 85% of the computation, 80% of the data references, and so on. A set of smaller nodes share the execution of the residual activities.

A system becomes more distributed as each node participates in a larger percentage of the total of the data processing work to be done. If a 10 node system distributes work so that each node does about 10% of the work, that system is intuitively more distributed than the system which is dominated by a single node.

8.   DEGREE OF DISTRIBUTION— CONCLUDING REMARKS

Although the concept of the degree of distribution is somewhat abstract it serves to show the richness and variety of distribution decisions which can be made in developing a system.

The concept has some practical importance in that different degrees of distribution may imply different kinds of development and operational costs. As more of the activity of a system is dispersed there may be impacts on operating costs, communications costs and programming costs as a function of the degree of distribution. Distribution of trivial data entry functions to a node of modest intelligence implies a different operational cost than distribution of application logic to a node with its own operating system and need for local operating and system programming personnel.

In a similar vein the size of required hardware nodes and the type of communications mechanisms are determined by the degree to which distribution is accomplished in a system.

Finally, a perception of how much one wishes to distribute, the granularity desired, the flexibility required, as suggested by organizational considerations, will provide an insight into what constitutes suitable software which in turn will suggest some basis for the selection of specific vendor product for the distributed system.

Chapter 8

System Structure—Shape

1. CONCEPT OF SHAPE

The "shape" of a system indicates the flow of data and control from node to node and suggests part of the idea of the general structure of the system. Shape is naturally closely related to the idea of degree since the specific pattern of data and control flow is determined by decisions about where to place particular functions and particular application activities.

There is a general tendency in the field to try to characterize systems as hierarchic, peer or compound. A hierarchic system is conceptually represented in Figure 33. There is a strong notion of a tree structure with a central site of control defined at the root. The root is felt to be in one sense or another the "master" system. A peer system, conceptually represented in Figure 34, is felt to be a cooperative joining of nodes of equal control. A compound system

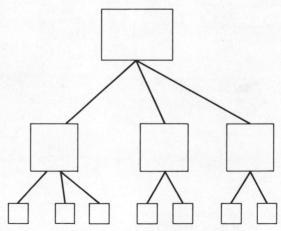

Figure 33.   Concept of hierarchic system.

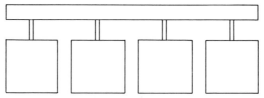

Figure 34. Concept of peer system.

contains elements of both types of structure. This is represented by the two diagrams of Figure 35.

Despite the widespread use of concepts of hierarchy and peer to characterize systems, the unqualified use of these characterizations does not really transmit much information about the dynamics of a system. Variations in design permit much more elaborate systems structures than what is implied by the characterization of a system as either a peer or hierarchic system.

As a first elaboration of the concept of shape, it is necessary to observe that the data flow of a system and the control flow of a system may not have the same structure. Any engineer of computing systems will verify that from a hardware design viewpoint control lines and data lines do not map directly on

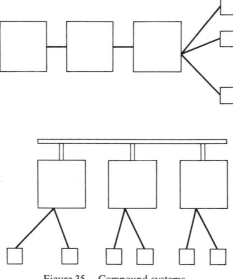

Figure 35. Compound systems.

each other in all systems. Neither do software structures which define data and control paths at higher levels of abstraction. Thus one needs at least a two part statement to characterize a system; a statement giving the shape of the data flow and a statement giving the shape of the control flow. A system may be peer by virtue of its data flow but hierarchic by virtue of its control flow. There are so many varieties of the concept of control in a system that control itself may have many different shapes. A system, as we mentioned in the section on autonomy in the previous chapter, may have centralized or hierarchic control over one resource and may have distributed or peer control over another resource.

Similarly, applications running on a system may exhibit different fundamental data flow shapes. One application may move transactions to regionally distributed data partitions in a peer manner. Another application may always go to a central point for data which it merely formats at an outlying processing node. Thus a system may assume multiple and parallel shapes as regards both its control and its application data activities.

Even within the context of a single application the flow of data and control may vary from hierarchic to peer on a transaction basis depending on various mappings of program population and data partitions across the system.

As an additional consideration the logical shape of a system need not coincide with its physical shape. The data and control flows of a logical system may seriously diverge from the physical structure. Thus a system which is drawn physically like a tree may support applications in which the interaction between applications elements spread across the physical nodes is essentially peer to peer. Another aspect of physical and logical divergence lies in the possible use of different mappings of physical equipment to function. This is particularly true in multiprocessor or virtual machine forms of distribution where the relationships between physical processors or virtual processors is entirely determined by the structure of programming logic and the data and control flow characteristics which come out of that logic.

This by no means suggests that we should abandon the concepts of hierarchic and peer, merely that they must be used with care and somewhat refined if the terms are going to convey real ideas about the nature of a system.

This chapter will discuss some fundamental aspects of hierarchic and peer structures in order to convey some operational ideas of how systems may be organized around the central themes. We will discuss six fundamental kinds of systems.

1. Functional hierarchic systems.
2. Application hierarchic systems.
3. Distributed control/application peer homogeneous systems.
4. Centralized control/application peer homogeneous systems.

5. Distributed control/application peer heterogeneous systems.
6. Centralized control/application peer heterogeneous systems.

2. FUNCTIONAL HIERARCHIC SYSTEMS

Figure 36 is a representation of a system which has been hardware decomposed into a set of reasonable hardware levels. The figure represents a system in which there is a "back end" data engine responsible for data access and which interfaces with a computational engine which holds application logic. By inference the data manager exists in the data engine and all record references and returns pass across the interconnection between the computational processor and the data engine.

At the other side of the computational processor is a front end processor which is responsible for various functions of path control, message handling between local terminals and some specialized local input/output file handling. Its file handling responsibilities lie in the area of printer, reader, punch and tape (source/sink) devices; the data engine handles only on-line data structures.

The front end processor interfaces with some number of network processors which are responsible for line control, basic message assembly and validation, protocol imposition, and so on. Each network processor controls a network that may or may not be dedicated to a set of users or to a particular set of applications.

The network processor talks to a network with some intelligence represented by concentrator nodes which serve to concentrate between transmission mechanisms of various types. Thus the input to a concentrator may be a large number of slow lines; the output is a single line of greater capacity representing a pipe to the network processor. It is common to find network processor and concentrator functions combined into a single physical unit.

The network processor on the other side of the communication net represent site gateways to and from families of work stations in business units or locations. These network processors communicate with intelligent controllers which in turn communicate with terminals. The function of the controller is to provide some degree of processor intelligence to support local data entry and storage and some, perhaps limited, ability to query local storage collections. The controller may in fact be a small computer. Its primary responsibility may be to provide dialogue and screen support for the terminals.

The terminals themselves may have varying degrees of intelligence in support of presentation formats on a screen. The terminals might be specialized for applications or general purpose in that they anticipate access to any number of applications from the same terminal.

This distribution is called hierarchic function because the application logic is

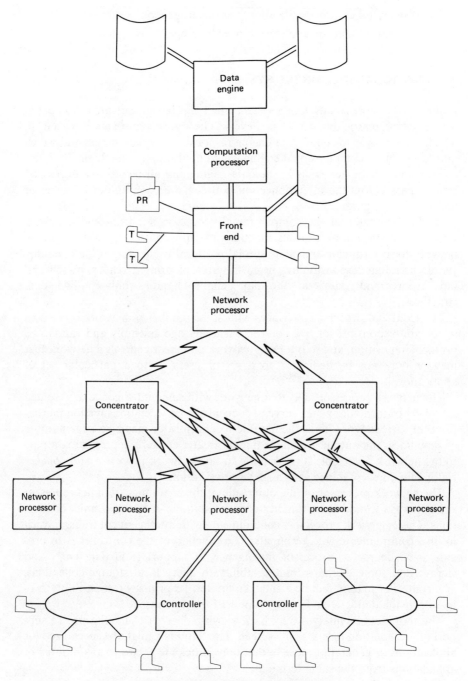

Figure 36.   Decomposed functional hierarchy.

left essentially intact on the computational processor. In addition systems control is vested in the central complex of boxes which as a group may provide data control, remote operation, remote start-up and program load and system recovery functions. The exact distribution of control functions between the processing nodes in the central complex will vary. Thus it is possible in some systems to involve different specific boxes in different control functions.

There are three interesting aspects of this system: packaging, location and control. Each of these represents a set of design choices which will influence the final configuration in detail.

2.1. Packaging

As drawn the system contains eight levels. Each level is dedicated to a particular function which conceptually corresponds to the type of software layer we discussed in Chapter 7. Here it becomes quite clear that the structure of software function will affect the degree to which we are able to accomplish the physical eight level hardware system.

It is actually possible today, using announced hardware product, to construct the physical system of Figure 36, but it would probably be very difficult to do because of software limitations and variations in the line protocols used by various vendors who would provide the various boxes.

Across the large population of system vendors there is a large set of permutations of packaging of the functions which are being offered. For example, IBM might offer the data engine, computational processor and front end as an integrated package running on a 3300 family processor. The network control function would be offered on a 370X processor. At a local site IBM might offer an 8100 system running the DPCX operating system. This node would offer combined local network processor, terminal controller and terminal interfaces to unintelligent terminals. Network concentrator services might be offered on a Series/1. A variation might propose the Series/1 as the local controller or a Series/1 as a local network processor. The Series/1 option might involve some greater programming effort on the part of the using organization.

We see that even from a single vendor there are choices in the way the functions of this system may be supported and different combinations of functions in different box populations. Across the entire population of vendors there is potential limitless choice; however, each choice will represent various degrees of risk and effort to achieve software interaction and box to box interconnection.

Some vendors perceive the network processor and front end functions to be suitable for combination on a single box. There are multiple variations on the theme of the interface between terminals and local controllers depending upon the intelligence available in the set of terminal offerings. There are combinations which package computational processor and front end but suggest the isolation of the data engine. In fact the choices are staggering and the effort of making a choice on a purely technological basis is probably beyond the resources of a using organization. One of the really large problems in the industry today is how to qualify vendors, how to qualify vendor interconnect capacity, how to evaluate what seems like an innumerable number of combinations of potential physical structure.

The factors to be involved in determining a physical shape of a system involve assessments of vendor reliability, processing node capacity, interconnect capacity, delivery schedules, software structures and function. All of these elements of choice must be considered within constraints of cost, reliability objectives, performance objectives, flexibility goals, and so on. The dramatic enlargement of the decision space that contemporary product offerings allow carries with it a considerable potential increase in the effort and cost to make a choice. This is true even within a system which is hierarchic by both data flow and control flow and which may be dedicated to a single application.

There was a time in the industry when the systems proposals were largely uniform. Major vendors in the 1960s tended to submit proposals which were structurally similar and which differed only parametrically from each other. That time has passed us; proposals now differ dramatically in their appreciation of system shape and dynamics and certain systems shapes can only be assembled using multiple vendor sources.

2.2. Location

Another aspect of this system is the configuration of the nodes as regards their physical location. Figure 36 strongly suggests that the data engine, computational processor, front end and network processor will be in the same location, possibly even the same room. The concentrators will be at some intermediate geographical point and the other nodes will be distant. However, in the future it is not clear that the data engines, as they emerge and evolve, may not be geographically remote from the computational processors or that the remote stations may not be as close as another floor of the building or in another building in the same industrial park. The use of concentrators may still be appropriate for short-distance intercommunication. They may appear more in the guise of switching units in such configurations.

If multiple functions of data engine, computational engine, front end and network processor are bundled into the same box it is possible that individual processors "under the skin" may be dedicated to these functions or it is possible that a single uniprocessor engine supports all functions.

Even in a hierarchic system there may be some distribution of control. Control may be organized hierarchically so that each level has an expanded zone of control and talks to a higher level only in case of error or the need to report information of global impact.

3. APPLICATION HIERARCHY

Figure 37 shows the structure of a hierarchic system which derives from a discovered natural hierarchic shape within the logic of an application. This natural application shape may derive from organizational structure in which clear levels of function and responsibility can be perceived across management levels.

The three levels of Figure 37 are an operational level, a mid-management supervisory level and a policy making management level. The hardware structure may involve a set of microprocessors at the operational level, a mid-sized or small processing node at the supervisor level and a large computational processor at the management level.

The microprocessors may be imbedded in a hostile environment, inaccessible

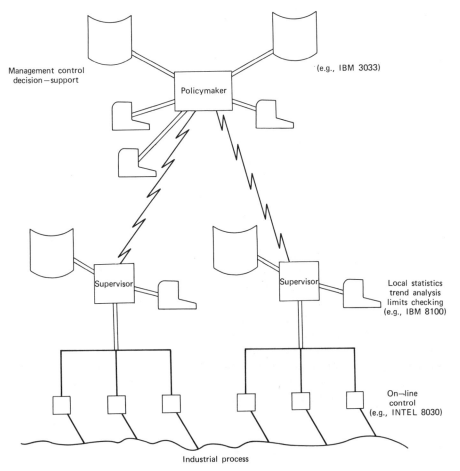

Figure 37. Application hierarchy.

to humans, or imbedded in manufacturing equipment. These processors contain programming to control the second to second operation of the process to which they are connected. Depending upon the nature of the process, each microprocessor may be identically programmed or may be differentiated to control a different aspect of the on-line process. If the processors are imbedded in the on-line operational equipment they may physically be chips containing processor logic and memory. It is also possible that they are external to the process and connect to it through an interface supported by an adapter unit. In this case the microprocessors may be packaged "single board computers" with adapter boards inside of a small box. In such configurations the microprocessors are "microcomputer systems" and may have some limited disk and peripheral unit capability.

The lowest level is an operational level on-line for the control of an industrial process. At some program designated rate the microlevel will transmit data to the supervisory level.

The supervisory level contains a small computer system, perhaps of the IBM Series/1 class, which has significant disk storage and which supports a supervisory interface through terminals and peripheral equipment. From this level adjustments may be made to parameters at the microlevel, displays of collected data may be defined, local reports may be produced to support the level of management decisions appropriate for the supervisory level.

The supervisory level transmits data to the policy level which is a computationally important processor with a capacity for the manipulation of large amounts of collected data and the support of decision making at the highest level. In addition the management level may provide "background data" on request from the supervisory levels in order to assist decision making at that level.

It is not necessary, of course, that such a system have only three levels. In the design of such a structure a decision about how many levels are appropriate must be made. Without violating the organizational structure additional levels may be interposed if network size and complexity justify an intelligent network. A concentrator or network controller may be interposed between the microlevel and the supervisory level or the supervisory level and the policy level. A system may have both application and functional hierarchic components.

Figure 37 suggests an industrial process which is stable, well understood and well partitioned. It is just such environments where the concept of fitting the structure of the computer to the structure of the organization achieves success. Although such environments are by no means constrained to on-line manufacturing or process control situations, it is in these situations where distribution of this type achieves the most success and is most widely practiced.

4. HIERARCHIC ORGANIZATION AND FLEXIBILITY

Within the broad concept of hierarchic systems we have shown a system structure whose distribution stresses functional dispersion and a hierarchic structure whose dispersion is based upon application logic. We have suggested that systems may distribute both and we have stressed the amount of variation which can occur within the notion of hierarchy.

Even within the structural concept of a tree, a design may make broad choices as to:

1. Where to place processing power and how much of it to place at each node. Boxes lower in the level may be small microcomputers or significant computer systems with operating systems of their own. No implication need be drawn about whether lower level boxes are locally programmable or must be programmed at the highest level box. In the strongest form of hierarchy the distributed component is completely dependent upon a large "host" system for its programs, operation, start-up. It is certainly possible that the distributed component may be locally programmed and may have a good deal of local control authority over its own resources. Thus the concept of application hierarchy, per se, does not imply the extent of autonomy or the dispersion or centralization of application skills.

2. There are large degrees of choice about how much local storage is to be associated with a processing node. Currently small systems offer storage capacity in the hundreds of millions of bytes with performance characteristics roughly similar to larger storage units available with very large processing units. Product trends have been particularly vigorous in removing storage constraints from small systems. Consequently the dispersion of function or application logic to a small system is much less limited by storage capacity than it had been in the past.

3. There is wide flexibility about the physical location of boxes and the degree of separation of function between boxes.

The growth of flexibility in designing hierarchic systems is a direct function of the improvement in the capacity and price performance of small systems and the development of software which provides both increased capability at a small node and increased capability for central nodes to communicate and provide services for local nodes. The direction is clearly toward increased generality and autonomy.

5. PEER SYSTEMS

The underlying concept of a peer system is that the participating processing nodes cooperate with each other as equals. In its purest form this means that application logic and system control is spread across a population of nodes without any observable or definable control point for any system function.

Such configurations may be created by the use of the memory shared multiprocessor in which each processing node has access to a single operating system through memory address sharing. Such systems may also be created by a set of processing nodes, each with its own operating system, which communicate with each other to achieve global control of the system.

The interconnection of processing nodes in peer environments, however, may not be pure from a control point of view. It is possible to define configurations in which there is a set of application processors which are peer related and a set of designated control processors or a single control processor which is responsible for a defined set of global functions such as scheduling, resource management, message management, data reference authorization and program or data synchronization. It is in the design of peer systems that the divergence of shape of application logic and control logic is most strongly felt in developing a configuration. The reader will recall the description of the system in Chapter 4. This is a good example of an application peer system with strong hierarchic control aspects.

Within the concept of peer there are, once again, innumerable variations. The variations occur in the methods used to interconnect processing nodes, in the dispersion of function and application activity across nodes and in the physical distance between the nodes.

5.1. Interconnection

The interconnection design between nodes is a serious design choice which is determined partially by a perception of interactive patterns and partially by the available technology and methodology for interconnection.

5.2. Single Connection Systems

Figure 38 shows a form of interconnect which depends upon a single connection between the nodes. This concept may be used for both local and geographical interconnection.

The single connection design is often used in connecting processors which are implemented on boards to other board processors within a single box. It may also be used to connect separate boxes. It has the advantage of reducing the circuit count and complexity of interconnection. It has the disadvantage of becoming a potential bottleneck or a vulnerable component of the system. If a connection of sufficient speed and reliability can be found it is an attractive solution for connecting processing units which are in the same room or which are within some small number of kilometers of each other.

A variation of the single connection design is the ring design. We discussed the essential difference between bus and ring designs in an earlier chapter. The bus tends to make all messages immediately available to all connected nodes; the ring introduces fixed time delays in transmission.

Single connect designs may be used to interconnect nodes at geographical distances. In this situation, however, the notion of "hopping" must be introduced. The current technology requires that node 1, of Figure 38, wishing to talk to node 3, must pass through node 2. Thus the time for message transfer is

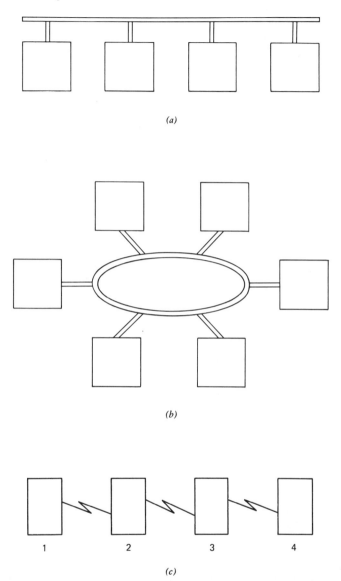

Figure 38. Interconnect structures: (a) common pipe; (b) ring; (c) hopping.

a function of the number of intervening nodes. How much of a burden this will actually place upon a system is somewhat determined by the configuration at each node. If each node has a network processor, or a front-end/network processor, then the passage of messages will not disturb the computational processor at each node. If, either because of hardware or software structure, it is necessary to refer to a computational node to undertake the forwarding, additional delay may be experienced. In addition the performance of the node on local processing may be disturbed.

5.3.   Multiple Connection Paths

An extension of the idea of a single interconnection involves the addition of connections where each supports a specialized kind of interaction. Figure 39 shows a multiple computer system in which each processor has a general message connection to all others. In addition, however, two of the processors in the system are dedicated to input/output operations. Each of the general purpose processors communicates with the storage management processor on a storage management bus and with the communications processor on a communications bus. There is nothing special about the interconnections between the specialized processors. The design intends to reduce the load on the general interconnect and improve the responsiveness of I/O processors by removing non-I/O traffic from the communication pathways. This kind of "multibus" architecture is common in systems which are geographically proximate and which have a high degree of single systems image. For geographically dispersed systems it is common for computational nodes to talk to each other over different interconnecting mechanisms from those used to support interaction between these nodes and terminals or controllers.

5.4.   Star

Figure 40 shows an interconnect scheme which is called a "star." Each computational node talks to other nodes through a switchlike node which provides a path from any node to any other node. Such a design is common in connecting processors to memory banks within a single system. It is also common in teleprocessing oriented designs. The advantage of the design is that it eliminates contention for pathways out of or into a node. The disadvantages of the design are:

1. The switch becomes a potential point of system vulnerability.
2. The switch may become a performance bottleneck.
3. The number of pathways increases as the number of units which are to be interconnected.

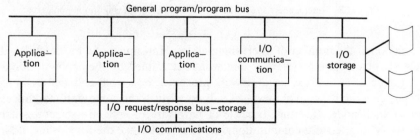

Figure 39.   Multiple bus example.

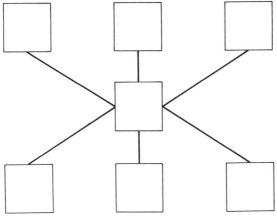

Figure 40.   Star.

5.5.   Mesh

The most elaborate form of interconnection is shown as Figure 41. This is called a "mesh." In a mesh each node has a distinct path to each other node. The advantage to the design is the elimination of contention on pathways between nodes and the ability to keep the network partially operational. There is no single point in the system where a malfunction can bring the entire system down. The disadvantage to the design is the enormous number of interconnecting pathways required. To interconnect N nodes requires on the order of N squared pathways. The design is used to interconnect processing units to memories in multiprocessor systems where it requires P times M pathways for P processors and M memories. The design may also be used to connect groups of processors to each other in geographically dispersed networks of fully capable computing systems.

The complete world of interconnect possibilities is by no means defined by the archetypical models. Systems may be formed with dynamic routing capabilities, pathway selection features, which may effectively transform them from a network of one shape to a network of another. It is also true that the existence of a physical path between nodes does not mean that a logical connection between the nodes exists at all times, that the nodes are always "in session" with each other.

5.6.   Interconnect Considerations

There are various considerations in designing an interconnected system. Speed, availability, reliability are basic. In addition there are considerations of cost, load and the specific characteristics of the interconnect mechanism. Some mechanisms are "full duplex" in that they allow interaction in both directions simultaneously. Some are "half-duplex" allowing interaction in both directions

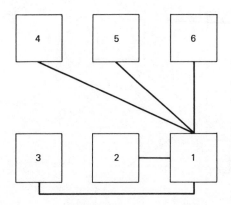

1 → 2 ⎫
1 → 3 ⎪
1 → 4 ⎬ Shown
1 → 5 ⎪
1 → 6 ⎭

Figure 41.   Mesh.

but in only one direction at a time. Others are "simplex," allowing interaction in only one direction.

A great deal of effort has been expended in studying the characteristics of interconnect mechanisms and the behavior of various interconnect topologies. Various systems structures have been proposed which would approximate the behavior of an "open network," an interconnection design which has the properties of a mesh, but which would not involve as many circuits and interconnection pathways.

One such design is called the "boolean cube." This design revolves around N*LogN interconnections, where N is the number of nodes to be interconnected. It operates with about half of the efficiency of a fully connected network. The concept involves visualizing a system of nodes as existing at the edges of a boolean cube. Figure 42 demonstrates for N equal to 8. This is a three dimensional system with the number of nodes equal to 2**3. Each node has a direct path to a set of nodes and an indirect path to another set. The indirect path requires movement through an intervening node which is part of the direct set of more than one processor group. The direct sets intersect so that some family of nodes provides connection across indirect paths. It is physically possible for every processor to talk to every processor in either one or two network cycles. However, because there are multiple indirect paths contention may develop in the network which will cause delays. Thus processor 1, wishing to talk to processor 6, may choose to go through path A or B. It does not know about other

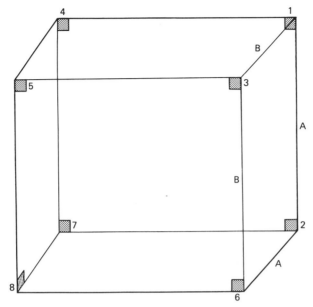

Figure 42.   Boolean cube. N = 2³ = 8. Direct: (1:2,3,4)(2:1,6,7)(3:1,5,6). . . .

traffic on the system and may run into a delay at node 3 because processor 5 has chosen a path through 3 to talk to 1.

This interconnect scheme may be used to interconnect complete computing nodes or elements of computing nodes to other elements. Thus one may visualize the corners as containing a set of computer systems or as containing a mixture of processing units, data storage units, communications controllers, and so on.

It is sometimes efficient to share physical paths by subdividing the total bandwidth of a path and allocating part of the resource to different intercommunicating units. This concept is sometimes called "virtual circuits." It is an extension of the idea of shared channels to the world of interconnection across longer distances. Thus a single fast pipeline may be either time division or frequency division multiplexed to form apparent multiple paths. The concept of "virtual circuit" undertakes to define a logical level of interconnection independent of physical paths.

Another aspect of interconnection is "alternate routing." Nodes in a system may have more than one path to each other. These multiple paths may be designed as a preferred path and a failsoft fallback path or as equally desirable paths depending upon instantaneous system load. Sometimes a fallback path may involve indirect passage through intervening nodes while the primary path is direct. Sometimes all paths may involve intermediate forwarding nodes, and the selection of one over the other depends upon the load on the path at any particular point in time. Other factors which may influence chosen paths are speed, cost, security and line quality during an interval. The load on nodes which handle the path may also affect the desirability of choosing one path over another.

The issues which are involved in network design lie outside the scope of this book. This section has intended only to introduce some fundamental concepts in interconnection so that the reader is somewhat aware of choices and possibilities.

6. A PEER HOMOGENEOUS SYSTEM

Figure 43 shows an interconnection between three processing nodes using a multibus design for interconnection. There is a bus subsystem which enables any terminal to reach any processor and another bus which interconnects the processors.

This system is characterized as homogeneous because all of the processing nodes contain identical programming and perform exactly the same activities. The data of the application running on this system has been partitioned geographically so that processor 1 handles northeastern data, processor 2 handles western data and Processor 3 handles other regions of the country. Each processing node is identical in hardware configuration and in systems software configuration, differing only in the regional data which is resident at the node.

One must be a little careful about the notion of homogeneity. At a conceptual level a system is homogeneous if all nodes are doing the same thing. This need not imply, however, that all nodes are physical duplicates of each other. It is possible that the amount of storage may vary because of regional requirements; it is also possible that the amount of memory on each processor may vary and that the speed of the processor itself may vary. The system may contain different configurations of the same architecture or product without violating a concept of homogeneity.

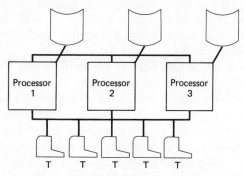

Figure 43.   Multiple bus peer system.

It is not clear how far beyond this one can go and still have an image of a homogeneous system. It becomes clear that a system which appears homogeneous to the logical designer of the application may not appear so to those responsible for physical planning or actual system integration.

In the opening sections of Chapter 1 we mentioned that it is conceivable for a system to contain different system software populations and it is possible for each node to be a different processing unit. It is conceptually possible for processor 1 to be an IBM 4300, processor 2 to be an IBM 8100 and processor 3 to come from another manufacturer. This might occur if a rigorous bottom-up and decentralized philosophy was operative within the organizational structure which supports this application.

Yet such a conglomeration of equipment would be considered by some to be a homogeneous system if each node was operating identical application logic. One of the problems of divergent node characteristics would certainly be the interconnection methodology across both hardware and software structure. The hardware problem would be in finding an interconnect hardware instrument which would talk to hardware nodes of various speeds and various interfaces. Currently the interconnection of diverse nodes is probably most realistically supported by teleprocessing methodology. However, even here differences in protocols at various levels may have to be resolved. The software problems involve the availability of software which creates some level of common system interface. In the current state of the art the argument for boxes as close to architecturally identical as possible seems rather strong.

6.1. Operational Scenario

The picture of Figure 43 shows no control point, this is a distributed control system. The operational characteristics of such systems vary, but we will describe one possible scenario.

Each processor "polls" the terminal bus looking for messages which are appropriate to it. A transaction entering the system is selected by one of the processors on the basis of an analysis of the data which the message will require. It is thought to be good design, currently, for all of the processing associated with a particular message, or set of messages forming a transaction, to be accomplished on a single node. High "local hit" ratios are generally thought to be desirable, although we have earlier described a system where this feature was not seen to be a requirement.

Each processing unit has its own operating system which controls the resources of its node and which is responsible for whatever node to node interaction may be required. Node to node interaction will be rather uncommon and is provided for a very small set of transactions which may reference data in more than one node. It is also provided so that in the event of malfunction an operating node can take up the messages intended for the inoperative node and provide a "can't do" message for the terminal.

6.2. Control Processor

Figure 44 shows the existence of a control processor in a system. The existence of this processor is consistent with the earlier statements that a system may be application peer but centrally controlled in some aspects. Figure 44 represents an application peer homongeneous/centralized control system. The control point may undertake a number of activities. It may be the transaction router, it may provide the central locus of operator control, it may be the mechanism for passing messages between processors, it may do some level of load balancing. If the processors, as they do in Figure 44, use a "shared DASD" design which enables different processors to access different data units, then the control processor may manipulate routing on the basis of availability. None of the functions of the control processor, however, changes the peer structure of the application. Although control flow has changed the data flow of the system remains logically unaltered.

7. PEER HETEROGENEOUS SYSTEM

The same considerations of degrees of homogeneity and control variation apply to heterogeneous systems. A system is application heterogeneous, in the view of this book, when each of the processing nodes has different local application logic. If data is partitioned so that inventory data is at processor 1, accounts

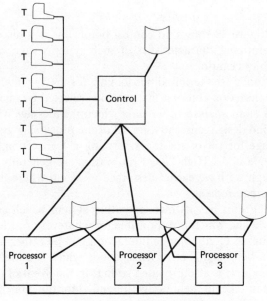

Figure 44.   Control point.

receivable data at processor 2, accounts payable data at processor 3, then the application logic at each processing node will reflect manipulations private to each type of data.

The degree of interaction between processing nodes may tend to be stronger in such systems than in application homogeneous systems, but good current design thinking still requires high local hit ratios and methods to reduce the degrees of interdependence between the nodes.

A source of examples for application heterogeneous systems are the worlds of industrial process control and distributed architectures in military vehicle control systems. A population of dedicated microcomputers, for example, is distributed around a vessel or aircraft in order to monitor the condition of a particular part of the vehicle. From time to time a check-in procedure is run so that the system can determine in a positive way that all of its components are operative. If a local processor finds a local malfunction, news of that malfunction may be broadcast throughout the system or reported to a control point which undertakes to initiate whatever action is required.

8. CONCLUDING REMARKS

This chapter has described a number of variations in the ways that nodes may be arranged and interconnected with each other. We have seen two major kinds of hierarchic concepts and a number of diverse peer arrangements. Mixtures of the two structural notions are frequent. The mixture occurs because of differences in the structure of control as opposed to application logic or data flow logic. The mixture may also occur when node clusters have peer relationships with each other but where each peer unit is itself a collection of functionally specific nodes.

There is probably no intellectual limit to the combinations which may be imagined in defining system shapes. There are, however, real limits in interconnect capacity, node capacity and software structuring.

Chapter 9

Distance

1. MULTIVARIOUS, MULTIFORMUS, MULTIPLEXUS

A survey of the literature of distributed systems will find that different writers take different views of the population of systems structures which may qualify as a distributed system. Some comments about this, and the definitional difficulties associated with this, were made in Chapter 1.

An underlying idea of "distribution" involves the notion of multiplicity of processing units. The idea of multiple processing units includes at one edge the idea of the generic multiprocessor and at the other edge the idea of geographically dispersed complete processing units with independent storage devices and teleprocessing intercommunication.

The world of systems structures, however, contains, as we have seen, a large number of potential intermediate structures. There are systems which contain processors which do not share memory but which share storage disks and may or may not also communicate with each other across channels much as they communicate with their own storage devices. There are systems, as we have seen, that are interconnected by interprocessor channels or buses which do not share storage and which are either in the same cabinet, the same room, or the same industrial site.

There are various notions of sameness and difference between the multiplicity of systems structures which may emerge. There are two fundamental viewpoints. One view is that systems which consist of teleprocessing interconnected distant components are fundamentally different from systems which consist of channel interconnections in the same room. The opposite view is that these systems are essentially similar, their logical structure is identical to an important community of users, and their physical structures differ in ways which are not important to an enterprise.

It is always difficult to calibrate measures of sameness and difference. One important difference between systems is whether or not the processors share a common operating system. A number of design problems develop in the coordination of processors when processes running with one operating system undertake to refer to processes or data running with another. This point of view

126

suggests that the memory shared multiprocessor does not fit into the class of distributed system. There are objections which can be raised to this, but it is a useful way to start considering issues of sameness and difference. We will use the term "multisystem" for collections of interconnected systems which may share disk storage, which are connected by channels and which are in the same data center. Some consideration of sameness and difference between such multisystems and geographically distributed systems will be undertaken from the viewpoint of technology, operations, business impact and application development.

1.1. Technology

In current technology (1980) processing units which share storage devices must have some local coordinating mechanism because there is no coordination available in the disk unit that they share. Since each processor has an independent path to the device and each processor runs its own operating system, that operating system must be extended to provide coordination of data references for data resources which may be shared between the processors. One approach to this problem is to interconnect the processors with an I/O channel and use that channel for coordination protocols and messages. No application data flows from one processor to another, but control information flows in the form of declarations of intent to reference a shared item, intervals of control over a shared item, and so on. This interconnection differs from many distributed systems in that in distributed systems there are important instances of data flow as well as control flow in the system. If there is no shared storage between the processors, then processors must send each other data if location independent access to data is going to be supported. This difference in the presence or absence of data movement between processors is an important difference between multisystems and some distributed processing systems.

However, many distributed processing concepts for geographically remote systems include the notion of a shared data node. A data node is a point in the system where shared data is located for access to all potentially sharing application processors. The difference between the shared storage device and the shared data node is the amount of intelligence at the shared data node which permits it to exercise coordinating functions. One speculative scenario for future systems is a structure which consists of a very high capacity data node used by sets of smaller application processors. In various versions of this systems structure data may or may not flow to the application node.

The speculation must be that systems structures of the future will support identical data and control flows whether they are geographically remote or geographically close. Computer and memory technology suggest that structural differences between multisystem and distributed systems concepts will begin to disappear as more intelligence is placed in all components of the system. The shared storage device of the future may well be a shared data node whether it is local or remote from the referencing application processor. This suggests that program structures and program interfaces to systems software should be independent of the geographical distance between processors and that software distinctions between multisystems and distributed systems need not and should not exist.

Another technology development which suggests a blurring of multisystem and distributed system distinction is the development of high speed communications mechanisms which have data rates as great as, or greater than, channels and which have geographical reaches of many kilometers. A fundamental question is whether the design conventions of teleprocessing based systems or the design conventions of channel connected systems should serve as the basis for support of such "in-plant" interconnection mechanisms. There is some speculation that such mechanisms can be used not only to interconnect processors, but processors to terminals, processors to storage devices, and so on, so that there is only one control and data interconnection mechanism between elements of a system which may be dispersed over significant geographical distances. This further supports the idea that multisystem concepts and distributed systems concepts are moving rapidly toward each other and as technology matures the distinctions will not be in any way clear from a system structure point of view.

1.2. Operations Management

If multisystems and distributed systems seem to be advancing toward each other from the point of view of potential technology, is there still some basis for making an important distinction between them? One such basis might be the impact on the operational environment which surrounds multisystems in the same room or distributed systems in a single establishment or enterprise.

This issue is addressed in Chapter 14. The essential question might be posed in this manner. If an installation has a single system of a given capacity and requires more capacity, what is the operational impact of getting a larger single machine, of interconnecting a second machine to the first in the same room, of interconnecting a second machine to the first from a remote location?

Chapter 14 suggests some way of assessing this issue. As regards the similarity or dissimilarity of distributed versus multisystems, the thrust of the question is how significant the differences in systems structure will be to the organization, staffing and costs associated with the operational environment. If multisystem interconnect leads to very different levels of complexity and cost from distributed systems, then it is valid to make important distinctions between them and to provide different kinds of software support. If it can be shown that various approaches to operations can minimize operational differences, then the distinctions between multisystem and distributed system will blur even further.

1.3. User Community

If technology suggests that multisystem and distributed systems are blending from the point of view of systems structure and if it is possible to create equivalent operational environments, is there some reason for the user community to make important distinctions between multisystems and distributed systems? This is a management style issue which depends on what the motivations for distributed remote processors truly are and to what extent the advantages seen for distributed may be achieved by, for example, department dedicated machines cooperating with each other in a single data center.

The remainder of this chapter addresses the notion of distance between processing units as a system variable, to be determined largely by the attributes of an application.

2. THE NOTION OF DISTANCE IN APPLICATION DESIGN

Distance is a concept which is important because of the implications that distance has for time. The current state of the technology is such that there is a tendency for nodes which are farther apart to require more time to interact with each other. This is partially a result of physical characteristics of interconnect mechanisms and partly a result of associated software structures.

The concept of distance refers to the time which is involved in an instance of node to node interaction. This time derives from the interconnection method which is used.

The idea of a time burden in interactions between nodes has been repeatedly alluded to in earlier chapters. It is important because the perception of time required to sustain an interaction event will influence the choices which are made about what functions or application actions may be distributed and how far away they may be placed from each other. If placing a program at a particular node increases the amount of time for communicating programs to interact, it is necessary to know whether that additional time is tolerable within limits of application performance. In effect a lower bound is placed on the granularity of distribution. This lower bound is a kind of "index of decomposability." This "index" is an as yet informal notion of the limits of distribution. We are undertaking to address the question of the granularity of distribution which is reasonable for any design. Should applications be dedicated to nodes or is it permissible to disperse individual programs of an application, finding more discrete partitions which may be spread across different physical nodes.

The list of interconnection vehicles includes various concepts and mechanisms. One may place on this list:

1. Cross-memory.
2. High speed internal bus.
3. External bus.
4. Channel.
5. Short haul interconnecting rings, loops and buses.
6. Teleprocessing lines.

Cross-memory refers to software structures in certain operating systems. In such systems programs may run in a software defined addressing space called a virtual memory. The size and structure of the virtual memory is somewhat independent of the size and structure of the real memory banks of the system. The intent of the virtual memory software design is to allow programs to occupy as much logical space as they require even if this means addressing through memory locations which do not in fact exist on the machine. The hardware of the system contains mechanisms that translate from virtual addresses to real addresses and that control the movement of referenced operands and instructions from a backing store to main memory as required. The mechanisms provide the illusion of larger memory spaces at the cost of some potential performance degradation.

In systems which use the virtual memory concept, a program or set of programs may run in a defined address space. If programs in one address space wish to communicate with programs in another defined address space some form of cross-virtual memory referencing must be provided by the operating system.

In the current state of the art such cross-memory mechanisms are limited to programs which are running in virtual memories defined in the same uniprocessor or multiprocessor system. Thus the distance which such a mechanism can reach is rather limited. From a hardware point of view, however, such a mechanism should be very fast since it involves the fast processor to memory interconnections of the machine.

A high speed bus, as used here, intends to suggest a very fast bus, perhaps on the order of 25 megabytes per second, which interconnects single board computer systems to other single board computer systems which exist in the same box or "cage." A class of systems is emerging in which complete computer systems can be packaged on a single board and multiple copies of these computers can be placed in a single box. The bus connections between the boards are very fast, but they have a limited reach. The distance between processing nodes is limited to the space in the box.

An external bus connects computer systems housed in separate cabinets. These buses are also very fast and have a reach of quite a few hundred feet.

A short-haul mechanism connects nodes which are distant from each other up to some number of kilometers. The mechanisms operate in the megabit per second range, are usually serial by bit and allow for multiple connections.

Channels are sometimes used to interconnect processing nodes although their major use is to interconnect processors and memories to input/output devices. The use of a channel to interconnect processing nodes usually involves some extension to channel logic which makes a processing node appear to another processing node as an I/O device. The IBM channel to channel adapter is an example of such hardware. The CTC permits IBM 360s and 370s to talk to other 360s and 370s on dedicated channels which are supported by the CTC. The reach of a channel is in hundreds of feet and they operate at speeds up to three or four megabytes per second.

Teleprocessing lines have almost unlimited reach but they are very slow compared to other mechanisms, operating in kilobyte per second rather than megabyte per second ranges. They also have operational characteristics characteristics which make them more sensitive than the other mechanisms. As a result more complex software may be involved in supporting teleprocessing interconnection than in using other mechanisms.

Transportation mechanisms which will provide geographical interconnection at megabit speeds are beginning to become a reality. We may look forward to the day when the speed of intercommunication will no longer be related to distance covered and when teleprocessing speeds will be in excess of speeds currently available with mechanisms of shorter reach. When this occurs many of the considerations in this chapter will become less important. In the current environment, however, the distance notion is important and the speed and reach of various interconnect mechanisms is an important design parameter.

3. INFERENCES, IMPLICATIONS, CONSIDERATIONS

The set of interconnection concepts and mechanisms described in the previous section implies a range of choices about where nodes may be placed in relation to each other. We see that nodes may be placed within a number of potential boundaries.

There are many situations, of course, where the location of a node is predetermined for historical or organizational reasons. However, in pure top-down design situations there may be some discretion applied to the actual location of the nodes of the system.

They may be placed within logical boundaries on virtual machine systems. They may be placed within "skin" boundaries by packaging multiple computers within a single box. They may be placed within room boundaries by using external buses or channels or short haul mechanisms. Nodes may be placed within establishment boundaries, within a multibuilding industrial park or on different floors of a skyscraper. Finally, nodes may be placed only within enterprise boundaries, communicating with each other at geographical distances separating various sites of an organization. This choice limits the interconnect mechanism to some form of teleprocessing.

Each of the possible interconnect mechanisms comes in various forms with its own range of speeds. Channels have an enormous range of speeds as do teleprocessing lines and interprocessor buses. Thus the choice of what mechanism to use involves the selection of a type of mechanism and a particular speed of that mechanism.

The choice of the physical distance to place between nodes of a system does not necessarily imply the interconnection mechanism. Their capabilities overlap and there may be reasons to use a mechanism which is not logically indicated. These reasons may come from characteristics of software, pricing structures, requirements for flexibility, and so on.

The suggestion that logical partitions of software function and data may be organized before physical locations are known seems counterintuitive to many people. However, there may be organizational reasons for preferring certain partitionings, or natural application structures which emerge from structured design. Many think it is good and necessary procedure to derive a conceptual system structure before defining a hardware base on which it is to run. Among the degrees of freedom in such a design approach is where to actually put the hardware. If the location of hardware is already determined, that set of locations and the times associated with interaction between the locations will naturally constrain the partitioning of the application.

The choice of where to place data processing nodes is only partially determined by available technology. It is influenced by various organizational concepts. Processing nodes may be made geographically remote from each other because the organization wants them to be at certain places where certain events occur. Nodes may be placed because various levels of management insist on having a local machine or refuse to have a local machine. There are many considerations which will influence the distance between nodes; not all of these will appear rational to a technologist but they are real nonetheless.

The remainder of this chapter will explore the relationship that the distance between nodes may have on application design and system choice.

4. THE INDEX OF DECOMPOSABILITY

The notion of the index of decomposability derives from a desire to discover a reasonable basis for determining the size of program structures which may be dispersed throughout a distributed system. It is closely related to the notion of the "level of profitable parallelism" which the author has described in other places.

As an introduction we will use a small example which is borrowed from earlier work in program decomposition for parallel operations. Many feel that the dispersion of components of a single program is not a realistic undertaking. However, there is much interest among programming technology theorists in methods to accomplish this in distributed or parallel systems. The reader should not be put off by the program decomposition example since the same kinds of considerations are relevant to application or cross-application interactions.

The limits of distributability may be demonstrated by the small DO loop of Figure 45. This loop is a unit of computational work which has been defined in an application structure. We have already decided that the loop is a module which can be placed at a particular node in the system. Present at that node are the arrays B and C and space for the creation of the array A which is the cross-product of B and C. We wish to determine if this unit of work may be profitably broken down further and its components spread to other nodes in the system.

```
DO I=1,10,1;
  A(I)=B(I)*C(I);
END:
```

Figure 45.   A potentially decomposable software unit.

The analysis proceeds in two stages. The first stage is to discover partitions of work which may be independent within the DO loop structure. An analysis of data reference patterns and iteration to iteration relationships reveals that the loop is a parallel loop. Each iteration of the loop may be run independently of any other iteration. Thus A(1)=B(1)*C(1), A(2)= B(2)*C(2), etc., may all be run concurrently. We know this because there is no passing of data between iterations and there is no sharing of data among iterations.

From a logical partition point of view we may arrange for ten processors to run one iteration of the loop each. This could be accomplished in a number of ways. A copy of the program which accomplishes the assignment statement might be placed at each node. The relevant elements of the arrays might be placed at each node. The result of the operation, a given value for a specific A(I), could then be passed to a node that would form the array A. The processor which recognized the DO statement might send a message to the other processors requesting that they execute the assignment statement on local data. Alternatively the processor recognizing the DO statement might have all of the data for B and C which it would selectively transmit to other processors when it requests the execution of code.

If we assume that the population of processing nodes involved in this event are connected over teleprocessing lines with speeds of 9600 bits per second and access to these lines through a massive telecommunications access method which may impose various queueing delays, etc., then the feasibility of such a distribution looks rather shaky.

The basis for objecting to the scheme of distributing the DO loop iterations comes from a perception of the time it will take for the necessary communication between nodes relative to the time it takes to perform an iteration. We have an intuitive sense that something is out of balance and that it would be more profitable not to distribute in this way, but to execute all iterations of the loop at one site. This would result in reduced systems load and in reduced elapsed time to perform the loop.

The distance between the nodes, in terms of time, suggests that the unit of work we are analyzing for distribution is beneath some reasonable lower bound for size. This concept of a minimally reasonable size for a distributed procedure is the idea of the index of decomposability.

The same scheme running on a boolean cube machine where each processor was in a single cabinet and processors interconnected across a 100 megabyte bus would look considerably more attractive.

The indices of decomposability for the teleprocessing interconnected system and the in same frame system vary because of our perception of the time it will take to perform the necessary initializing and coordination functions between processing nodes. The faster the interaction, the more frequent interaction events may be tolerated and the potential distributability of program logic increases.

There is a similarity between the index of decomposability which suggests the size of distributed procedures and the level of profitable parallelism which suggests the size of procedures which may be run concurrently. Much of the work in analysis of programs for concurrent operation will apply to analysis of programs for distribution.

Every system of nodes will have an index of decomposability which determines the minimum size of a distributable unit of work. This idea can be useful in understanding the emerging structure of an application under consideration for distribution. It is also a useful idea in determining where processing nodes may be located.

5. A CONCEPT OF SYSTEM COMPARABILITY

One of the problems in systems design has been the lack of methodologies for comparing systems of different structure and different types. Much work has been spent trying to define taxonomies of computer systems and characterizing them by interconnect attributes. The problem remains, however, that no commonly used structural classification system exists.

This problem is more than intellectual and academic. Because no classification scheme exists we are constantly surprised by the variety of system shapes which contend for the same application dollar. Uniprocessors, multiprocessors, locally distributed nodes, geographically distributed nodes all seem to provide potentially suitable bases for a large set of applications.

The idea of the index of decomposability provides a simple conceptual tool for a first approximation of a mappping of application structure and systems structure. Consider Figure 46. The X axis is calibrated by the size of a program in terms of the number of instructions which it should run between instances of node to node communication. The Y axis represents the burden on a system of each instance of node to node communication in terms of instruction times required to support the interaction. The burden time includes the number of instructions required to handle the transportation mechanism and the time on the mechanism expressed in instruction execution times which elapse while messages are en route.

Every configuration which may be a candidate for the support of an application will find a place on the Y axis. Every potential program module will find a place on the X axis. Earlier work in decomposing programs for parallelism suggests that a reasonable lower bound for a program to run before it must talk to another program is the time that it takes to effect that communication. Using that as a guideline and starting point we decide that a unit of work which will

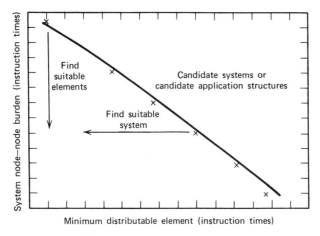

Figure 46. Index of decomposability.

run on a single processor for a time smaller than the time required to talk to another node is a unit of work which is beneath the index of decomposability.

Figure 46 shows that if one is given a candidate set of configurations for an application one may infer the size in time units of execution of the smallest program which should be considered a distributable element. Conversely if one is given a set of application modules one may infer the interconnect characteristics desirable in a selected configuration. Application modules may already exist because of a design which indicates that a high degree of modularity and concurrency is necessary to fulfill performance requirements. Or the modules of the application may already be defined if this is an old application being analyzed for possible distribution.

There is no fixed relationship between the amount of time a program will run autonomously and its physical size in terms of byte space required in memory. Thus it is difficult to project the actual number of modules which an application will decompose into. Yet the mapping of execution times and communication burden times does give an initial perception of the general size and population of distributable program elements which may be used in structured and composite design to guide idea of module strength and module coupling.

The index of decomposability also suggests a tradeoff between node power and telecommunications speed. If the work units defined for an application are to be large in order to avoid excessive communicsation, the processing nodes must necessarily be larger and faster in order to meet performance and response constraints.

The index of decomposability participates in the decision about where to place processing nodes. Given degrees of political freedom, one can choose the locus of nodes as a result of understanding the distance implications inherent in various types of interconnecting mechanism. Thus if application logic impels a particular application structure and that structure cannot meet performance requirements across teleprocessing lines, then positioning nodes at places where they may be reached by faster interconnect mechanisms is a necessary solution.

The separation of logical partitioning and physical structuring is inherent in the idea of an index of decomposability. As the characteristics of interconnection mechanisms change over time, modules that could not be profitably distributed geographically may become profitably distributable at those distances. It is desirable to be able to move programs to more remote nodes without disturbing the program structure and interfaces. In order to accomplish portability, interfaces to systems software must be provided so that no reprogramming of program to program or program to data references is necessary if the interconnection mechanism changes.

Changes in business style and the relationships between applications may, as well as technology, suggest that programs far from each other should be moved closer, or that programs clustered at a node may be dispersed. It would be very convenient to permit the movement of program populations without changes to the program interfaces.

In order to achieve populations of portable programs it is necessary that systems software provide service interfaces which are insensitive to the transportation mechanism being used. It is also necessary that the logical structure of a program or application be determined independently of an eventual hardware base. However, some kind of guideline must exist in order to impose bounds of the size of individual modules and to discover roughly the number of distributable elements which will exist in the program or application. A rough appreciation for interaction times inherent in different interconnect mechanisms will serve this purpose.

6. SUMMARY OF EFFECTS OF DISTANCE

The distance in time between nodes will influence the basic perception of the design of an application. Depending on how long instances of interaction will require, different degrees of modularity and different interaction relationships will be defined.

The size of a program will be influenced by decisions that derive from the distance notion. In turn, the autonomy of a node, the rate of interaction between nodes and the units of interaction will be influenced.

In a politically unconstrained environment it may well be best to determine where nodes will be placed after a considerable amount of analysis of application structure has been undertaken. A reasonable approach is to determine the functions which must be performed and determine the packing of functions into modules in a way best suited to application logic, and only then should a decision be made about where to put the nodes. This decision is based on the interaction delays which the application may tolerate in its attempts to meet performance constraints.

Naturally this approach is reasonable only when there is no existing equipment already installed. However, it may be reasonable whether or not an old c new application is being considered for dispersion to hardware not yet selected.

This chapter has discussed the location of processing nodes from the point of view of the intensity of interaction which may be required by an application and the constraints on the interconnecting mechanism that is consequently implied. There are other considerations relating to the placement of nodes which will be discussed in later chapters. For the sake of completeness we will mention here that the geographical distance between nodes of a system may also seriously affect the operational costs associated with each node. Nodes in the same cabinet will generate different operational burdens and requirements from nodes in different cities.

Certain changes in program development costs may also occur because of distances between nodes in a system. Remote debugging, testing and maintenance requirements may or may not be available within the context of a particular distribution.

An additional constraint on location exists as a result of the fact that not all hardware/software offerings make all interconnection options available. Thus a particular system offering may only support teleprocessing interconnection or only support high speed bus interconnection. If a different distance is required for node interconnection than offered by available software, it is necessary either to change the location of the nodes, provide the software or choose an alternative set of vendor offerings.

There is also a relationship between the notions of single systems image and distance. It may be that different levels of transparency are meaningful or useful at different distances. One level of single system image may be available for nodes in the same cabinet, another for those which are geographically dispersed for different classes of users or professional staff.

Chapter 10

Allocation

1. ISSUES TO BE CONSIDERED

This chapter will consider some of the issues involved in decisions about the location of program, data and control elements of a system. We will try to identify some available techniques, some decisions which must be made and some problems which must be resolved. The state of the art is not yet far advanced and not all of the analytic techniques which are emerging are yet mature. Yet there is a general direction indicated which suggests the kinds of analysis and decisions which must be made.

2. DATA AND PROCEDURE RELATIONSHIPS

The dispersion of elements of a system involves an analysis of relationships between users of a system, the units of work which represent their use of the system, the data to which users refer and relationships between groups of data. This analysis is required whether an old application is being considered for dispersion to a new physical structure or a new application is being designed for a distributed physical base. The analysis will reveal the closeness of coupling between various systems elements and suggest how partitioning is most reasonably accomplished.

There are a number of levels of analysis which may be undertaken to discover logical clusters of systems elements, and each of these levels may be repeated a number of times in order to discover good partitions. There is, however, a fundamental analytic tool which may be used to determine element relationships. The use of this tool, in various forms, combined with a good deal of judgment, will suggest the essential shape of a distributed system.

A system is a set of objects and operators. Objects are those things which are operated upon; operators are those things which modify objects. Figure 47 shows a matrix representing columns of operators and rows of objects. This matrix serves as the base of analyses for distributability at many levels. De-

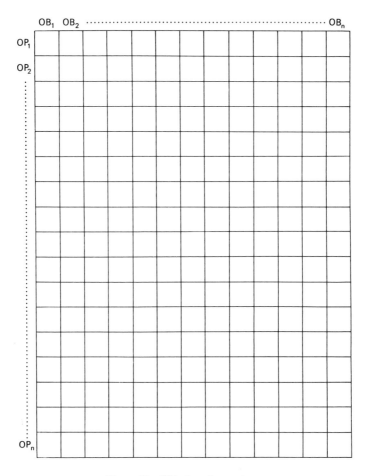

Figure 47. Objects and operators.

pending on the specific set of operators and objects which are chosen and upon the information recorded at the intersection of an object and an operator, various insights into a system may be gained.

The matrix may be used to relate users and the applications that they use. This would suggest the placement of applications relative to locations of users. The matrix may be used to relate programs to data, transactions to programs, and so on. It is at program to data level that we will demonstrate its use.

2.1. Forming Programs and Records

We will begin with the assumption that a new application is being investigated for which no data exists and for which no programs yet exist. We wish to discover what a natural set of data structures and program structures might be for this application.

The objects represented on the matrix will be the elemental fields which are defined for the application. Each field represents a value or a key which must exist within the framework of the application. The names of the operators are the primitive operations which must be performed upon the fields. The definition of operators requires some careful consideration. One temptation is to name all of the fundamental functions performed on the field. Thus functions like add, compare, multiply might serve as a list of operators. However, such a list would not reveal the fact that such functions may be performed at different points in the application structure. The operator list must relate more closely to the logic of the application. We wish a list such as calculate weekly pay, test for reorder, find highest on list and so on. The operators might be well chosen at the level of description which would appear on a program flow chart or on a well documented program listing. It is important that the operator list be granular enough so that the operations represented do not represent programs but activities which will be imbedded in programs.

Within the matrix a mark is made to represent the data which is referenced by each operation. Figure 48 shows a matrix of check marks for an arbitrary set of operators and operands. The check marks tend to indicate a population of programs and a set of record structures. Thus the operators which reference the same fields are candidates for inclusion in the same program structure. The fields which are referenced together are logically placed in the same files or records.

This sounds rather straightforward, but it is not. It may be necessary to redefine operators a number of times before clear clusters of programs and clear record groupings or file groupings emerge.

If no clear groupings develop, it might be possible to discover program and data structure by adding information to the matrix. This information would indicate the kind of reference which is being made and the intensity of reference which is being made. A denotation for READ and for MODIFY would indicate which functions only referred to the data and which functions actually changed it. This might suggest a pattern for operator grouping where the sites of change might be minimized. If there is no way of avoiding multiple program reference to the same field, it might be convenient to cluster change operators in a single program if possible. This will eventually reduce the program to program synchronization problem in the running application.

If there is some data about the intensity of reference, even to the point of denoting whether an operator is a low, medium or high user of a field, this might be helpful for operator grouping.

The intent of this exercise is to discover the programs and data structures of the application. Readers with a long history in the industry will remember the days when the goal of an application design was to keep all of the "runs" in tape time. Thus the programs which formed the application had operations assigned to them in such a way as to minimize total application time. If one

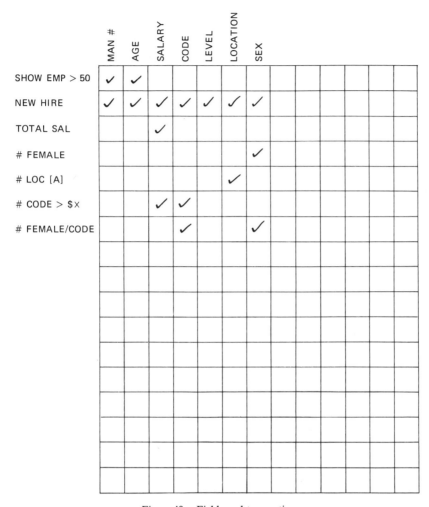

Figure 48. Fields and transactions.

program ran 3X tape time and another program was seriously I/O bound, then operations were moved from the compute bound to the I/O bound program. The spirit of this analysis is the same. There is a certain degree of freedom in the grouping of operations among programs. The goal here is to minimize the number of programs which refer to the same fields. Similarly, data structures are formed to minimize the number of files or records to which a program must refer. We are seeking, at a module definition level, a maximum partitioning of program logic and data reference.

One suggested convention for operators on the matrix is the use of the concept of a transaction. If the transactions which can occur in a system are defined, then each transaction represents a reasonably primitive operator and a mapping of transactions and field references will suggest data grouping and transaction grouping.

There is some tendency in the literature emerging in this area to use the word transaction as a substitute for the word program. This implies that each transaction type will have a one to one relationship with a particular processing program. In general this is not necessarily true. Transactions may require multiple programs for processing and a single program may handle multiple transaction types. An understanding of the data requirements for each transaction will suggest the structure of the program population by indicating which transactions should be handled by the same program structure because of commonality of data reference.

There is a relevant body of material in software technology, program structuring techniques and module definition techniques that should be understood as part of the procedure for defining program populations. Outstanding in this area is the work of Glen Myers in Composite Design.

2.2. Old Applications

In many situations the program and file/record structure definition process will already have occurred. An application may be already in production in a centralized environment and the analysis is undertaken to determine whether, or to what extent, the application may be profitably decomposed to run on a multinode system. In such cases the program population and the data structures are already known.

The advantage of such a situation lies in the fact that it is possible to develop statistics on the intensity with which various programs refer to various data structures. This can be done with statistics gathering mechanisms available with some data base management systems. This assessment of reference must be approximated, in new designs, by judgmental evaluations of high, medium and low reference. The matrix can be used to determine feasible distributions of programs and data. If a program is the sole user of a named data structure, then that program and that data structure are jointly distributable. If a program is an intense user of a data structure and a population of programs are light users, then it is possible to distribute the data with the intense user and allow the light users to refer to the data remotely. If there is a population of intense users, then that population should be kept together in the same node with the data.

There is another dimension to be considered. This involves the type of use which a program makes of data. Some programs will merely refer to data; other programs will modify data. In general it is good practice to keep data near its source of change. Programs which change data should be left together at a site where the data that they modify exists. Programs which only refer to data are more safely removed to remote sites.

There must be, of course, a good deal of judgmental balancing between intensity of reference and type of referencing in reaching dispersion decisions. There are a number of diverse solutions to problems of multiple program reference to data. Under certain conditions data may be left in place and referencing programs moved. Under other conditions data may be partitioned and moved to various sites. Under some conditions data may be replicated at various sites. Data which is referenced only within the structure of an application may be replicated without introducing too much systems complexity. Data which is changed will introduce some coordination problems when it is replicated. The section on distributed data will address considerations in data location more completely.

2.3. Summary

This section has undertaken to discuss the first step in understanding the distributability of an application. For new applications a program population and data structures must be developed by analyzing the logical relationship between the operations of an application and the data objects which are involved. When programs are defined and data structures are developed, then a similar kind of analysis will indicate how programs and data may be physically dispersed through the system. If an old application, with an already given set of programs and data structures, exists, the analysis is limited to how to disperse the already formed population of objects and operators.

3. DISTRIBUTING PROCESSES

There are considerations in the distribution of processes which go beyond their relationship to data. Any given distribution of process/data combinations will give rise to a set of relationships between processes. Processes may relate to each other in a number of ways. They may be related because they share data. Such a relationship implies that they make reference to the same data but not to each other. Thus either program may make data references to the same data, but they never send messages to each other or call upon each other for services. Such relationships must be coordinated by some kind of data reference synchronizing mechanism in the operating system or in the data manager system.

Processes may also have direct relationships with each other. These relationships may be of two fundamental types, synchronous or asynchronous. In a synchronous relation a process sends a message to another process and then waits for the response of the other process before it may continue. In an asynchronous relationship the process initiating the conversation may continue to work during the interval that is required for a reply, or no reply may be expected or necessary.

In addition to variations in the relationship between processes there are variations in the unit of interaction between them. Thus some processes may talk to each other by short messages; others may communicate by passing large files to each other. Finally, process relations will differ in the frequency with which they communicate with each other.

The combination of considerations of how the processes are logically related, what the unit of interaction is and how intensively the processes communicate will determine the distributability of processes throughout the system.

3.1. Packing and Dispersing

One of the critical decisions, particularly important in an environment where smaller machines are involved, is under what circumstances two processes should be placed in the same node and under what circumstances they should be dispersed. Another way of stating this is to put the question "To what extent should nodes be single function dedicated nodes and to what extent should they be multifunction?" This decision may be made within the programs of an application or between distinct, but interacting, applications.

There are some guidelines for this kind of determination. If node cost is low, then dedication is attractive because the replication of systems is not expensive. If node costs are high, however, it is desirable to pack as much function into them as is reasonable within constraints of good response times and reasonable levels of performance analysis costs. The cost of multiple small nodes of a certain type versus the cost of a single larger system can be approximately calculated and a tendency to single or multifunction based partially on that calculation.

The degree of data sharing and common reference will also influence the dispersion. If data sharing is low, then multiple nodes become more feasible than if data sharing is high. Similarly the rate of process interaction will influence whether a distribution across nodes is desirable. Finally, as we suggested in the chapter on distance, the fundamental speed of the interconnection mechanism as a constraint on permitted rates of interaction is very important. The three fundamental constraints on distribution, then, are: the rate of process to process interaction, the speed of the interconnect mechanism and the degree of remote data access.

It is very important to consider this issue carefully. One wishes to avoid situations in which it is necessary to redesign or reprogram because errors are made about node or interconnect capacity. What is really lacking are known techniques which reduce the cost of changing one's mind.

3.2. Reasonable Distributions

The question of whether to put processes in the same node or different nodes is a limited form of the question "What is a good distribution of a population of processes across a population of nodes?"

We have seen that the placement of processes may be constrained by data elements which they reference. There may be political and technological con-

PROCESSES
A   Nonportable from Site 1
B
D
E
F
G   Nonportable from Site 2
H   Nonportable from Site 3
I
J
K
L

Figure 49.   List of processes discovered in logical partitioning.

straints as well. There are organizational issues which may bind a process to a specific node even if that process and its data are jointly portable. Figure 49 shows a population of processes for which a distribution decision must be made. There are four aspects to the distribution decision:

1.   Which of the processes are portable?
2.   How many nodes should there be?
3.   How should processes be grouped together?
4.   How far apart should the nodes be?

Of the programs in Figure 49 only a subset is movable at discretion. Some may be bound to a site by data; others may be bound to a site for reasons of node capacity, operating system or data manager interfaces, machine compatibility, etc. The dispersion decision starts with a set of nonportable processes around which other processes must be grouped in some way.

The number of nodes defined by the population of nonportable processes is the minimum number of nodes that the system may have. The maximum number of nodes is the number achieved by placing each process in a unique node. Thus the system of Figure 49 may have from three to twelve nodes. The determination of the number of nodes is part of the determination of how processes should be grouped together.

The factors of rate of interaction and unit of interaction combine to form a concept of burden on the system due to interaction. This burden achieves a certain level as a result of the distance between the processes. Given a certain interconnection mechanism, a flow of data associated with each process to process interaction, and a rate of such interaction, a number representing the amount of work the system must do to support interactions can be developed. For any particular interconnection mechanism a matrix may be formed which

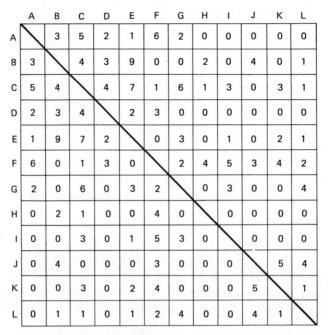

	A	B	C	D	E	F	G	H	I	J	K	L
A		3	5	2	1	6	2	0	0	0	0	0
B	3		4	3	9	0	0	2	0	4	0	1
C	5	4		4	7	1	6	1	3	0	3	1
D	2	3	4		2	3	0	0	0	0	0	0
E	1	9	7	2		0	3	0	1	0	2	1
F	6	0	1	3	0		2	4	5	3	4	2
G	2	0	6	0	3	2		0	3	0	0	4
H	0	2	1	0	0	4	0		0	0	0	0
I	0	0	3	0	1	5	3	0		0	0	0
J	0	4	0	0	0	3	0	0	0		5	4
K	0	0	3	0	2	4	0	0	0	5		1
L	0	1	1	0	1	2	4	0	0	4	1	

Figure 50. Burden number—same box.

represents the burden of supporting interaction between processes. Such a matrix is shown in Figure 50. The matrix represents systems burden if all of the processes are in the same box. A similar matrix may be formed for burden across a set of alternative interconnection mechanisms. Figure 51 shows the burden for a teleprocessing interconnection where every process is assumed to talk to every other process across teleprocessing lines. Values in both Figures 50 and 51 are normalized numbers intended to show relationships. A preferred distribution of process is one that minimizes systems burden within constraints of node size and system responsiveness.

Consider Figure 52. This shows two possible distributions of the processes A through H. In Figure 52a the total burden is 259. In Figure 52b the total burden is 224. Distribution B is preferred to distribution A. The technique is to place processes in such a way as to minimize the total system burden for process interaction. Thus processes have a kind of magnetism for each other which is a result of the burden number.

It may be that the minimization of the burden numbers still does not yield a system which will meet its response requirements. It is here that the concept of distance can be useful. If response requirements cannot be met by teleprocessing interconnection, it is possible that a desired logical distribution will be

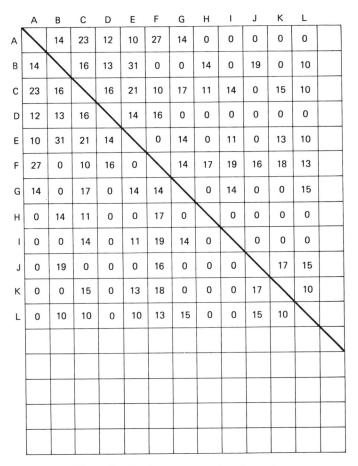

Figure 51. Burden—teleprocessing dispersal.

sufficiently effective if a faster interconnection is used. A faster interconnection may involve locating the nodes physically closer to each other so that they may take advantage of faster mechanisms with shorter reach. It is very desirable to save the logical structure of the application, if possible, since logical analysis is expensive and complex work. It is preferable to decide where to place the physical boxes which will support a logical structure after a burden analysis is completed. Thus it is desirable, if politics allow, to decide to geographically distribute or locally distribute very late in the development of an application and not as the first decision which is made. The goal of design is not geographic dispersion but a well partitioned system with performance predictable elements giving good responses.

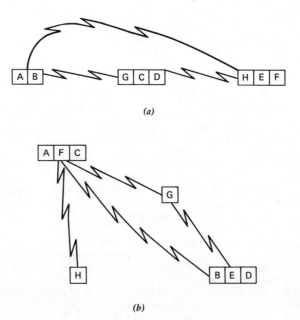

Figure 52.   Two distributions.

Naturally there will be situations where the physical location of nodes is predetermined and not a result of the design process. In such cases movement of nodes to improve performance is not feasible. If physical nodes are not portable, then it is particularly important to structure applications so that components of the application can be moved from one site to another without disturbing the basic structure of the system.

4.   DISTRIBUTING DATA

Of all of the aspects of distributed processing the distribution of data is the most complex and multifaceted. There are issues of methodology in separating data, issues in the structure of software to support distributed data and even a fundamental question about whether distributed data is an important goal for a system to achieve.

There are two points of view about the importance of distributed data. Some hold that distributed data is an important aspect of a system in its own right. Business units, locations, users, want certain data to be physically located at their sites. They wish control over the media and absolute control over how the data is handled.

Another view is that distributed data is not, per se, important. The important goal, this view holds, is efficient, reliable access to data wherever it may be located in a system. Thus distribution is only one means to an end. It is a mere technique for overcoming the difficulties involved in reliable, predictable, efficient access to data at a central point. The true goal of systems design is to permit remote nodes access to data as if it were local. The data should be held at a single site where rigorous mechanisms for integrity, security, recoverability may be applied.

These two views represent positions which are influenced by whether one holds a top-down or bottom-up view of systems development and whether one sees distributed processing as the dispersal of some function from a data center or the interconnection of processing nodes which have legitimate data environments of their own.

4.1. Basic Methods for Distributing Data

Two basic methods for dispersing data through a system are partitioning and replication. Partitioning tries to define various segments of data which are appropriate to a particular node and place them where they are most intensively referenced. Replication undertakes to make data available to all using nodes with some set of rules for controlling the synchronization of the various copies.

4.1.1. Partitioning

There are a number of fundamental methodologies for partitioning data. These methods emerge from various decisions about:

1. The level at which a data partition is defined.
2. The criteria used to define the partition.
3. The permanence of a partition of data at a logical node.

Data may be partitioned at a file level or at a subfile level. In a system with a set of well defined files it is possible to disperse these files across nodes using reference analysis of the type discussed in earlier sections. It is also possible to disperse at a record level so that some parts of a file may be at one node and other parts at another node. Subfile partitions may be preferable when there are nodes which tend to refer intensively to a particular part of a file but not to all parts. When subfile partitioning is undertaken the various dispersed parts may become logical files to the system. Whether a system views a dispersed single file as such or as a new set of smaller files is a specific system characteristic deriving from the details of the software package. Most small data manager subsystems would use the convention of naming the parts of the large file as individual small files at each node.

There are various criteria for defining partitions of files. One partitioning criterion is by some attribute of the data. This attribute may be geographic location. For example, regional data clusters may be allocated to regional nodes. This kind of data "splitting" leads to application homogeneous systems similar to the first banking industry example.

The partitions may also be defined across applications. Thus there might be, in a system, an inventory node, an accounts receivable node, an accounts payable node, and so on, in the spirit of the commercial example of an earlier chapter. By its nature, this kind of splitting leads to application heterogeneous systems.

It is natural to think of split systems as essentially peer in their structure. Figure 53 suggests that the use of certain attributes might lead to structures which were not clearly peer structures. In industries where an event entered into the system tends to receive intensive attention, declining over time, and where the entry describes the event, systems of the shape of Figure 53 may emerge.

The attribute chosen for partition definition in this demonstration is time. Thus entry records which are most current remain on the lowest level processing nodes for a week. After a week interest in these events diminishes and they

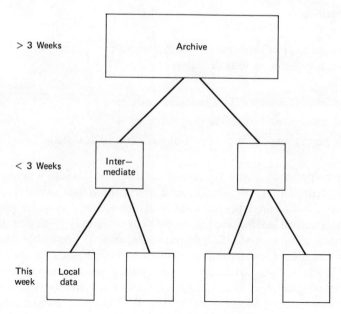

Figure 53.   Archival hierarchic data.

are percolated to the next level. After three weeks they are percolated to the last level.

Whether this system is appropriately drawn as a hierarchic system depends upon some details of control of the data flow. If each level determines what is to be sent up and the time when it is to be sent up, then the system, although it looks like a tree, is not hierarchic as regards control. If higher levels demand the percolation and the data that moves to them can only be retrieved with their logical permission, then the system becomes more conceptually hierarchic in its nature.

An approach to partitioning at a subfile level is called "extraction." We saw an example of this with the service application example. An analysis of what a node requires for operation may reveal that only some fields of a record are required. These fields may then be extracted from a central file and placed at appropriate using nodes. If the data so extracted is not represented at the node with the larger record structure, a partitioning has occurred. If these fields are allowed to exist at both places, then a replication has been undertaken and various synchronizations must be applied.

Sometimes the difference between a replication and a partition can be subtle. If summaries or images of the extracted records are sent to another node from time to time, then if the design allows any period of time in which record images at sender and receiver are both usable in any way, the design moves closer to replication. For reasons we will mention when we discuss replicated data the differences between partitioning and replication are not always as clear cut as simple categorization may imply.

It is possible to put partitions of data permanently at a particular node so that that node is always the possessor of a particular set of data. It is also possible for partitions of data to be moved from one node to another as demand develops. Partitions of read-only data may be moved to multiple places; effectively replicated, partitions of data which may change will commonly be moved to a single place at a time. The level of movement may be an entire file or set of files, or a selected set of records from a file. When the using node is finished with the data it may retain it until another node requests it or it may send it back to some central distribution point.

4.1.2. Data Replication

Multiple copies of data may be placed at different sites in a system. The first form of replication we will discuss is permanent replication. When data is permanently replicated there are duplications of records, fields and other data structures at multiple nodes of a system.

The essential problem with replicated data is the distribution of changes and the closeness of synchronization between various copies of the data.

There are various levels of synchronization which may be appropriate. An application should be able to determine which level of synchronization is appropriate for its operation.

1. *Immediate synchronization with controlled reference.* This requires that all copies of data at all nodes be identical and that no reference of the data, even to read, be allowed during the time required to effect a change and to distribute the change throughout the system. The lockout of reference may be made at a file or a record level. If reference is not permitted at a file level, then no record of the file may be referenced while any part of the file is being changed. If lockout is maintained at the record level, then only the changing record is controlled.

2. *Immediate synchronization with permitted reference.* This requires the immediate broadcast of changes but allows read-only reference to data under change while changes are made within the system.

3. *Batched or queued synchronization.* This permits a node to make multiple changes to a file and transmit changes in a batched, queued manner to another site where data of the same kind resides. The decision of when to transmit may be made by the changing node or by the receiving node. Similarly the physical location of the queue holding accumulated changes may be placed at either node. The mechanism for transmitting changed information may be a copy of a change notice transaction, a copy of the image to be placed in the record at the other node or some form of summarization transaction.

The synchronization of replicated data is a system requirement which may be designed in various ways. We will discuss some methods shortly. It is important to be able to recognize exactly when some form of synchronization becomes a requirement. It is commonly believed that synchronization problems occur only with replicated data. This is not entirely true. In a system which has data partitions defined by application it is necessary to synchronize the values in related fields even though no fields or values are replicated. Thus if one node represents the number of items on hand, another node represents the number of order and a third the number scheduled for shipment, it is necessary to coordinate these three fields as closely as if they were replicated data. It is necessary to design so that they are current to the same time period and that they are part of the same scope of recovery, checkpointed to the same place when a system error has been discovered.

4.2. Synchronization Techniques

Synchronization may be achieved in various ways which depend upon the immediacy of the synchronization required and upon other aspects of system design. Figure 54 shows a hierarchic system in which there has been both partitioning and replication. A discussion of design alternatives will enable us

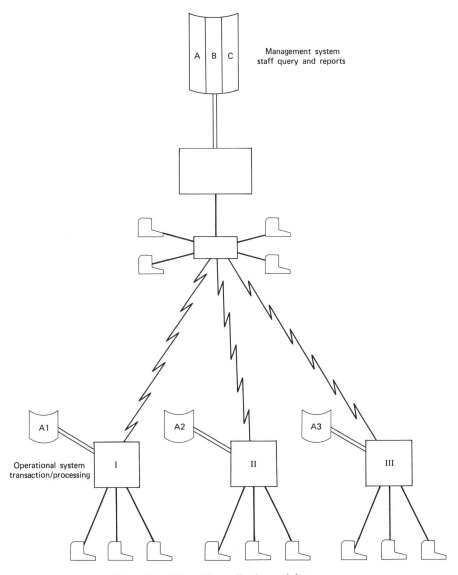

Figure 54. Hierarchic application and data.

to bring together various issues of system synchronization, data design and application design.

The data of the system has been partitioned at a file level. An analysis of what is required to process a transaction at the lower level of the system has determined that only file A is required for 95% of transactions. In a retail environment the lower nodes can confirm purchases without reference to the higher level node in the vast majority of cases. Files B and C are changed only to reflect transactions and are not involved in determining whether or not a transaction can be permitted. In addition to bringing A forward to lower level nodes, A itself is partitioned into A1, A2, A3 to reflect a regional or store level partitioning. Beyond the two levels of splitting there is also some extraction. An analysis of transactions determines that 90% of the transactions can be authorized by reference to only 10% of the fields of file A. Only those required fields are brought to the lower level nodes.

Replication occurs in the system because the fields brought to the lower level nodes are duplicated in the original file A. This permits staff members at the site of the larger node to make inquiries and to produce reports on data at that node.

4.2.1. Asynchronous Batched

One possible design is to permit the small nodes to process transactions asynchronously and at selected times send change notices to the larger machine. These change notices would be applied to the large node copy of file A at a time when small node use of file A was not permitted. At this time necessary changes to files B and C would also be applied.

This design has some attractive features. Because the lower level nodes are sending secondary transaction notices to the larger node it is possible to allow different data structures at each node. If naming conventions are applied system-wide, there should be no constraint on the nature of various data managers in the system. It is also possible to use communication lines efficiently by proper batching of transmission and timing of transmission.

The transmission of change notices may be at the discretion of the lower level or the higher level node. If there is no question of transmission efficiency, the queue for transactions may be put at either node level.

In order to be effective the environment of the design must have certain features. Most important is the tolerance of the staff at the larger node for less than current data. Many headquarters staffs have such a tolerance if the data they can use is consistent as of a certain designated time. In addition the staff must be able to tolerate the constraint that they have read only access to the data.

To be operationally effective the lower level nodes must have sufficient storage to hold developing batches and particularly to continue to operate if the higher level node is not available when expected. If the higher level node is "down," the lower level nodes must be able to continue to collect batches until the larger node comes "up." At that time the larger node should request transmission of batches and establish local queues for processing when the files are actually changed.

A very interesting aspect of this design is reflected in the question of where system control effectively lies in this system. Although the system is drawn hierarchically, it can be argued that effective control lies in the lower level nodes. It is these nodes that commit the company to a transaction. They must have sufficient computational power to make local determination of the acceptability of a transaction to the enterprise. Those transactions that must be referred to the larger node because of reference to nonlocal data may be done on a "will confirm basis." The lower level nodes accept the transaction on the contingent confirmation of the higher level machine. In this design that would be done on a next day basis.

4.2.2. Synchronized Messages

If users of the large node have no tolerance for obsolete data or if the number of transactions requiring confirmation from the large node is very significant, then this design is inappropriate. The increased rigor of the synchronization requires that each transaction be simultaneously reflected at lower level and at higher level nodes. The lower level node may undertake to process transactions but will not respond to a user terminal until it receives confirmation that the larger system has accepted and recorded the transaction. There is the concept of a two stage commitment involving mutual confirmation and synchronization from both levels of node. While a change is being made at the larger node, permission to read a record under change may or may not be granted. In the most stringent design no record may be read while it is under change and no record may be changed while it is being read.

A variant of the synchronization may involve a preliminary reference to the larger node before the lower level nodes modify their files. This is appropriate if confirmation from the larger node is a serious aspect of the predominant number of transactions.

4.2.3. Refreshment

Another variant of design considers that the local data of the lower level nodes is a scratch or memo file. Each morning the larger node sends a "current as of" copy of all locally used data to lower level nodes. This design is appropriate when the possibility exists that the local nodes may make incorrect assumptions about what can and cannot be done or what is and is not available. Local and higher level files are allowed to diverge for limited periods of time and are brought back to identity each morning. Such a design may be influenced by legal and regulatory constraints on a particular industry which define what is an "official" file and where an "official" file may be located.

4.2.4. Multiple Points of Change

In all of the possibilities discussed so far there is still only one originating point of change. If data is replicated so that any node at which it is located can be a source of change, additional design needs to be undertaken. There are two basic approaches. One approach allows each node to make a change in its local copy and then promulgate the change throughout the system. The proper sequence of events is for the node which wishes to make the change to send out to all nodes a request for a "lock." Each node receives the name of the data structure which the originating node wishes to change. Each node inspects the local condition of that data structure. If the data is not currently under change, then the requesting node is notified that it is permissible to change the data. Each node then applies a local lock to that data structure. This local lock will either prohibit changes or prohibit all reference depending on the stringency of the synchronization. When the originating node receives status reports from all other nodes it applies the change. After the change is applied the originating node informs other nodes of the change. The distribution of the change (and the scope of the initial lock request) may be limited to those nodes which have an interest in the changed data.

If a node determines that a lock request affects a data structure which it is currently changing, that is, a local lock has been applied, a refusal of change rights is sent to the node initiating a lock request.

Such mechanisms are easier to conceive than to implement. Difficulty of implementation depends somewhat on the nature of the interconnection mechanism. There must be assurance that the sequence of lock request, sending of permission, broadcast of change and removal of locks are coordinated with sufficient care. Provision for simultaneous or effectively simultaneous lock requests, permissions, and so on, must be made so that pathological sequences cannot occur. Design features which define system status in case of system malfunction during the sequence are especially important.

An alternate design allows changes to occur only at one point in the system. Each node is a designated change point for a particular set of data. Copies of data structure may be dispersed through the system but only read access is allowed. When a change is desired a node requests change at the proper change point. The change point node either refuses or accepts the request. If it accepts the request, it may notify all nodes that a particular data structure is to undergo change so that all reference to that structure is locked. When the change is complete a copy of the changed structure is promulgated to all nodes with a copy.

It is possible to develop a system with transient replication of data. Nodes which wish to refer to selected data structures request copies for periods when they wish them. A designated control point for each file or structure distributes copies or partial copies as required. Changes may be restricted to the control point using a synchronizing mechanism essentially identical to that described above.

4.3. Software Structure and Distributed Data

The sections above have addressed various ideas about how data may be placed around a system. There are some other considerations in distributed data which tie closely to issues in software structure.

The current state of the art involves the distribution of data within the context of data managers. Thus each site which has partitions or copies of data has a complete local data manager of some type. Data may be distributed among multiple copies of IBM's CICS, or IMS, for example. An image of a single system is achieved by building into the data manager some directory or map of where particular data structures are located across a population of nodes. CICS, for example, will determine if a referenced data structure is at its own node or if it is at another node. It will request transmission of remote data if necessary, and the application program need not be aware of where the requested data was located.

What we will soon surely see is the possibility of heterogeneous data managers interacting with each other in a transparent manner so that, for example, an application program running in a CICS environment may have access to data under control of a local or remote IMS data manager system.

What is less certain is that we will soon see the concept of the distribution of complex data structures among nodes. Hierarchic data structures with complex indexing pointer structures are not, at this moment, distributable in any system known to the author. There is distributed data but there is no distributed data base. Finally, the concept of distributing a data base manager among nodes by dispersing various functional layers has not been explored to the point where we may expect early fruition. The major direction of work seems to be to add network data management function to existing data manager structures or to add a network management layer somewhere in the system.

An interesting set of design questions relates to where in the software structure a concept like network data manager should be placed. Figure 55a shows a network data manager as a software layer on top of a local data manager. This network data manager provides an interface to application programs which allows them to reference data elements. It determines the location of referenced data structures and selects which local data manager it wishes to communicate with. The local data manager at the node with the data sends the data back to the requesting copy of the network data manager. This approach is attractive if the logical image of data which a program sees is close to the physical structure. If this is true, the network data manager may select a single local data manager and receive the entire requested data structure.

Figure 55b shows a network data manager underneath the local data manager. This approach becomes attractive when the data structures of the system become rather complex. It is desirable to have the local data manager provide the interface to the application program and to resolve the physical structure of the requested data before the network data manager is invoked. It is possible that the idea of distributed data base might be supported in this way. The local data manager would develop a physical "pick list" of the structures involved in a complex data reference. The network data manager would determine the node location of referenced physical structures, request data from all appropriate nodes, collect the data and present them to the local data manager for presentation in proper form to the applications.

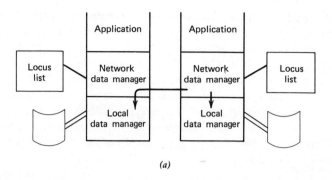

(a)

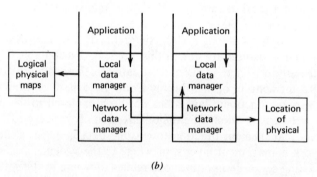

(b)

Figure 55. Data manager software layers.

4.4. Finding Where the Data Is

If data is dispersed among a set of nodes, there must be a mechanism for telling where a particular file or data structure is located. This section will discuss various approaches to this problem in the simple context of distributed files.

The system has need of a directory function. A directory, for our purposes, is a list of files, locations of files and who may refer to the files. The placement, partitioning and functions of nodes with directories may be organized in various ways.

We must be very clear in the distinction between the location of directories and the location of the data to which the directory points. It is possible for a node to have a file but not to have a local directory which enables it to know that that file is resident locally.

4.4.1. Control Point

Figure 56 shows a strongly centralized data directory system where there is a single copy of a directory at a "data control node." A user at any application

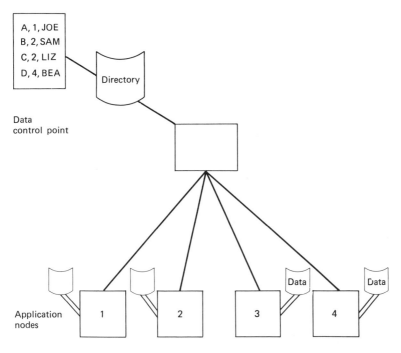

Figure 56.   Data control node.

node requests access to a particular file. The application node communicates with the data control node to determine if the user has authorization to use this file. It also will request information about where the file is so that it can develop local tables which will give access to the file. An important detail is that the data control point has the right of refusal. It can refuse to tell the requesting node where the desired file is located. It may do this because the requesting user does not have proper authorization or for any other reason which seems appropriate. Other reasons may be that the requested file is already in use and is not sharable, or that systems load will be adversely affected if access to that file is permitted at this time. The discretionary right of the data control point to refuse information and access is its essential quality as a control point. If it had no right of refusal it would not truly be a point of data control.

4.4.2. Replicated Directory

Figure 57 shows a system in which all nodes have a complete copy of the directory of all files in the system. A particular node may determine whether any local user has access rights to a file and also the location of the file. The system has the advantage that it would be possible for processing nodes to ask permission to use each others' directories if a local directory was unavailable

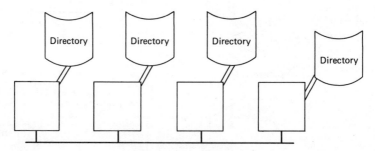

Figure 57.   Peer directories.

for any reason. It has the disadvantage of the cost in space of replicating directories and the associated requirement that the directories be kept in synchronization when changes to the file population are made. A variation of this design allows a local directory to diverge and describe a set of files which are to be known only to local users. The system might provide a command which a user might use to broadcast the name and status of a file to other nodes when he wished access to the file to be permitted from those nodes.

4.4.3.   Shared Directory Services

Figure 58 shows a system in which each application uses a centralized directory node to find the location of files. This system differs from Figure 56 in one very essential detail. The node which has the directories is not a control point. It is a services processor. It has no right of refusal to a request from an application node. Authorization checking has been moved onto the applications processors, which do local determination of file access rights. This movement of the authorization from the site of the directories to the application node essentially changes the structure of the system.

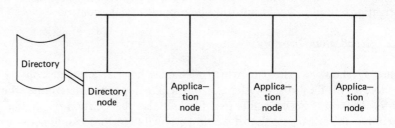

Figure 58.   Global service directory node.

4.4.4. Local Directories

Another approach to directory siting is to place a directory for all local data at each application node. Any node may inquire of its peers whether or not a file is located at that place. There are various methods for accomplishing the inquiry. The preferred method depends upon the nature of the interconnection mechanism and the interconnection topology. With an interconnection where each node talks only to a right and a left node it is necessary to ask for the location of a file with multiple uses of the interconnection facilities. The initiating node asks its neighbors for the file. If they do not have it, they pass the request on to their neighbors until all nodes are visited. The node with the file sends a positive response to the initiating node by some route. Usually some kind of a time out mechanism sets an upper limit of time before which a response must be received or the initiating processor will assume the file does not exist. Alternatively, individual negative responses can be sent hopping down the lines.

In mesh networks, or in single bus short-haul networks, it is possible to broadcast a request to all nodes. In a mesh the name of all nodes must be known and individual messages sent. In a single bus structure it is possible merely to broadcast the request. Depending upon concerns for line loading each node may make a negative response or the system may depend on a single positive response before a period of elapsed time.

It is possible to design subareas of data where certain nodes have access to some data files but not to all. Figure 59 shows a system with such boundaries. Each boundary is enforced by either not placing the name of a file in nodes beyond the boundary or by maintaining lists of permissible referencing nodes. Users must go to nodes within a particular boundary, depending on the work they wish to do and the data they must access.

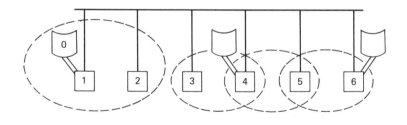

Domains: node 1, 2
                    3, 4
                    5, 6
                    4, 5

Figure 59. Domains of node reference.

4.5. Transparency

We have mentioned ideas of transparency a number of times throughout this text. The essential idea is that a user or an application program need not know where data is located in the physical system. Its advantages are portability, reconfigurability and ease of program development.

In the above section all of the systems had the ability to take a file name and search a directory for its location somewhere in the system. The user requesting access was not expected to know where the desired file was located. We have not been clear on whether a program needed to know where the data is. There are many who feel that the application should be as protected from this information as a user. There are some who feel that transparency of this type, while offered as a feature, should not be imposed on an application program.

The issue has two aspects. There is the question of whether an application programmer should know, at program creation time, where data is located. There is the related issue of whether he should use this knowledge in the transcription of the program. The question of knowledge is by far the more important.

It seems clear that two application development scenarios may be envisioned. In the first the application is expected to evolve over time in imperfectly predictable ways. A maximum degree of flexibility is desired in supporting potential physical reconfigurations of the application logic. In the second scenario the application is expected to be absolutely stable over its lifetime.

In the presence of a continually developing application it is legitimate to pay some performance penalty for flexibility. It is convenient for the system to determine where data structures and program populations are held. In the presence of a stable application it is worthwhile to trade flexibility for performance.

An application programmer may structure his application in a very different manner if he expects 200 millisecond responses to data references or if he expects 2 second responses. His entire notion of program structure, the manner in which he organizes data references and distributes logic is sensitive to an appreciation of performance differences of the magnitude involved in going to a device or going through a teleprocessing line to a device and then experiencing the return. Consequently it is important for many applications programmers to know where the data is going to be located. This will remain true until the time differences between local and remote references narrow.

Whether it is useful for the application to submit data commands which specify the location of data is less important. As long as he has been able to use the information in planning the application it is not necessary that he transcribe locations into code. However, if the knowledge is there and there is conviction that the data will not move over the life of the application, some performance benefit will accrue by providing the statement of location.

A reasonable system would allow two forms of entry for an application program. One form would contain no information about the location of data

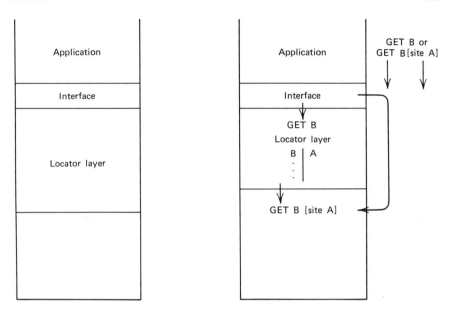

Figure 60.   Around the transparency issues. If [site A] present GET bypasses locator layer.

and rely upon the system to locate it. An expanded form would provide data location information. Such an interface is a modern mapping of the old idea of permitting various levels of service for I/O requests depending on whether an application required record or block level services. Figure 60 shows the structure of a system which resolves issues of the desirability versus the limitations of allowing programs to specify where data is located. Applications developed for this system can make tradeoffs about the need for flexibility and the need for performance and on this basis determine whether the location information will be provided with the data reference.

4.6.   Data and Process Movement

There are various ways to react to the fact that a program wishes to manipulate data that is not local to it. The decisions involve whether data is to be moved, whether transactions are to be moved and exactly what the split of work will be at either node.

4.6.1.   Files to Programs

A file may be sent to the program. This involves a complete transmission of the entire file structure from the place where it is located to the place where the program wishes to operate upon it. The advantage to such an approach is the speed of the program when it begins to operate. However, such a design maximizes the amount of data transmission in the system, particularly in systems which involve "hopping" (the necessity of going through intervening nodes to reach a final destination) In addition to adding to systems load, moving complete files may delay the start of the program by a nontrivial amount of time. In interactive environments this is less tolerable than in batch environments where a program can be scheduled to run when its data arrives.

If complete file transmission is undertaken, a number of design decisions must be made. Primary among them is the recognition that sharing of the files among multiple nodes is probably not practicable. The control of multiple copies transmitted to different nodes introduces synchronization problems which might be more effectively resolved with other data movement strategies.

The movement of file copies in exclusive use mode will still involve some decisions about whether the new copy or the original copy is "the" file. It is possible to pass complete control and responsibility for a file to a receiving node. At notification that the file has been received the sending node deletes its copy. The receiving node becomes responsible for the file, for back-up copy creation, integrity, and so on. Files float from node to node on demand.

It is possible to designate a home point for files. When a file moves to another node from its home point all manipulation rights are given to the receiving node, but until the receiving node successfully transmits a returned new file the copy at the home point is the master copy.

4.6.2. Records to Programs

An alternative to moving entire files is to move data on a record basis. A program issues requests for records which are satisfied by the home point node. When copies of records are outstanding the home point may lock reference to these records for change or for read until the record is returned. The advantage of this design is that it reduces the amount of transmission required. In addition it permits shared use of the file from different nodes by reducing exclusive locking to a record level. The disadvantage is that the running program may experience delays because of remote data reference while it is operating.

Any scheme which moves records to remote locations is a form of dynamic replication. When a record is so moved it is locally locked and marked as invalid if changes are expected to be returned from the remote location.

4.6.3. Avoiding Data Movement

In order to avoid data movement many designs prefer to move the program to the data in one way or another. In batch environments this may involve actually transmitting a program stream to the network until it reaches the data. Programs, control statements and network directives are formed into a stream which passes through the network. This job networking environment is represented by such software as IBM's JES subsystem. Various systems allow various amounts of flexibility in specifying where a job is to be executed and in directing the return of output.

In a system of heterogeneous nodes there will be limitations as to the degrees of freedom in program movement, depending upon the local operating systems, the local hardware architecture and what adaptive mechanisms are included in the system.

In on-line environments the equivalent of batch transmission is called distributed transactions. A transaction submitted at a node is sent to the node where its data is for application processing. Figure 61 shows two nodes. Each node has a message handler layer, an application layer and a data management layer. Distributed transactions are accomplished by passing the transaction up into the application layer which has the data.

Variations of this can be designed. It is possible for different application programs to reside in different nodes. If there is a direct mapping of transaction type into application program, then the routing is based upon the location of the application programs which are functionally specific for the transaction.

It is also reasonable to replicate application programs at various nodes. If there is no clear association of site with transaction, then it must be possible to

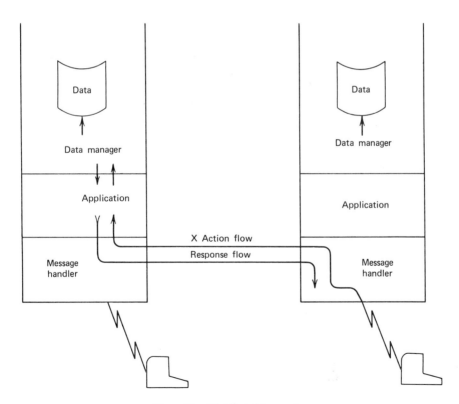

Figure 61. Distributed transactions.

process transactions in different places. Thus all programs of the application are in all nodes and a particular program runs not on the basis of transaction type but on the basis of where the data is.

It is possible for a transaction to enter the application layer at the node where it is submitted and have the application layer analyze what its data requirements are. This is necessary if it is possible for a transaction to refer to both remote and local data. The message handler layer may not have sufficient logic to determine where the transaction should be routed. Local application logic may then either request data to be moved or it may be able to develop a list of directives for a remote data manager to apply to local data. For example, the application layer may be able to develop a list of all fields to be modified and in exactly what way they are to be modified and send this list to a remote data manager.

Figure 62 shows the passage of the transaction through the application layer. This application layer forms a data manipulating list of commands which it forwards for execution to a remote data manager.

If application logic is sufficiently complex, it may be necessary for an application program at one node to talk to an application program at another node. This "appl" to "appl" communication is shown on Figure 63. It may come about because of the way data is partitioned or it may be inherent in the perception of the application logic.

4.7. Back-up Replication

Sometimes the motivation for replicating data is to provide back-up copies in case of some system malfunction. This malfunction may be a user error which destroys or distorts data or it may be the unavailability of data at a particular node.

Back-up, archiving and data replications are related to each other in distributed systems design.

It is common for systems to provide both transparent and visible mechanisms for back-up and archiving. The visible mechanism is the user's ability to make copies of file and place them in his own library. The transparent mechanism is some automatic copying of files at designated times by the system. These files may be kept on-line if space permits or they may be dismounted and stored in an off-line archive.

The distributed design must address the location of system created back-up files and the means by which users can access and address them. In many distributed systems some of the nodes are too small to provide meaningful local back-up and must depend upon some larger node. It may also be desirable to depend upon a larger node if professional operations staff is not to be located at the site of a node. In this case all back-up copies are sent to the larger node and, when necessary, retrieved from the larger node. This mechanism may be invisible to a user.

It is possible to give a user an ability to designate which files are to be

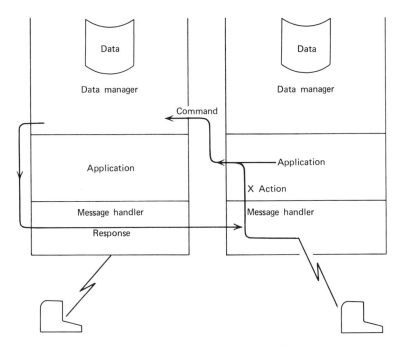

Figure 62.   Local application processing.

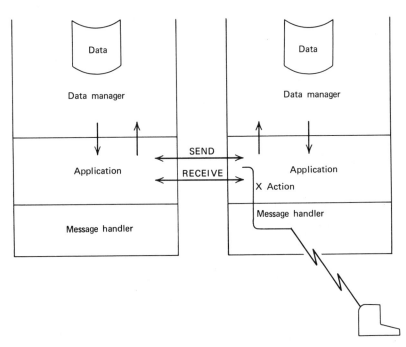

Figure 63.   Application to application.

ımatically backed up at a remote node by defining a back-up profile prepared by a user or by a systems programmer on his behalf. It is also possible to design a system whereby a user is explicitly responsible for sending copies to a remote node. Full support of this concept involves establishing library space for a user at both the local and remote nodes. Currently many interconnected systems have commands which provide for the transmission of files; fewer provide for local and remote library space for a user.

If primary copies are kept at a local node and back-up copies are kept at a remote node a number of possible systems features emerge. Some of these represent extensions of the idea of replication and define an intersection between ideas of back-up and ideas of access.

If the location of copies of files are nontransparent, a user may have the ability to decide which copy of a file he wishes to consider primary. He may apply some ideas of version across the two nodes which are specific to his needs and use.

It may be desirable to provide a systems feature which is called "pass through." This enables a user to logon to a system and either use its local data or use data which is located remotely. When referring to remote data the local node is used essentially as a terminal controller.

A user may have a collection of small files which he wishes to keep locally and manipulate locally. He may wish collections of small files to be kept remotely but sent to him on demand for local manipulation. He may wish to keep data remotely and manipulate it remotely in pass through mode. These abilities may be provided transparently or explicitly on reference to the file, but there is a clearly implied ability for a user to decide where a file is put.

5. DISTRIBUTING CONTROL

The issue of distributing control is made more complex than it might naturally be because we have never defined exactly what we mean by control. We have a vague notion that control has to do with the synchronization of reference to resources, with allocating resources, increasing utilization, and so on.

Systems differ widely in what they consider the control responsibilities of various systems elements and of application elements. This section will undertake to treat the concept of control as an intuitively understood set of functions which are provided in some way by systems software elements.

5.1. Elements of Control

Control contains three elements: data required to make decisions, algorithms required to manipulate data to make decisions and access to control data and algorithms.

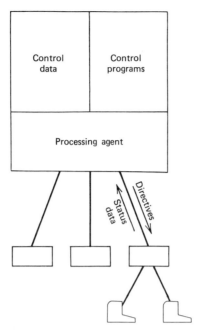

Figure 64.   Centralized control.

In the most centralized kind of control design data and algorithms are placed at a single point and only a single system node has access to them. In a multi-node system a pure master/slave relationship exists between the node which can operate on control data and the other nodes. Figure 64 shows a system, naturally drawn hierarchically, where a single node is controlling the activities of all other nodes. These smaller nodes undertake tasks solely as permitted or directed by the central node. This is a usual perception of a single processing system built around a uniprocessor central processing unit.

5.2.   Distributed Access

In distributed designs involving multiple nodes some additional control functions must be placed at a center to control the outlying slave nodes. This may involve remote operators, remote problem determination, remote program loading and reconfiguration. All of these functions may be put at a central node which either generates or demands from outlying nodes the data which is required to control the system as a single unit.

Control may become more distributed by permitting more than one node to access the data and algorithm which is collected at a central point. This con-

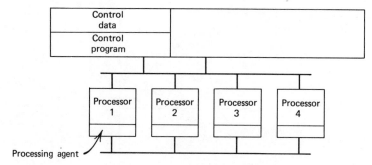

Figure 65.   Distributed control access.

cept is common to multiprocessor designs. Figure 65 shows a multiprocessor with a single operating system. This operating system has data required for system control and the algorithms required to manipulate the data. Any processor in the system is permitted to access the control structure. This is possible because the memory locations which hold the operating system are equally accessible to all processors.

It is possible to tilt this system structure toward a centralized design by permitting only one designated processor at a time to execute operating system control programs. This processor may execute control on its own behalf and on behalf of other processors which submit requests for control actions to the designated control processor. This is sometimes called "floating control." If the control processor malfunctions, then another processor will pick up the control function. The design keeps control centralized but provides a fallback capability in case of system malfunction.

The multiprocessor version of distributed control is to allow any processor to execute the operating system when it requires control function. Depending upon the program structure of the operating system, it may be possible for many processors to be executing various portions of control programs at the same time.

Despite the distribution of access, however, the system is still centralized in that there is only one place in memory where necessary programs and data are available. Also, each processor makes systems-wide decisions on a global basis. Whichever processor is executing control code is using global data and makes decisions which affect shared elements of the entire system.

5.3.   Control Partitioning

A further distribution of control becomes possible by partitioning the concept of control into discrete control functions. Thus control may be partitioned into memory management, program management, I/O management as shown in Figure 66. This partitioning is accomplished by restructuring the programs of

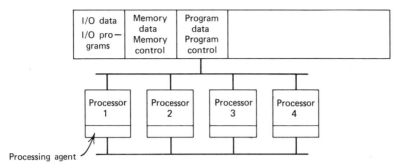

Figure 66. Structure in control.

the operating system into a set of specialized service elements. When the operating system is so restructured it is possible to allow all processors to address any control element. It is also possible to designate particular processors as responsible for various functions. This can be done by permitting access to only particular locations in the memory. The memory protection mechanisms of most multiprocessors could provide support for this design. From this point it is an easy conceptual step to move data and program associated with a particular control function into a memory physically associated only with the processor responsible for that control function. In fact this might naturally occur in machines which have "cache" memories. A cache is a small private memory which is managed by the hardware of a system to contain those programs and data which a processor is currently using. In a cache machine references to data and programs are tracked by system logic in order to determine the current subset of references.

It is interesting to notice that the control structure of Figure 67 is essentially the same as the control structure of Figure 66 despite the fact that one figure is a multiprocessor and the other is more recognizable as a distributed system. This observation supports the notion that the logical organization of control structure is independent of the physical structure.

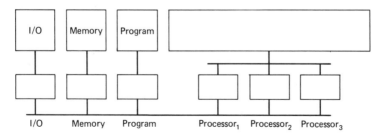

Figure 67. Distributed control elements.

5.4. Global Control Processors

Figure 68 will serve as the basis for the discussion of this section. It shows a family of applications processors combined with a set of functionally specific control processors. The functions of these processors represent control functions which are appropriate for a distributed system. We have a global system scheduler, a message interchange processor, a data manager processor. Each processor has the data and program necessary to perform its specific function. These functions are performed at the request of the application processors or at the discretion of each control processor.

Data at each functional processor is global for its function. An application processor wishing to start a program at another application processor will send a message through the message interchange processor to the global scheduler. This message will request the start of a program and provide a set of preferences about the type of processor the program will run upon. The global scheduler knows the assignment and status of all processors and programs in the system. It can select a good mapping of program and processor. It has enough information because the application processors constantly send data about their status and activity and because all changes in status are brought about by the global scheduler.

Each application processor may have some local control over the mix of work to which it has been assigned. Local time-sharing and dispatching decisions are applied by local processors because the global scheduler is too far away to manage the multiprogramming mixes at each processor at a sufficient rate.

The system has a control distribution in which there are a set of specialized global sites for designated functions and a set of sites which exercise some local control.

The advantage of such a design lies in the ability to exert levels of global control without interfering with the work of application processors. Only if the path to the global processors becomes a bottleneck does the rate of application processing fall off. A disadvantage of the system is the ability of the failure of a global processor to bring down the entire structure.

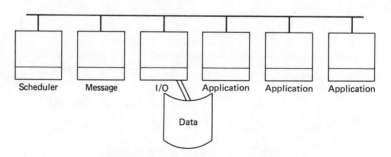

Figure 68.   Global function processors.

The difficulties in designing such a control structure lie in the partitioning of control function into neat elements. The compartmentalization of function is not always obvious. The definition of the extent of local versus global control is not easy. However, systems concepts of this nature are beginning to emerge in the literature and in experimental systems.

5.5. Cooperating Peers

In the purest form of distributed control all data and all control algorithm is dispersed throughout the system and replicated at all points. There is no global data at any point in the system. Each node has a complete operating system which is responsible for local control and for interacting with other nodes to achieve some form of system-wide control. Figure 69 shows such a system. A detail of Figure 69 which is important is the interaction processor which is associated with each application processor. A node is a processor pair. The interaction processor performs those functions related to internode interaction. The intent of the interaction processor is to allow the applications processor to continue work on applications while conversations between nodes are undertaken. A set of difficult design decisions must be made about what elements of an operating system should be in the application processor and what elements should be in the interaction processor. For example, should the command"SEND a message to another program" be processed by the interaction processor whether or not the receiving program is at the same application processor as the sending program? Should SEND be used both locally and remotely but be processed in the interaction processor only when another node is being referenced? Should a different command be used?

The spirit of the system of Figure 69 will be demonstrated by the request to start a program at another node which we used to describe the global scheduler.

A processing node wishes to start a progam which resides at some number of

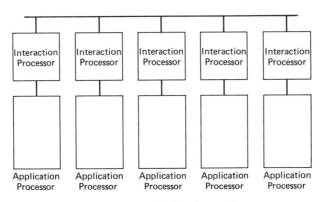

Figure 69.   Pure distributed control.

nodes in the system. It sends its interaction processor a message which specifies the name of the program and a set of constraints which describe attributes of the processor most desired for the work. The interaction processor broadcasts the request to the interconnection bus. Each interaction processor takes the message. Each interaction processor knows the status, type, load, and so on, of its local processor. It is possible to send this information to the requesting interaction processor and let it choose a most desired processor. It is more distributed, conceptually, to have each interaction processor determine how close a fit its processor is with the constraints, determine its own interest in getting the available work and submit a bid to the requesting processor. As the bids come in the requesting interaction processor maintains a record of the highest bid and its source. When all bids are in the most interested processor is notified that it has gotten the work and the other processors are notified that they have lost.

Load on the interconnection mechanism may be reduced by suppressing null bids and by suppressing negative notification. A node not interested in the work makes no response. The initiating node cuts off response acceptance after a designated time. Similarly, if a node has not gotten a "go ahead" after a certain time, it assumes it will not get the work.

One detail which must be designed is the way that an interaction processor treats new requests for bids during the interval between its bid for work and its notification of success or failure. It wishes to modify its bid for work based upon some guess about whether outstanding bids will bring work to it. One approach to this is to assume it will get the work if its bid is beyond a certain urgency level and assume it will not get the work if its bid is beneath this level. If these assumptions are wrong, there will be misassignment of work and disinterest in work which should be taken on. This may or may not disturb the system depending upon the frequency of node to node requests and how finely tuned the system is.

It is in design areas like this that we realize how much at the edge of the art we are. Most work of this type is in a somewhat investigative and experimental stage. We need some new insights for the control of processors which are peer cooperating this closely.

It is fruitful, of course, to mix the ideas of interaction processors and global processors to discover most reasonable systems structures. For example, scheduling might be done globally but messages handled through interaction processors, depending on which approach seems most appropriate for a particular control function.

Many of the issues in control structure are not of direct interest to using organizations because their vendors have made control structure decisions upon which they rely or by which they are willing to be constrained. However, in many application areas systems are being designed at a level where control structure decisions must be made. In addition these topics are interesting because they give us an insight into the possible directions of the industry and its arts.

PART THREE

ORGANIZATION AND ECONOMICS

Chapter 11

The Perspective

1. GENERAL

The dominating characteristic of the current computer industry is the wide variety of choice which organizations have in developing approaches to data processing. Data processing solutions of very different attributes are offered by multiple vendors or even by the same vendor. It is possible to develop highly centralized organizations, systems structures and operational environments or highly distributed environments using hardware and software product from a single marketing division of a single vendor.

In the face of such diversity of organizational and equipment choices there is a developing feeling that methodologies must be discovered which will enable enterprises to make reasonable and safe data processing choices. The development of such methodologies depends upon:

1. The identification of factors which are relevant to data processing decision making.
2. The discovery of relationships among these factors.
3. An assessment of the importance of various factors.

There appear to be three kinds of relevant considerations. These are organizational factors, applications factors and systems factors.

Organizational factors include such issues as:

1. The centralizing or decentralizing tendency of an enterprise as regards its mission oriented decision making.
2. The defined power roles involving data processing management and business unit and location management.
3. The risk/reward assessment stylistics of an enterprise which will influence it to be "value-" or "cost-" driven in decision making.
4. The distribution of data processing skills within an organization which determines where application recognition, evaluation, development and operation may reasonably occur.

Applications factors include:

1. The relationship between the data involved in an application and the enterprise organizational structure.
2. The structure of the application logic and how well it lends itself to various kinds of system distribution.
3. The previous history of the application which determines the extent to which design of the application is constrained by already existing programming and data structures.
4. The future of the application. The extent to which it will evolve and be modified over time as opposed to its tendency to remain stable during its useful lifetime.

System factors relate to:

1. Price/performance characteristics of various computer system offerings.
2. Price/performance characteristics of interconnect mechanisms.
3. Programming expenses associated with various systems offerings.
4. Operational expenses associated with various systems offerings.
5. The rate at which changes in computer economics influence the pattern of commitment to various offerings.
6. Systems manageability, the degree to which coherent systems may be built, operated, maintained and evolved from various collections of offerings.

The major issues to be addressed in any consideration of the economic aspects of distributed processing involve ideas of value assessment and cost assessment constrained by organizational issues and applications history. Figure 70 is an only partially facetious representation of the problem. In the form of a possible job description for someone responsible for assuring that data processing delivers maximum profitability to a company, the tasks and its problems, a broad outline of the status of the current world of computing is suggested. How does one relate issues of changing technology with issues of organizational dynamics? And how is this relationship organized to reduce risk in the face of subtle technical problems which can render a broad plan infeasible?

2. CONCEPTS OF VALUE

The function of management concerned with data processing is to maximize the profitability of data processing to the enterprise. The profit of data processing is the difference between the value of data processing and its cost. While there are approximate notions of cost, notions of value are currently very ill defined and classed as "intangibles." Methods for quantifying the value of

Maximize the net profitability to the enterprise of data processing:

- Determine real total costs of data processing activity including hardware, software, communications, staff, end user interfaces and efforts.
- Quantify real values of data processing.
- Consider full range of data processing alternatives across buy, make, rent, and different levels of product integration.
- Determine best relationships between data processing functions.
- Consider rates of technology change and implications for the future.

Faced with:

1. Organizational issues:
   - Organizational framework and set of relationships.
   - A rate of enterprise change.
   - A feeling for values of information.
   - A feeling for information flow.

2. Technology:
   - Set of hardware offerings.
   - Set of software offerings.
   - Set of service offerings.
   - Set of communication offerings.
   - Rate of technology change.
   - Rate of change in cost relationships between hardware elements of system.
   - Rate of change in cost relationships between operational and programming costs and hardware.
   - Rate of change between hardware and communications costs.

3. Intersecting organization/technology issues:
   - Set of available enterprise data processing skills.
   - Set of potential enterprise skills.
   - Set of costs associated with organization of skills.
   - Set of relations between value and cost.
   - Set of "User" anticipations and standards of acceptability.

Problems:

- Hidden irrational constraints in vendor hardware and software.
- Inadequate tools for performance measurement.
- Difficulty in value assessment.
- Difficulty of predicting future.

Figure 70. An idealized job description.

computing are very vague and much computing equipment and service is acquired on a "cost avoidance" or "cost replacement" basis. The intent of this section is to bring to the attention of the reader the importance of ideas of value.

A discussion of the possible sources of value in data processing will reveal some of the nature of the value assessment problem.

2.1.   Displaceable Cost

This is the most well understood source of value for computing. A system or application is justified, over its lifetime, on the basis of the costs that will be reduced with its existence or use. The cost of an activity currently performed is determined on the basis of direct and indirect costs in space, personnel, administration. The cost of a computer based alternative is compared. The system is justified if, over time, the cost of the computer is lower. The computer system is seen as a way of achieving volume insensitivity, reducing staff, avoiding increases in staff, by replacing expensive and inflation prone personnel costs with a stable hardware cost.

Except for the problem that computer costs may not be as carefully and completely assessed as might be desired, methodology for this is reasonably well understood. After a period where computer system development cost is totally additive the installed system begins to reduce cost until there is a total net payback for the system or application. Figure 71 illustrates this simple concept.

2.2.   Increased Productivity of Personnel

The issue of productivity is many faceted. There are considerations which are relevant to the ability of a group of computer users to perform their jobs at less cost or with greater effectiveness. The computer system is seen as a way to

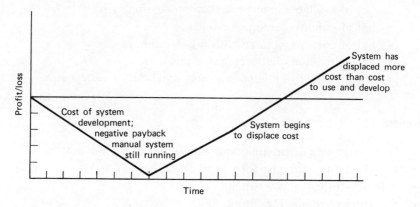

Figure 71.   Application payback.

reduce trivial work components for highly skilled employees, as a way to reduce the administrative burden of error detection and as a way to increase the rate at which simple tasks are handled.

In its most direct form the issue of productivity is related to displaceable cost. If a group of workers can be made more productive in simple tasks, then smaller groups can handle higher demands.

There is an aspect of productivity, however, which is less directly related to cost avoidance and more closely associated with vaguer concepts of value. When personnel involved are highly skilled professionals whose activity relates to the mainstream of an organizational mission, proper levels of data processing support may imply more than directly quantifiable cost benefits.

The ability of a company to design, produce and distribute product is directly affected by the quality of computer services which are available. Instances of unavailablity, undesirable variations in responsiveness, awkwardness at human interfaces can have major impact on the profitability of an organization when computer dependent activities are critical to its product line and market stature.

A group of design engineers will produce high quality product on schedule when they are adequately supported by computing devices. If there is inadequate computer support their designs may be deficient, their schedules may be prolonged and the posture of the product in the market may be seriously affected. If a product is late to the marketplace its revenue producing potential will be reduced. If it exhibits operational characteristics which lead to high maintenance costs its lifetime profitability may be drastically curtailed. If carefully analyzed and understood, these potential costs will far outweigh the costs of various levels of computer service. Economies practiced to reduce computer hardware or software budgets may be very false economies if a reduction in quality of critical work is a result. The cost of an underutilized machine may be far less than the costs of an overloaded machine which is affecting the productivity of critical skills in an enterprise.

Yet it is very difficult to numerically assess whether it is worthwhile to provide under 1 second response time for a product design group. It requires an understanding of organization, marketplace and product life opportunities and costs which are more complex than an assessment of the cost of a bigger computing system. Because of this the "safe" or "conservative" position has been to manage to minimize computer costs. Concepts of value in key personnel productivity are difficult to quantify in other than trivial terms like increased work units per day.

2.3. Time Value of Information

Figure 72 shows a concept of the decrease of the value of information over time. The true value of data processing is best understood in terms of the dollar value of information which data processing systems deliver to an organization.

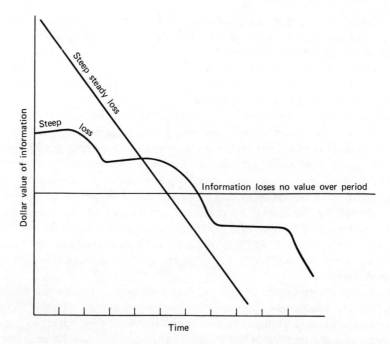

Figure 72.   Cost of information delay—various value decay patterns.

The quality and amount of information made available at key times can affect the profitability of an enterprise very directly in a number of ways.

Information which is timely can reduce inventory requirements and the amount of corporate resources which must be committed to acquiring and storing required parts or finished goods.

Increased timeliness of information can reduce judgment errors in management decision making. In industries where prices are volatile and contracts must be made frequently a knowledge of latest prices can justify very large expenses in computing services.

Finally, more timely information can increase the decision reaction time of an enterprise, allowing it to respond more quickly to changes in its supplier or finished goods markets.

A sensitivity to this kind of thinking has led many to attempt to understand organizations in terms of information flow. The exact path of information through an enterprise is determined in some studies and the time of arrival of such information is mapped against possible errors in policy and practice which occur because too little information arrives too late. The dollar value of computing is the savings achieved by avoiding decision errors or by reacting more quickly to serious situations.

Any reader will recognize that quantification of "benefits" of this kind is very difficult except on a very judgmental and "soft" basis. Yet it is critical that such benefits be given the importance they deserve. The resource is not computing; the resource is knowledge of the status and capability of an enterprise on a timely basis.

2.4.   Place Value of Information

Closely associated with the timeliness of information is the question of where information should be sent and why it is sent there. Figure 73 shows an organization chart in which each node is a decision point. The place value of information is determined by the dollar value of decisions which can be made upon it at various points in an organization. A piece of information moves from one place to another on the assumption that it is moving to a decision point where it will take on greater value. It takes on greater value because it joins a conglomerate of information which has a greater value than its parts. For example, the knowledge of the inventory level at all warehouses is more valuable than the knowledge of the inventory level at a particular warehouse. Information may take on greater value because decisions which are made against it at one node have higher potential negative or positive effect on an enterprise than decisions which may be made against it at a lower point.

Place and time value may be used to plan the logic of a data processing system in many ways. A decision to move a piece of information from one place to another is based upon its increased value at the receiving point. The decision about when to move it and how quickly to move it is based upon the rate of decay over time. Thus a piece of information may have a cost of delay such that it is worth the same at a place whether it arrives in three seconds or three days. Such a transmission should be accomplished at the lowest possible cost and could not justify a high speed telecommunications line. If the cost of

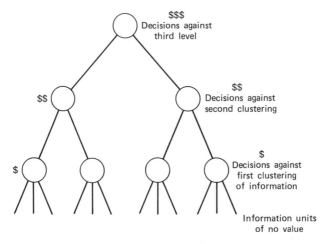

Figure 73.   Place value.

delay is steep then the difference between its value in three seconds and its value in three days can be spent in communications facilities which will get it there in three seconds.

2.5. Concluding Remarks on Value

What must be clearly understood is that the value of data processing may be orders of magnitude beyond its costs when the values are well understood.

Unfortunately it is difficult to quantify values in a way that is satisfying for people whose responsibilities lie primarily in controlling hardware expenditures for computing systems. We have a methodology problem and an attitude set which is retarding the profitable application of computers to critical applications which do not involve obvious cost avoidance.

3. COSTS OF COMPUTING

The other side of the economic coin, of course, is cost. In the area of cost there are two fundamental problems:

1. How to determine the true costs of computing to an organization.
2. How to manage to minimize cost in an era of rapid cost changes in all of the elements of computing which contribute to cost.

The determination of the true costs of computing is a more subtle art than our practices reveal. One aspect of the problem is identifying the costs which accrue to all parties involved in computing. Figure 74 shows a matrix which has as its columns some elements of computing cost. It has as its rows a simple division into data processing department costs and user costs. Too often the costs of computing are seen only in terms of line items for a data processing center or organization. Costs associated with the use of the computing service which occur in using organizations are not reflected as part of the cost of computing.

In deciding between centralized, decentralized and distributed organizations and systems it is necessary to know the total cost of various solutions accruing to users as well as to the data staff and management. Different systems solutions may distribute costs differently and may reduce the total enterprise cost while appearing to increase the cost because the data processing department budget must increase. Alternatively, some systems structures may look attractive because they reduce data center costs but really lead to higher total costs which are not understood because some expenditures are hidden in operational departments. A true cost assessment must look for all computer related costs regardless of the departments in which they occur.

In the current state of the art it is not uncommon for organizations to not know the true cost of computing even at the data center. Controller sensitivity

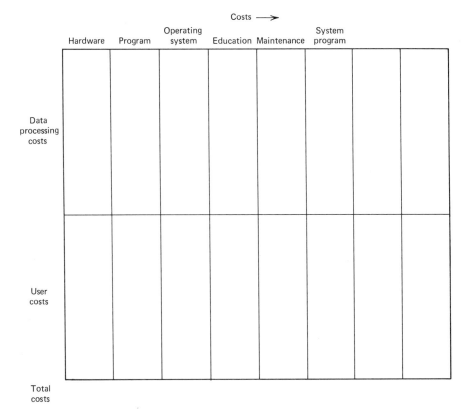

Figure 74. Full representation of costs.

to cost may be related only to hardware component cost. Costs of operational staffs, systems programming expertise, planning, application development, and so on, may not be considered at all in controlling data processing expenditure.

Surely in the selection of system solutions, in comparing one system structure against another, it is necessary not only to know the hardware bill, but the total cost of a system in terms of the professional staffing necessary to implement, operate and maintain a system over its lifetime.

Another aspect of cost which is critical is the constant rate of change in both the absolute costs of different elements of a system and in the changing percentages of total system cost attributable to various components of a system. This instability affects the comparative costs of different systems structures. It also affects investment decisions which relate to the timing of investment in computer resources and the basis on which the resource should be acquired.

The elements which contribute to system cost may be classified into a number of broad classes. The following sections describe the general nature of each class of costs.

3.1. Computer Hardware

This is the purchase, lease, or rental cost of processing units, memories, random access storage devices, channels, printers, terminals, control units. Associated with these costs are costs of power, cooling, installation preparation and physical maintenance which may be different from system to system.

Although the fundamental component hardware costs may be listed easily it is sometimes difficult to properly assess the full cost of computer hardware without considerable expertise. Various vendors offer various packaging options and configuration choices. It is not always clear, except to an expert, why a particular control unit is desirable or necessary, or why a particular adapter is preferable to another.

There may be subtle secondary costs associated with different hardware. A unit which has a quiet printer may be less expensive than a unit which has a noisy printer if it is necessary to spend money to insulate personnel against the noise.

3.2. Communications Hardware

Communications hardware includes the interconnecting paths between processing nodes and whatever nodes exist in a network primarily for message and data handling. Short-haul buses, loops, rings, teleprocessing lines, concentrators, multiplexers, modems are clearly communications hardware expenses. Channels used for interconnect, front end processors, gateways, may be thought of as computer or communications hardware depending on details of function and vendor source.

Frequently the vendors of communications hardware, even when this hardware is very much like a computer, are a different set from the vendors of computer hardware. Configuration of networks and intelligent units to control networks is a special function frequently somewhat disassociated from computer system design. It is not yet clear to what degree communications system design and computer system design should be integrated in system planning and to what degree they should be recognized as different activities.

3.3. Systems Control Software

Software products consisting of operating systems, telecommunications access methods, data management systems, network control packages and a large set of other programs are available from various vendors. Commonly the manufacturer of computer hardware or communications hardware supplies the software necessary to establish an operational environment for applications system. The facilities delivered by these software components provide for distributed data, resource allocation, synchronization and recovery to various degrees.

There are various aspects of cost associated with systems control software.

Some products are given with the hardware; others are separately priced. Various vendors take different approaches to licensing and use. Various vendors take different approaches to issues of multiple use by a single enterprise, charging the same for each license or offering price relief in various forms for secondary users.

In addition to the cost of acquiring a systems control software element there are various costs of use. These include specialization for a particular application or system, installation, modification, performance tuning and adjusting. Users of packages must be aware that there is a continuing cost involved in such software that takes the form of professional expertise involved in supporting systems programmer functions associated with a "package."

Various vendors offer various options concerning how specialized a particular system may be. An organization which does not wish to invest serious effort on optimized systems may accept a preconfigured option of a software package. This is a vendor prepared version of the software which is more easily installed than a system which must be specialized by the user.

The maintenance of systems control software, in terms of finding and correcting errors in programming, may be assumed by a user organization or by the vendor. There are very different styles of support associated with different software packages. Some vendors support software for an indefinite period of time, until a version becomes obsolete; others offer a limited time period guarantee.

In the sections on degree of distribution, in Part Two, we discussed the fact that choices must be made about exactly what software components should be acquired in light of the kinds of distribution which a user wishes to undertake. One choice a user has is to write certain elements of his own. The risk and feasibility of this depends on how complex the element must be.

3.4. Application Software

There is a fuzzy line between applications software and systems control software. Some would classify data managers and other subsystems as applications and not as system control elements.

Beyond this classification issue there is clearly activity which is specific to the logic of an application. This logic may influence how much and what kind of system control software is desirable for a system.

A user may invest programming effort and activity in the development of application programs or he may try to acquire "canned" application packages. The amount of design, programming, testing of new programs which a user must undertake is a function of the uniqueness of the application and a user's perception of what constitutes effective use of professional skills. In any case some investment must be made in selecting packages, in making the decision to make or buy and in installing the programs in an operational environment.

The efficiency of applications development may relate very closely to aspects of the systems software and the degree to which it supports applications development by providing productivity tools and enough function to minimize the amount of programming which must be done.

3.5. Operational Costs

These are costs associated with the running of a computer installation. They include console operators, data media librarians, user/center interface specialists, schedulers, data entry specialists. In addition they include systems programming type activities associated with the operation of the system. Such activities involve parameterization of packages and modification of software environments to accommodate new releases or changes in physical environment. Other functions include error analysis and fault determination, interfacing to software vendors to apply changes and corrections, performance tuning and performance analysis.

There are a host of standard and recurring expenses: paper for printers and terminals, binders for output, carts for distribution of certain output, and so on.

3.6. Management Costs

Management cost has two aspects. The first is the cost of providing an organizational framework for program development, daily operations, hardware maintenance, and so on.

The second aspect of management cost is the provision of direction and leadership. Systems planning at a level which provides an enterprise an enterprise level of data processing direction is one function. At more pragmatic levels there is database design to support applications development, software components selection and evaluation, hardware component selection and performance evaluation, system change management and systems maintenance. Various enterprises hold various opinions about whether it is best to centralize or decentralize these functions and the amount of investment which should be made in the required skills.

3.7. User Costs

These are the costs which a user experiences in using a data processing system. There are costs of education, of physical access to the physical system, submission of work, retrieval of result, preparation of data. There are costs that result from system failure or unsatisfactory performance. These are costs beyond whatever kind of apportionment a data center makes for the use of computer hardware and professional services.

4. COSTS AND DISTRIBUTION

The issue before us is illustrated by Figure 75. Across a set of possible systems configurations how are costs minimized? Figure 75 takes the broad view that

	Centralized uniprocessor	Centralized multiprocessor	Physically close multiple systems	Geographically remote peer multiple system	Geographically remote hierarchic system	
Processor memory channel						
DASD storage						
Communication hardware						
Operations						
Application development						
System modification						
Other						

Figure 75. Costing solutions.

not only must hardware costs be considered, but all aspects of cost must be analyzed. Only in this way can true cost comparisons between very different systems structures be made.

The remainder of this part will introduce issues of centralization and decentralization in order to show some of the considerations relevant to how systems management may be organized. Then we will discuss some aspects of hardware, operational and programming costs which influence choice of system structures.

Chapter 12

Decentralization and Centralization

1. INTRODUCTION

Chapter 6 of Part Two made a distinction between distribution and decentralization and indicated that there are degrees of freedom in the movement of management, application skills and hardware/software elements from a central point. Distribution is a technology and system design concept. Decentralization is an organizational and management concept. Hardware components, software components, data structures and even operational controls of various kinds can be dispersed without necessarily creating a decentralized environment. It is only when the "staff" skills of system planning and development, systems planning and decision making begin to be dispersed that decentralization occurs.

There is one essential element whose dispersion in various forms is central to the topic. That element is cost. There are various views about whether data centers should be run as profit centers or cost centers. But in either approach it is common to distribute the costs of data processing to a group of users. A consolidated workload data center characteristically charges back elements of cost associated with using the computer equipment or using professional skills. The exact algorithms used for this charge back will encourage or discourage computer use and will enforce a kind of priority in systems use. Supposedly more important operations will have more budgeted funds for computer use and may buy more time from the data center.

The effect of distributing costs is that the user experiences data processing service as a budget item. As a budget item the cost of using data center services may suggest to an aggressive user that he may exercise other options. He may wish to be able to decide how he wants to use funds allocated for data processing service. He may wish the ability to contract with outside service bureaus which are offering attractive levels of service at attractive prices. He may also decide that he wants his own machine.

A data center must resist tendencies to withdraw from the use of its services for the same reasons that a public utility must resist private generation of power. As use goes down larger portions of cost must be retrieved from the remaining user set. As costs for this user set go up, the tendency to withdraw goes up and there is a spiral which eventually leads to the potential collapse of the data center.

2. SYSTEMS MANAGEMENT

The heart of the centralization/decentralization decision lies in how one wishes to organize and operate those tasks associated with setting data processing policies, plans and standards.

It is important to note that tendencies to decentralize data processing systems management need not be consistent with issues of decentralization or centralization in the organization of the mission of an enterprise. A company with strong entrepreneurial instincts that tends to define maximum roles of responsibility and decision making in its structure may or may not choose to centralize or decentralize data processing. An analogy, not attractive to data processing professionals, lies with secretarial services. A highly decentralized enterprise may still support operational business units out of a centralized secretarial pool. A highly centralized enterprise, strongly controlled from the top, may allow each department its own secretarial staff.

Just as there are degrees of freedom between dispersing systems elements and staff elements, there are degrees of freedom between the essentially centralized or decentralized tendencies of an enterprise and its organization of data processing.

It is not easy to give a complete statement of what the system management functions are. However, the following partial list will give the reader an insight into their nature.

1. *Business Standards.* All applications are reviewed and analyzed to assure that the business operations implied by the application conforms to the policies of the enterprise. Levels of auditability, styles of customer interface, and so on, are required to be in accordance with business practices which the enterprise management feels desirable.

2. *Benefits Assurance.* All applications and systems are reviewed to determine that they will result in economic benefit to the enterprise. Values and costs are determined and applications are supported on the basis of greatest value to be gotten from resources available for data processing development and operation.

3. *Feasibility Assurance.* All systems and applications are reviewed to assure that the proposed project is feasible in reasonable time at reasonable cost. Risks are assessed, possible imperfections in concept or design are revealed and technological soundness is assured.

4. *Planning.* The development and evolution of data processing is planned. Application possibilities are uncovered, new systems approaches are developed, capacity growth is projected over time.

5. *Standards.* Standards for hardware systems, software systems, communications systems are developed and promulgated. Programming and documentation standards are supplied to application development groups. Standard operational environments may be defined and organizational structures recommended for sites with data processing equipment. Skills standards and requirements are defined for various data processing roles.

This short list of what is involved in systems management suggests that there are fundamental issues of who is in control of data processing in an enterprise. A single group with the powers and functions mentioned above would represent a highly centralized approach to data processing control. Dispersion of these functions or abandonment of some of them represents steps toward decentralization.

3. DATA PROCESSING SKILLS

Another way of looking at the organization of data processing is to list the skills which are involved in the use of computing systems. There are a number of fundamental skills:

1. Recognize a possible application.
2. Design an application.
3. Design a system for support of an application.
4. Assure the quality and feasibility of designs.
5. Acquire hardware and software components.
6. Implement the system and application.
7. Operate the system and application.
8. Maintain programs.
9. Maintain hardware.
10. Manage use of system and application.
11. Plan evolution and eventual replacement.

The distribution of skills throughout an enterprise means that operational business units or locations have personnel with the talents to perform some or all of the fundamental functions of data processing listed above. If all of the skills are dispersed and if there are no constraining standards applied to the skills, then one has complete decentralization. If only some skills are dispersed and there are constraining standards, then there will be residual centralization. For example, a business unit may have the skill to recognize and implement an application. These tasks may be done within standards imposed by a centralized staff. Other tasks, like acquiring equipment, may not be within the capability of the business unit.

It begins to appear that decentralization vs. centralization is a rather subtle issue. There are various shadings of control, various levels of independence, a rather rich and complex set of potential power relations between data processing center staffs and users. We will explore this more fully in a later section.

An interesting detail about the distribution of skills is that the exact nature of skills may change depending upon whether they are centralized or dispersed. If there is a tendency for the center to employ large uniprocessors using complex operating systems the skills required are the program support skills associated with the operating system. Getting an application "on the air" in this environment requires a set of special knowledge of the conventions associated with software packages. The act of getting an application on in a business unit using a small machine may involve very different kinds of skills. This skills difference is only potential; there is no one to one relation between machine size and skills dispersion.

The last two sections have given us a reasonable idea of the kinds of powers and activities which are involved in discussing centralization and decentralization. We will return to the skills list in a later section and try to provide a method for measuring tendencies to decentralization and centralization.

4. THE ARGUMENTS FOR CENTRALIZATION

Some of the arguments for centralization are general, in that they apply to centralization or decentralization of any function. Some of the arguments are unique to data processing organization. A partial list of considerations which influence people to centralization will give the reader a sense of what is involved in these considerations.

1. *Visible, Controllable Organization and Expenditure.*   Data processing expense is significant and it must be explicitly managed. Even as hardware costs decrease, it is necessary to manage data processing because of the potential value of such systems to the enterprise.

2. *Quality of Staff.*   Data processing design and development is a complex task. It is fundamentally difficult to do. It is necessary that good people be attracted to the enterprise. These people can only be attracted and held if there is an organizational structure which shows career path. Centralized systems management is the only way to provide a professional with growth and future. The dismemberment of such a staff will result in a general decline in skills in the enterprise because business units cannot hold and advance data processing specialists.

3. *Size of Staff.* Regardless of whether there are economies of scale in hardware, there are economies of scale in personnel. A centralized organization permits the sharing of skills among applications and systems and minimizes the per application and per system cost of professional activities.

4. *Enterprise-Wide Viewpoints.* It is essential that the interests of the enterprise be represented in data processing planning and development. Individual business units will design for their own interests and these interests may or may not coincide with the enterprise's wider requirements. Provisions for interdepartmental system communication may not be made, data sharing may not be undertaken, proper planning for evolution may not be done unless system control is in the hands of people responsible for the data processing growth of the enterprise. The costs of retrofitting autonomous applications and the costs of seeing that units are related to each other too late are very high. These costs can be avoided by centralized systems coordination and planning.

5. *Standards.* The implementation of applications and systems involves risks which can become tolerable only if certain standards of performance are applied. There must be centrally imposed standards of hardware, software, programming language, data design, if projects are to be successful and their costs controlled.

6. *Negotiating Position.* Relationships with vendors will be best if the vendors deal with a central agency which represents the economic power of the entire enterprise. Prices, delivery schedules, quality of support from vendors is improved for an enterprise which centralizes its interfaces to sources of data processing supply.

7. *Economies of System Scale.* This argument is obsolete in the minds of some, yet it is still strong for others. Larger hardware systems are more economic than collections of small systems. In order to use large systems well it is necessary to have highly skilled professional staffs. These staffs are equipped to handle the complexity and to maintain high utilization levels by consolidating workloads in shared environments. These high workload levels reduce the cost of computing to individual users.

In summary there are economies in staff organization scale due to skills sharing and due to higher levels of more effective people that can be organized in a centralized staff.

5. THE ARGUMENTS FOR DECENTRALIZATION

The arguments for decentralization fall into two general categories. The first category consists of "positive" arguments which address the general benefits to be gained by decentralizing. The second category consists of "negative" arguments which display dissatisfaction with data processing centers and the kinds of service they provide.

5.1. The Positives

These arguments for decentralization apply to decentralization in general:

1. *Fixing Total Responsibility and Entrepreneurial Control.* It is important that managers be totally accountable for the profitability of their operation. In support of this all of the significant functions and services they require must be put under their control. There must be no way for a responsible manager to point to an outside unit as the reason for his failure to perform. If computing power is a requirement for successful operation, then the business unit manager should have absolute control over, and responsbility for, this computing power. Additional costs are more than compensated for by additional management accountability.

2. *Avoid Interdependency.* Interdependency between business units leads inevitably to conflict. It is not just a question of "communications problems." Units may well find that as they understand each other better their conflicts increase rather than decrease. It is worthwhile to avoid conflict management if possible. Organizations should be structured to minimize interdependency even if that means redundancy and duplication. The costs of such redundancy may be less than the cost of constant issue escalation and conflict resolution between departments with naturally different goals.

3. *Avoid Perception of Loss of Automomy.* Managements and staffs are badly affected by perceptions that their area of decision making is constrained. They become less aggressive and less effective. The benefits of an aggressive entrepreneurial attitude outweigh the costs. Perceptions of loss of autonomy and self-determination should be kept at an absolute minimum.

Some of the characteristics of a business unit and its work which lead to preferences for the decentralization of computer decision making are:

1. The work is highly specialized with minimum intervention from higher management.

2. The work of the computer is essential to the unit which depends upon the computer to accomplish its fundamental mission.

3. The computer system required requires low levels of computer skills or these skills are available on a contract basis from an outside source.

There are real constraints in how much decentralization may be undertaken. It is necessary to remember that not all business unit managers desire control over computing and the responsibilities which go with it. Some business units cannot accept control and responsibility because acquiring the skills is too costly and difficult. Frequently a business unit does not really understand how to recognize an application. It does not know the vendors, it does not know the offered services, it does not understand the risks and so on. These limitations may be overcome by transferring the skills into the department. But they should not be put there unless the departmental management wants them there.

5.2. The Negatives

These arguments for decentralization come from a perception of an unsatisfactory relation with the data processing organization. There are many who argue that whether one likes it or not one must decentralize. It is easier in corporate America to decentralize computing than to get good computing services from a data processing center. Those who hold this view claim that these centers are under constant pressure to hold down the hardware budget. This results in a preoccupation with utilization levels and a disregard for responsiveness. Lipservice may be paid to user satisfaction, but when decisions are made it is the effective utilization of hardware which seems most to influence decisions. Decentralization disperses the hardware figures and reduces the temptation to manage the hardware budget.

Regardless of the truth of this view, there is a nontrivial level of user organization dissatisfaction with data center services. There is a perception of unreliability, awkward interfaces and a lack of responsiveness to user needs for programming resource and machine service. There is an apparent preoccupation with "systems" rather than application issues. There is an atmosphere of a closed "fortress data processing."

It is not at all clear to what extent the accusations leveled against data centers and centralized staffs are reasoned and to what extent they are emotional. If true, it is not clear whether the discontent between user and server is inherent in the way we have understood our objectives or if there has just been insensitive management practice. The following sections undertake to provide a context for exploring user/d.p. relations.

6. DECENTRALIZATION/CENTRALIZATION LEVELS

We have listed a number of basic activities which are involved in data processing. Section 3 provided a list of fundamental skills. Using these skills and adding another dimension, we can develop a context for discussing the power relationships between users and data processing staffs.

Figure 76 is a skills/decision matrix. The columns represent the skills listed in Section 3. The rows represent levels of authority which a data processing management has over the exercise of those skills. Four levels of authority are represented. These levels suggest a reasonable calibration of power in the hands of data processing management. Naturally finer or grosser granules of authority can be defined in any particular organization.

	Recognize	Design application	Design system	Assure design	Acquire hardware/software	Implement	Operate	Maintain programs	Maintain hardware	Management use	Evolve
None	✓	✓	✓	✓	✓	✓	✓	✓	✓	✓	✓
Assist											
Insist											
Enforce											
Impose	✓	✓	✓	✓	✓	✓	✓	✓	✓	✓	✓

Decentralize ←

Centralize

Figure 76. Skills/decision matrix.

6.1. None

At the None level the data processing professional staff does not exist. There is complete decentralization. Every business unit and every location has complete control and complete responsibility for every data processing activity. From the concept of an application through to its phase out everyone is on his own. If it is necessary to coordinate the computer systems of various departments this is done by cooperative negotiation between these departments. All risks lie with the user, who has total power over his data processing destiny.

6.2. Assist

This casts the professional data processing staff into the role of consultants. They exist to offer guidance, on request, to any business unit which requires or desires that guidance. At any point in the discovery or implementation or operational phase of an application or system the user can go to the data processing consultants for advice. He uses them as a mechanism for reducing his own risk. The decisions are up to him. He has absolute right to ignore them; he has absolute rights of nonconcurrence with no responsibilities for justification (unless he fails).

There is a great deal of interest in using professional and management talent in this way. It is a way, for example, of contending with the hidden minicomputer problem. It is obvious that the way to contend with hidden machines is to remove any motive for hiding them. If the professional data processing staff stops trying to be an agent of suppression, then there will be no motive in hiding systems. A user interested in a system can approach the staff. The staff recommends the use of a center machine or the acquisition of a user machine. It offers assurance of design, negotiates with vendors, provides technological material and education. There is maximum motive to come to such a staff in order to reduce the risk of failure with a private machine and to discover what is really the best way to use computers for a particular application.

Professional data processing staffs will come to recognize that their function is to provide good solutions and not to feed a machine center. The effect of this is to maximize the enterprise's return from computing and to enable it to be aware of what is going on in business units and locations.

6.3. Insist

This level is very much like the assist level except that the recommendations of the professional staff must be more seriously considered. Exceptions to the recommendations must be justified and documented, although they may be permitted on the authority of higher levels of business unit management.

6.4. Enforce

At the enforce level the using organization is constrained to live with the rec-ommendations, standards, procedures of the data processing staff. Disagreement must be resolved at management levels beyond the staff. The user may retain data processing skills but his actions are constrained by the requirement for data processing staff concurrence.

6.5. Impose

This is complete centralization. There are no skills in the using organizations. Applications are conceived, developed, installed by the data processing organization.

7. THE MATRIX

Figure 76 shows that all of the checks are at the impose level for complete centralization and at the none level for complete decentralization. The matrix particularly suggests that there may be widely divergent mixes of skills and power and that the centralization/decentralization question is not only more finely calibrated than the binary nature of the phrase but that there may be power variations for each of the skills. It is interesting to draw different patterns of check marks in the matrix and develop scenarios which describe the pattern. The surprise is that there are very few which seem to be, per se, absurd. One potential use of such a matrix is to have various organizations describe their impressions of how levels of authority operate across different skills and then undertake to explore difference in opinion and perception within an enterprise.

8. CONCLUDING OBSERVATIONS

This chapter has attempted to explore the nature of opinions about centralization and decentralization. It has also introduced a framework for thinking about the topic in broader terms. It is useful to repeat that these issues relate to but are distinct from issues of system structure which apply to discussions of distribution. In the following chapters we will return to questions of systems structure and cost, touching on decentralization only as an issue in the cost of distributing operational skills.

Chapter 13

Hardware Costs

1. PERSPECTIVE

The intent of this chapter is to explore the question of whether it is reasonable, from a computer hardware cost viewpoint, to construct systems out of aggregations of processing nodes. Its viewpoint is not completely general in that it addresses the choice between the acquisition of a very large single processing node to support an application or the acquisition of a set of smaller machines with roughly equivalent aggregate power.

The reader is reminded that computer hardware costs represent only a fraction of the total data processing expenditure which includes management, planning, operations, education, and other items as indicated in the last chapter. Chapters 14 and 15 will explore nonhardware cost issues. In this chapter we will try to determine whether, from a hardware cost basis, there is significant motivation or inhibition for distributed processing.

Computer hardware costs now represent 30% to 40% of a data processing budget. Currently the amount of money being spent for computing hardware is considerably larger than the amount of money being spent for communications hardware. However, because of the continuing rapid decline in prices for computing elements and the much more gradual decline in prices for communications the ratios of expenditure will shift rapidly over the next decade. The greater expenditure for computing equipment applies only when it is compared to the expenditures for data communications lines. When compared to total expenditures for communications, including voice, the computer hardware expenditures seem modest indeed.

In general there has been a rapid increase in capacity for computing devices and a rapid improvement in price/performance. Estimates have been made that a processing unit with the capacity of a 1960 machine would cost only 0.5% of that machine in the mid-1970s and that by the mid-1980s price/performance will improve so that an almost equally dramatic increase in economies will occur.

Mass storage devices show a similarly dramatic improvement in cost per megabyte stored since 1960. Dramatic improvements in storage devices may occur because technology will lead us into an era when we do not depend on electromechanical elements for large storage units, although this is by no means a certainty.

On the other hand the price history of communications is less certain. Price reductions since 1960 have been gradual and they promise to continue to be gradual over the next decade. There seems to be dramatic technological change about to come upon us in this area, but the impact and direction of these changes is somewhat uncertain.

The rapid and continued drop in prices for processors, memories and storage devices has caused a change in some people's perceptions about the effective use of computers. The attitudes appropriate for the use of a precious, scarce, expensive resource are beginning to dissolve to some extent.

1.1. Old Perceptions

Central processing units and memories have traditionally been the major components of systems cost. The effective utilization of this expensive equipment was a preoccupying concern for the first decades of the industry.

Associated with the absolute cost of processors and memories was a perception that the industry priced to provide significant economies of scale. The price of the system which was the glory of its time was considerably less than the price of an aggregate of smaller systems which could deliver equivalent power. In addition the price of even small systems was very great so that the entry level for computing was significant.

The existence of economies of scale leads to the acquisition of large systems because of their price effectiveness. These large systems laid the basis for the idea of the "consolidated workload" machine. In order to realize potential economies of scale it is necessary to utilize the large system at high utilization levels. These levels can be frequently achieved only by bringing to a data center workloads which are unrelated and which are processed in the same center only to provide for machine efficiency. Generations of software were developed to support the notion of consolidated workload machines being used at very high levels of efficiency.

These perceptions should not be characterized as obsolete, but there is much less certainty about their fundamental assumptions. Some people have already abandoned this view of effective computing for something very different.

1.2. New Perceptions

Some workers and thinkers in the industry have a very different view of systems economics. They maintain that in systems structures the cheapest element of a system is its processing units and their memories. Dramatic changes have occurred in the percentage of total system cost contributed by a processing unit. Therefore systems can be constructed which can afford to use processing power rather carelessly, and there need be little concern about the effective utilization of processing units.

There is a growing case for the economies of dedication over the economies of sharing. Small systems have low entry points and they can be used to solve problems regardless of whether or not there is economy of scale. Because of a change in relative costs between hardware and professional skills it is more efficient to buy hardware than it is to buy skills to run hardware well.

This view holds that there is, in fact, no economy of scale in processor and memory hardware. Given the constraints of partitioning work and some constraints in handling peak loads, aggregates of small machines at various levels of cooperation will out price-perform the largest available systems and demonstrate advantages of configurability, reliability and stability of performance.

These are the contending hardware viewpoints. They lead to very different system acquisition and design policies. The remaining sections of this chapter will undertake to explore this issue in a reasonable way. The conclusion will be that the issue is not clear. However, the benefit to the reader will be that he will no longer make unsupported assumptions and can convince financial people that there are new alternatives worth considering.

It is important that the reader remain aware that this chapter is investigating only the issue of whether or not hardware costs represent an inducement or a constraint to distribution. Other cost issues, such as operational and programming costs, will be investigated in later chapters.

2. ARE THERE PROCESSOR HARDWARE ECONOMIES OF SCALE?

The question is almost impossible to answer. It is one thing to determine whether pricing for a particular system structure made of small machines is more attractive than pricing for an equivalent system of one large node. It is quite another thing to determine whether that pricing reflects an underlying technological economics and an underlying industry trend.

The economic preferability of one set of hardware over another comes from comparing the price/performance ratios of the two systems. In order for the comparison to be meaningful both the number used for performance and the number used for price must be correct. The following difficulties arise:

1. It is difficult to determine the true performance of a system. This difficulty is extreme when evaluating a system for an application which is not in condition to bench mark or when comparing different structural concepts of an application appropriate to different machines. It is, in general, very difficult to characterize the power of a system because it is sensitive to workload specifics and to subtle interactions between resources which occur as a result of workload characteristics. It is in general almost impossible to make reliable universal statements about the relative performance of two systems which may be operating under dif-

ferent operating systems, constrained by details of configuration whose significance is not appreciated. Only the grossest kinds of comparisons can be made. When the comparison is between a single large system and cooperating smaller systems it is difficult to even approach comparable measures of performance.

2. Even if some reasonable figure of merit for performance can be achieved the price/performance ratio may not be an indication of economy of scale because the pricing policies of vendors are different from system to system. Vendors use different pricing strategies. Prices are only partially determined by the cost of developing and manufacturing a system. They are also determined by the vendor's appreciation of his position in the marketplace. Consequently the relative prices of large and small machines do not represent inherent economies of scale which are natural to the data processing industry.

3. Sometimes one is comparing an older machine to a newer machine. This is difficult because there may be a technology change that makes any pricing comparison invalid. It is also likely that the older machine has developed a price history and is in a state of its life cycle where it is available at reduced prices.

4. Even if one were to attempt to determine if there were economies of scale on a cost rather than a price basis, it would be very difficult to do because vendors use different cost accounting techniques to determine their costs to design, develop, manufacture and support systems in the field.

So we are deprived of any real hope for determining whether or not processor economy of scale is a factor in this industry. However, we may informally explore the issue with reason and hypothesis. The author reaches a tentative conclusion that there are no economies of scale in processing units and memories, but that there are for random access storage devices and other input and output devices.

3. SIMPLE EXERCISES

The determination of hardware economics involves assessments of product price and product performance. The exercises to determine prices are easiest, naturally, because there is general knowledge of product prices available from vendors or independent sources.

It would be possible at this point to provide a list of current product prices from various sources. We are not going to do that because these prices are too volatile to have meaning by the time this book is published. Instead we are going to describe a set of simple exercises which the author has undertaken and a set of conclusions which the author has reached.

In determining whether or not economy of scale exists, it is necessary to identify the components of a system which are to be subjected to the analysis. This is not as simple as it may seem because vendor packaging practices differ from system to system as well as between vendors. Some vendors offer processing units priced with no memory included; some offer processing units priced with different sizes of memory and some basic controllers or minimum number of channels included in the basic price. Some vendors include the price of software, or some elements of software, in a basic price.

It is necessary to take care to assure that equivalent functional units are being compared and this is sometimes very difficult to do. A reasonable approach is to select a standard minimum configuration which includes a processor, a console, a minimum memory size and a minimum I/O interconnection configuration. This configuration should be defined for processing units in the 50,000 instruction per second, 100,000 instruction, 300,000 instruction, 500,000 instruction, 1 million, 2 million, 3 million, 4 million instruction per second ranges. A little later we will discuss the topic of comparative instruction power.

The initial list should be developed for at least two processor architectures. It may be that not all architectures straddle the entire performance range but the list for all architectures should contain as many points as the architecture provides. For example, the 370 architecture group should include the range from the 4331 through to the 3033.

A second list must be formed which represents larger configurations of the set of processors. This is important because there is a relationship between the actual speed of a processor and its memory size. A nominal 500,000 instruction per second (500 KIPS) processor will not be able to execute 500 KIPS with its minimum memory configuration. To determine how much memory a processor should have the author used the very rough index of 1.3 megabytes per million instructions. This ratio is an educated judgment by the author, based upon some typical configurations. The ratio leads to a memory size of roughly 400,000 bytes for a machine in the 300 KIPS range, 2.5 megabytes for a machine in the 2 MIPS range, and so on. If vendors do not supply such memory sizes, one uses the memory size that comes closest to meeting the ratio.

The full list of processor/memory systems now looks like the list of Figure 77. For two architectures, A and B, for all members of the processing family there is a minimum and probable configuration.

The next step is to associate prices with each of the configurations. After this divide the prices by the stated raw power of the processor in thousands or millions of instructions executed per second. This figure gives an index of the cost to execute an instruction on that configuration. A comparison between indices will reveal a very rough notion of whether there is economy of scale in hardware pricing. Only the probable memory configurations are meaningful in this exercise. The comparison is meaningful (so far) only for probable memory configurations within the same architecture. Economy of scale exists within an architecture if the cost per instruction executed for the larger machines with

Architecture A		Architecture B	
Processor Rate	Configuration Price	Processor Rate	Configuration Price
50 KIP, MIN M		N/A	
100 KIP, MIN M		N/A	
300 KIP, MIN M		300 KIP, MIN M	
500 KIP, MIN M		500 KIP, MIN M	
1 MIP, MIN M		1 MIP, MIN M	
N/A		2 MIP, MIN M	
N/A		4 MIP, MIN M	
50 KIP, 64K		N/A	
100 KIP, 128K		N/A	
300 KIP, 396K		300 KIP, 396K	
500 KIP, 700K		500 KIP, 700K	
1 MIP, 1.25 MEG		1 MIP, 1.25 MEG	
N/A		2 MIP, 2.50 MEG	
N/A		4 MIP, 5 MEG	

Configuration price/MIPS = Power Index for Processor/Memory

Figure 77.　System list.

their probable memory sizes is lower than the cost per instruction for smaller machines with their probable memory sizes.

The minimum memory size configurations are useful only to gain an insight into the impact of pricing of memory as distinct from processor pricing policies.

In order to compare architectures it is necessary to develop an algorithm which expresses the power of one architecture in terms of the other. Processors have different instruction sets which determine how many instructions must be executed to perform the same function and how much memory these instructions will occupy. In addition some processors manipulate only 16 bits at a time, other processors manipulate 32 bits at a time, and so on.

A simple approach to equivalence in architecture is to determine the instructions required to move data from one location to another and to perform branch instructions. Some architectures will move data by sequences of load and store register instructions; others will have memory to memory move instructions. The branch logic will also be different from architecture to architecture. Consequently different specific instruction sequences will be required to perform identical move and branch functions.

A very rough index of the relative power of two architectures may be obtained by a two step process. First, for the data unit length which seems most appropriate, count the number of bits which are moved from memory into processor and out again to perform the functions. Second, multiply each bit count by the percentage of machine time spent executing these functions. The percentage of machine time executing data move instructions depends upon compiler stylistics. The multiplier which the author used was 20% of machine time for instructions which moved data from one location to another. The intensity of instructions used to support a branching operation was estimated to be 30% of machine time. Justification for these multipliers is pure judgment based upon experience with various instruction mix determination algorithms for various compilers. I believe they stand the test of reasonableness and it is only this test one wants to pass. To pretend more would be misleading. The entire exercise intends only to establish some broad judgmental basis for an opinion about economy of scale. One very great gap in the work is the fact that processor power has not been adjusted for "I/O interference." This interference is a function of the way that storage and other devices are interfaced with the processor/memory complex. Different interconnection techniques and different configurations of I/O devices will result in different reductions in processor power. Some systems route data going to and from memory through the logic of the processor. For those periods of time during which I/O operations are being performed, the processor cannot execute programs. Other systems route data directly to the memory, using a connection technique called direct memory access. In these systems the processor can execute instructions while data is flowing into the system. However, some delays in execution may occur because the processor and the input/output units try to access memory at the same time. This results in delays in program execution because the processor, in all designs known to the author, waits for the I/O memory access to complete.

An approximation of the power of an architecture can be developed because the number of bits which flow across the memory/processor interface is a function of the number of instructions which must be performed to accomplish a certain function. A relative power of two architectures, which is admittedly naive, can be developed by dividing the architecture with the lower bit count into the architecture with the higher bit count. This gives a ratio of architectural power. This ratio can be used to express the MIPS rates of the architectures in equivalent terms by multiplying the more powerful architectures rate by the ratio. The price/performance cost to perform an instruction can then be adjusted by dividing the new MIPS rate into the price. Figure 78 shows the steps of this process.

We are still in a very preliminary state. We have a raw price/performance ratio unadjusted by influences of operating system performance and structure and with no elements of other systems costs such as storage devices, communications units, and data processing peripherals.

On the basis of exercises of this type on various vendor product lines the author has reached the following conclusions as regards economies of scale in processor/memory sets:

1. Over the last 15 years the economy of scale price curve has become considerably flatter for most vendors from the top of the family to the bottom.

Architecture A		Architecture B	

FUNCTION: Move 32 bits A to B

MOVE A, B	48 bits	LOAD REG 1, A	32 bits
Data	0 *	STORE REG 1, B	32
		Data	64
	48		128

* Memory-memory move

FUNCTION: Compare A:B, 32 bits

LOAD R1, A	32	LOAD R1, A	32
COMPRE R1, B	32	LOAD R2, B	32
BRANCH	16	COMPRE R1, R2, M	32
Data	64	Data	64
	144		160

FUNCTION FREQUENCY ADJUSTMENT

% TIME EXECUTING MOVE FUNCTION: 20%
% TIME EXECUTING COMPARE FUNCTION: 30%

TO WEIGH EFFICIENCY OF FUNCTION BY FREQUENCY

ARCHITECTURE A	ARCHITECTURE B
$.20 * 48 = 9.6$	$.20 * 128 = 25.6$
$.30 * 144 = 43.2$	$.30 * 160 = 48.0$
52.8	73.6

FORM A:B POWER RATIO APPROXIMATIONS

74/53 = 1.4 ARCHITECTURE A IS 1.4 AS POWERFUL AS B

ADJUST POWER INDICES

BOTH A and B ARE NOMINAL NATIVE 300 KIP UNITS

BUT: 1.4 * 300 = 420 KIPS.
    A IS A 420 KIPPer IN TERMS OF B

ADJUST PRICE/PERFORMANCE

ARCHITECTURE A	ARCHITECTURE B
$150,000	$135,000
150/300 = .50	135/300 = .45
150/420 = .36	

Figure 78.   Equivalent architectures.

2. There is currently a two-tiered pricing structure in the industry. Processors up to a given level of capacity exhibit price/performance advantages over processors beyond that level by ratios ranging from nearly 2:1 to 4:1. This holds both for within vendor and for cross-vendor comparisons for machines beyond the critical level. The reader is reminded that price comparisons are perturbed by variations in the amount of software which is included in the price of a processor/memory complex. It is a situation where we are trying to compare apples and oranges. Unfortunately it is often necessary to compare things which are different in many ways. Such comparisons may be basic to systems selection in the future.

3. Within the two tiers there is modest economy of scale. The very smallest versions of a system do not perform as effectively as larger versions up until the critical point is reached. Machines beyond the critical point exhibit a very slight tendency to economy of scale. This tendency is abruptly terminated, however, in the world of the "super-computer."

These conclusions are pictorially represented as Figure 79. The explanation of these conclusions lies partly in the dynamics of the marketplace and partly in the technology of the industry.

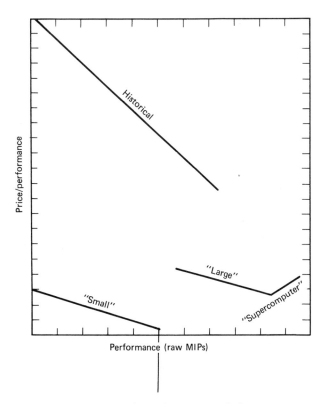

Figure 79. Price performance conclusions.

We have before mentioned the many ways that these conclusions can be in error. Still, the author's conjecture is that the current discontinuity in pricing exists, that it will disappear over time, but that processor economy of scale will not reappear in the next decade. Pricing perturbations, based on software bundling practices, naturally may remain a factor in actual systems comparative pricing.

4. INTERPRETATIONS

The (to some) surprising observation that there are no longer economies of scale in processing units is worth some discussion. We wish to gain an appreciation of the potential future. Are we in an unusual period or are pricing practices in the future going to be what they now seem to be? One wishes not to get caught in a "perturbation" which will adjust itself when one is trying to plan data processing hardware policy for long periods of time. Figure 80 raises the legitimate concern that we are currently at point A and that in the reasonable future the "normal" conditions of points B and C will be reestablished.

Figure 81 suggests that over a long period of time the price/performance of all classes of processor, maxi, midi, micro, have been steadily improving over time, but that the smaller machines are improving at a faster rate. Does the

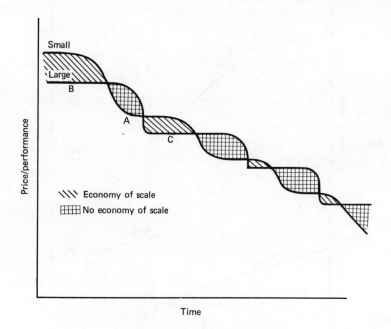

Figure 80.   Price/performance cycles.

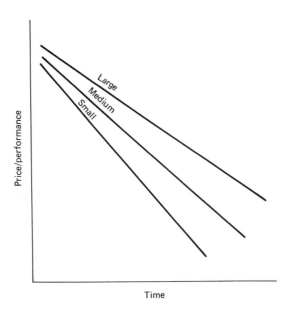

Figure 81. Long term price performance.

industry and its basic functions suggest that this will continue or should we expect a reversal?

The interpretations and predictions offered in this section are strictly the author's own views. They are presented to the reader in order to establish a conceptual framework for considering the issue.

If processor hardware economies of scale are to return, it is necessary that they have some basis in cost. The costs of designing, manufacturing and supporting computing devices do not, in an intensely competitive market in which no one organization controls the rate of change, completely determine price. Yet it is impossible to consider that prices are determined by algorithms entirely insensitive to cost elements.

It is therefore reasonable to ask whether the cost generating processes of the industry support a notion of economy of scale. The author's view is that the curve of Figure 82 applies. This curve suggests an explanation for the apparent two tiered nature of the pricing structure in the computing industry. The curve suggests that in any technology time frame there is a "knee." The technology itself determines where that knee exists in terms of raw performance. It may exist for a time at 1 MIPS, for a time at 2 MIPS, and so on, as technology and related manufacturing processes mature. The left side of the knee represents the fact that disproportionate increases in price/performance may be achieved with little elaboration of design or manufacture. The right side of the knee suggests that beyond a certain point very disappointing improvements on general price/performance are achieved by additional elaboration of design.

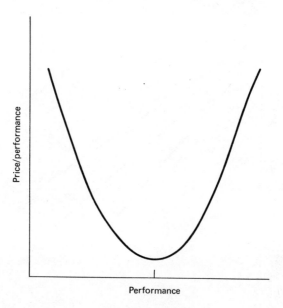

Figure 82.   Knee.

In order for there to be consistent economies of scale from small versions of a processor to large ones it is necessary to experience economies in technology, design, manufacture and systems support of installed units. It is very expensive to develop, test and prepare new technologies for manufacture. Machines to the left of the knee tend to be technologically more conservative than machines to the right of the knee. Associated with technology is design and manufacture. The design of a very high performance machine, a machine at the edge of the computational art, is very costly. This is especially true for the very fastest versions of a particular architecture. Such machines at the top of the line are acknowledgedly not optimum price/performers but exist to deliver maximum performance where that performance is required for a class of problems regardless of price/performance characteristics. Similarly, very fast processors contain many unique and specially designed parts. These parts are manufactured in small production runs on expensive production equipment. Consequently they do not experience economy of manufacturing scale.

On the other hand, smaller units may be made up of larger numbers of simpler parts which are replicated in the physical embodiment of the system. These parts may be optimally designed and manufactured in very large numbers, profiting from economy of production scale.

The reader is cautioned against making assumptions about where in a product line the pricing curve becomes discontinuous and must inspect various models of various architectures to determine where he has crossed into the "performance" only zone, where he would be motivated to acquire a system because it was the only way to achieve a required raw power. It is almost impossible, from the point of view of a hardware component price, to determine where a knee occurs. The knee will be constantly moving to the right, over time, as computer technology, design techniques and manufacturing technology improve.

In the area of system field support there are economies of scale natural to experience. The investment in maintaining operational hardware for a smaller number of large systems is more efficient for a vendor than maintaining large numbers of smaller systems.

With this background of observation a number of reasonable predictions can be made. First is that economy of scale pricing for traditional uniprocessors will not return to the industry. Second, it is possible that economies of scale will reappear in a new form because of some technological directions. This new form is of direct interest to those involved in ideas of distributed processing.

In addition to a general decrease in hardware price over time there has been another important phenomenon. The percentage of systems costs contributed by the electronics which make a computer a computer has been steadily decreasing as a percentage of total system cost. The relative contributions of power, cooling, cabinets and so on, have been steadily rising. It is therefore profitable to share as much of the "other" costs as possible among computer logic components. This is consistent with much industry practice already beginning to emerge. Outboard channels in their own boxes are being brought underneath the skin of processing units and the concept of central electronic complex as a marketable unit replaces the concept of central processing unit.

It is possible that by the end of the next decade those elements of cost which involve noncomputer logic elements will triple their contribution to total system cost. This observation, when combined with earlier comments about the cheapness of processing units, the existence of a "knee" and trends toward higher and higher circuit densities, suggests two things. First, the day of the large processor as a single processing unit is over. Most systems of the future will be multiple processing units in the sense that they will have at least a set of specialized engines, communications processors, I/O processors, memory hierarchy management processors, and so on, in addition to the visible problem state computational processor. All of these processors will be developed to exist in a single cabinet with a strong single systems image.

Beyond this, various trends in interconnection mechanisms and packaging practices suggest the emergence of a class of machine in which multiple problem state processors exist underneath the same skin, either as multiprocessors or as multiple processor sets where each unit has its own operating system. New concepts for what is shared and duplicated in a system will emerge to reflect new economics.

Consistent with observations made in the chapter on distance, and other observations relative to economies of operation, closeness of cooperation, and

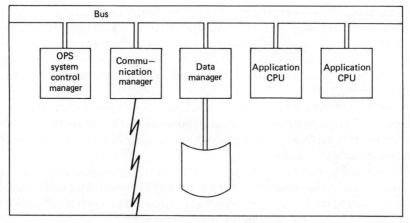

Figure 83.   Future structure.

so on, there seems a future for a class of machine like that drawn in Figure 83. A distributed use of such a machine is to dedicate sets of processors to various departments or business units in such a way as to guarantee reliability and stable response times. Intelligent terminals at outlying areas will be able to reduce communications flow and support excellent user interfaces with reasonable amounts of local storage.

5.   STORAGE DEVICES

A discussion of hardware economies of scale in computing devices would not be complete without a mention of the situation in disk storage devices. It is very easy to demonstrate that there are serious economies of scale in random storage units. A review of the pricing of such devices reveals that there is an almost 6-1 difference in the price effectiveness of devices which can hold billions of bits when compared to units which can hold millions of bits. Again, of course, the reader must assure himself, at the time of his reading, of what the current ratios are. But it seems, in general, safe to say that the total cost of a system consisting of a single large processor and a reasonable storage complement will be less than a family of processing units with the same amount of storage distributed among them.

There are two considerations important to include in this area of discussion. First, there is no natural relationship between storage capacity in an on-line storage unit and processing unit speed. The amount of required storage is largely an aspect of an application and does not seem as directly connected to processing unit speed as the amount of desirable main memory. Second, the economies of scale in large storage units is achieved when the space is intensively used. Underused large disks will not show the reduction in cost per megabyte stored. There is a kind of unit price versus unit efficiency tradeoff in these electromechanical devices.

Many small processors can share storage devices or can interface to large storage devices originally intended for use by larger processing systems. There may be some performance degradation, naturally, when sharing is implemented due to contention for access and the need to synchronize access among processing units. In determining the split and spread of storage devices, a designer must consider price, of course, but he must also consider reliability and performance. References to disk storage may contribute the dominating time elements affecting performance. Arm movement times are significant sources of response delay and limit the extent to which large disks can be effectively shared. Similarly, multiple smaller disks may serve as the basis for limiting the scope of a system failure.

6. DATA PROCESSING PERIPHERAL DEVICES

For essentially the same reasons that there are economies of scale in storage units, there are economies of scale in printers, tapes, card readers, and so on. In contemporary peripheral devices the contribution to cost of electromechanical components provides a base for economies of scale.

7. TOTAL SYSTEMS HARDWARE COSTS

A summary of the above comments suggests that from a processor/memory point of view a family of small processing units will currently have the potential of outperforming a single large node. From a total system cost point of view the disk storage and data processing peripheral prices will seriously balance this tendency. This can be easily confirmed by the reader. The secret in minimizing hardware costs seems to lie in designs which permit, within performance constraints, sharing of high cost storage and peripheral elements by families of processors performing at or below the knee. In the next chapter we will explore operational and software considerations which are relevant to this observation.

8. MULTIPLE SYSTEMS

If there is a suggestion that families of small processors can be price effective when compared to a large processor, there is still quite a bit of disagreement about the relative effectiveness of performance in comparing a single large processor to multiple slower processors.

Queueing theory indicates that a fast single server performing at a certain rate will outperform a set of slower servers with the same aggregate power.

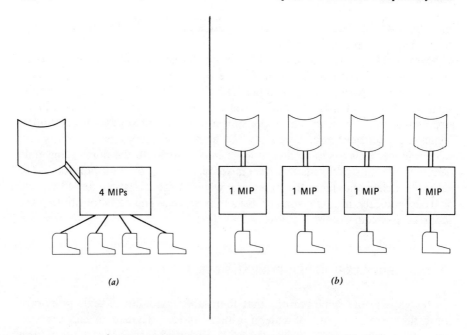

Figure 84.   Large/small system.

Figure 84 suggests why. Consider a 4 MIPS system which is serving a population of users each of which can consume from 600 KIPS to 1.2 MIPS of the
system resource, roughly 15%–30%. When all of the users experience a simultaneous peak, then 120% of the total system resource is demanded and responsiveness to user work will decay. However, notice that when two of the users
are operating at 15% and two are operating at 30% the large system can accommodate the load without decay in performance. As different demands are made
upon the large unit it can dynamically reallocate its shared resources to respond to variations in demand. Thus peak load conditions can be more frequently handled without disruptive effects if multiple users tend to peak at
different times.

Consider the system of Figure 84b. This is an aggregation of four 1 MIPS
processors with the same nominal aggregate power rate of the 4 MIPSer. Each
of the using units, generating their loads of 600 KIPS to 1.2 MIPS, is placed on
a single one of the four smaller units. When each user is requesting beneath 1
MIPS the system works reasonably. Consider the effect, however, of just one
user reaching a peak. The responsiveness of the small processor will be seriously affected. Although the other three users are only generating demands for
600 KIPS when the single user generates his demand for 1.2 MIPS, and the
total delivered power of the four systems is only 3 MIPS out of a potential 4,
the effectiveness of the four processor system goes down. This could be overcome if underutilized processors can pick up the load, but such a design re-

quires particular application characteristics, particular software features and particular interconnect mechanisms to be effective. The dynamic reallocation of resources is more difficult to achieve, given the state of the art, across multiple slower units than across a single unit operating under a sophisticated operating system.

Thus we see that it is reasonable to suspect that more aggregate power will be required from a set of smaller units to match the performance of a larger single unit. In the example of Figure 84, we would require four 1.2 MIPS boxes, with an aggregate power of 4.8 MIPS, or five 1 MIPS boxes with a different distribution of user load. Of course, to preclude any decay in performance one also needs a 4.8 MIPS single node, but its service will only decay when three of four users are in peak period and seriously decay only when all four are in peak. Further, it can track finer degrees of granularity in changes in user load.

There are other reasons why the single larger unit may be more effective that have to do with the increased simultaneity of resource usage. Higher degrees of parallel compute and I/O, shared operating system code between users and shared data may lead to an ability of the larger system to sustain better performance at higher utilization levels than smaller units. It is a quick rule of thumb that a large unit of contemporary design does not experience serious performance loading problems until it is utilized well into the 80% level, while smaller processors begin to experience performance perturbations at load levels beneath 60%. This is, of course, another arena of "astonishing counterexample." For every scenario in which a clear demonstration of the superiority of a single large node is made, there is an equally astonishing counterexample.

Whether or not an application or a set of users can be meaningfully split across multiple systems are issues having to do with load and use analysis. Whether or not the increased requirement for aggregate power will lead to a more expensive system depends upon contemporary pricing of processor/memory, storage, interconnect and peripheral components as well as upon the specific configuration of the multiple node system.

In the spirit of "astonishing counterexample," we will now present the argument that a family of small systems can be as effective or more so than a single large system.

9. COUNTERARGUMENT

The counterargument in the area of smaller versus larger processing units rests upon three assumptions which primarily relate to software characteristics rather than hardware characteristics. Software on large systems, the argument states, is richer in function and complexity than software on small systems. As a consequence, large systems may not be as much faster than small systems as they appear. Contemporary queueing analysis, some state, has not represented certain features of large systems in the modeling done to date.

Large systems, some claim, experience performance degradation when compared to small systems because:

1. A larger percentage of the time in large systems is spent undertaking global systems management. Thus significant reduction in processing capability is experienced because of the operation of highly sophisticated operating systems algorithms which allow the distribution of large system resources among unrelated users. This decay is inherent in the concept and is not a pathology of a particular operating system. Some percentage of system time and resource is "nonproductive" because it is devoted to determining systems status in ways that are not directly profitable to a set of users.

2. Large systems software is more functionally rich and general than small systems software. As a consequence of this it takes more instructions to do more things. More time must be invested in determining what a user wants to do, in determining its impact on the system, and in protecting users from possible bad effects. A large, general purpose software structure for a large system may require many more instructions to provide a function for a user. For the limited functions they perform, therefore, small systems software structures are fundamentally more efficient.

3. The large system suffers from "large systems effects." This means that for those system switching and control functions common to both large and small systems more time will be taken on the large machine. This is because the larger load will require them to be performed more frequently and there will be longer queues and lists to analyze when they are performed.

Figure 85 shows this argument. The 30% overhead for global system analysis is a figure the author thinks would satisfy the small processor enthusiasts. This figure represents activities of the system invested in the analysis of system use and status which are not directly related to servicing a particular user. A figure of 30%, in the judgment of large system advocates, is probably very high.

The 25% "path length" burden (number of instructions needed to perform a logical function) is applied on the assumption that it will take five times as many instructions to perform a function on the software of the large system as on the software of the small system. However, these instructions are being performed four times as fast (the machine is four times faster) so the net effect is a 25% burden. This path length penalty is applied to reflect the fact that it requires more instructions to select and determine what has to be done, more instructions to determine authority, more instructions to determine availability of resource, more complex interfaces must be supported, and so on.

The 5% large system effect burden accounts for longer queues and lists to inspect when it is making task switch and resource allocation decisions.

	System A Nominal 4 MIPS	System B Nominal 1 MIPS
Raw speed	4 MIPS	1 MIPS
Effective speed after:		
30% Global management	2.8	n/a
25% Path length	1.8	n/a
5% Large system effects	1.6	n/a
5% Unutilized	1.4	n/a
50% Unutilized	n/a	.5
Large system at 95% utilization delivers less than 50% of power to application, effectively a 1.4 MIPS system?		Small system with trivial operating system, essentially dedicated, with no penalty shown for limited I/O overlap

Figure 85. Large system effectiveness for identical processor architecture. The large system at 95% is effectively only 1.4 MIPs.

The result of the numbers of Figure 85 is that a system which is nominally four times faster than another system does not really deliver its power to applications processing if there is significant sharing and coordination required between independent users at high utilization levels.

It is time for another word of caution. Systems which are constructed from aggregates of small processing units may experience many of the systems management burdens which exist on large, multiprogrammed single processor systems. Shared data or device access, dynamic workload balancing, communications management may contribute large systems effects to an "aggregated" computer system.

In the figure the small systems are given an effective speed of 500 KIPS on an assumption of minimal software control burden on the system. There would be no global analysis, short functional path lengths and no large systems effects. The population of users would be small and require less management. In order to sustain acceptable performance in this kind of a software environment the load on the system is kept down to about half of its nominal capacity.

The assumption of 50% utilization is justified for two reasons. First, to accommodate "peak to average load" ratios so that there is sufficient slack for the systems to respond to peak demands without serious perturbation of response times. Second, the fundamental hardware structure of smaller systems, particularly as regards input/output interfaces, will tend to reduce processor utilization levels in the presence of simple software control algorithms. One of the things we may expect to see very soon are systems in the 1 MIPS range of the examples used here that have structures which would permit considerably higher CPU utilization because of elaboration of the I/O-CPU interfaces. Some small system advocates would object to the assumption of 50% utilization levels for small systems.

In any case, the effects of the adjustment of raw power that is represented by Figure 85 is impressive when it is considered in the light of the exercise of Figure 84. Although the small systems can be used only an average 50% of their capacity, the set of them can sustain a 2 MIPS rate and peak, reasonably to 2.8 MIPS. The total application's deliverable power of the single 4 MIPS system is 1.6 MIPS. Apparently, under certain circumstances the set of small systems can deliver more power than the large system. This raises some questions about earlier conclusions about the relative efficiences of small and large systems.

You can well imagine that there is animated argument in this area. There is no general agreement on the amount of time a large system effectively spends doing global analyses, there is no general agreement about path length ratios, which are themselves arenas for counterexample from system to system, and many deny that significant queues build in large systems. In addition, it is possible that many of the large systems effects will occur in systems which are constructed of small processors.

It is the unhappy requirement for a design or a policy that is going to make assumptions about these issues to explore at least the outer edges of the question of multiple machine performance and the large system to multiple small system performance analysis question.

10.   THE MARKET

The number of vendors offering important products in various combinations has been alluded to in an earlier chapter. There is an amazing amount of hardware and software available with equally amazing gaps.

For some years the distributed versus centralized hardware question was part of an issue drawn along vendor lines. Large systems vendors competed with small systems vendors in defense of traditional systems concepts.

Although there is still variation in pricing practice and an apparent discontinuity in processor class pricing, a number of important changes have occurred within the last few years.

1.   Large systems vendors have announced a variety of small systems for use with large systems or with each other.

2.   The idea of interconnected systems is now seen to include large systems as well as small systems.

3.   Software for all classes of system has considerably matured.

4. Notions of dedicated function surrounding small systems are beginning to dissolve as these systems become more powerful. There is a greater use of small systems in multiapplication environments.

5. Small system functional architecture is beginning to be less distinct and resemble contemporary large systems more closely. The addition of cache, memory interleave and I/O overlap has made smaller machines more useful in more areas. Structure and performance reform in large systems has made large systems more useful in more areas. The net result, of course, is a maximum difficulty in decision making for an enterprise.

There is no question that the population of small systems in the world is growing rapidly. As of this writing there are probably in excess of 300,000 small systems in use. Of these, around 75,000 are mixed together with larger units to form complete systems. Numbers of systems of all sizes are interconnected into networks of various degrees of cooperativeness, and interconnection facilities are maturing at a rapid rate.

Behind this comes the phenomenon of the growing "microcomputer," its contention for a spot in the "mini" computer world and its claim to be a building block for very large systems and for terminal devices and instruments of all sorts.

11. CONCLUDING REMARKS

Hardware trends seem to indicate that there is no longer any processor economy of scale but that economy of scale exists in storage and peripheral devices. Processors are contributing smaller percentages to total system cost and electronics are contributing smaller percentages to total computer costs. Communications costs will gather a larger and larger share of total systems costs. All computer related hardware is experiencing significant and continuing improvements in price effectiveness.

From a systems performance point of view the balance which must be struck is between the inefficiencies of partitioning and the inefficiencies of heavy contention for shared resources.

This is the condition of the present. What does the future suggest?

1. Technology will define a set of building blocks which will serve as the basis for all system construction.

2. A new range of processing power placement decisions will become available and significant systems will be buildable out of multiple processing units in the same cabinet.

3. The heart of future systems design will be the interconnection mechanisms. Higher degrees of configurability around an interconnect structure will be available and rates of interaction will be considerably improved.

4. In many situations the economics of replication and dedication will appear superior to the economics of sharing.

Future "large systems" may be aggregates of smaller systems with different vendors taking different approaches to how clearly the building block components are seen by a using organization.

As computer hardware costs become lower the focus moves from concerns about how to effectively use hardware to concerns about how to use hardware to control other costs. There is a growing awareness that software development, computer operations, user interface, enterprise information value are areas of cost and benefit which are more critical than hardware costs. The next chapters undertake to introduce these cost issues.

Chapter 14

Operational Costs

1. INTRODUCTION

The intent of this chapter is to introduce issues of cost which involve people who are performing tasks not directly related to applications development.

Operational costs is a phrase which can be taken narrowly to mean the costs associated with the physical operation of a system. In this sense it involves the salaries and facilities associated with console operators, media librarians, data entry specialists and others whose salaries contribute to the control of a "shift."

However, such a narrow use of the word is not profitable. There are other functions which are legitimately attributable to an operational environment. The tasks of scheduling and prioritizing work requests, tuning and adjusting an operational system, installing and maintaining "system" code are all part of operations. Thus there is a considerable body of software expertise which is associated with general operations.

There is a rather fuzzy intersection between operations costs and systems management costs. This can be observed in many ways. Professional systems staff and senior software specialists perform functions of planning and evaluation which are not truly operational costs. Planning the data design for use of a sophisticated data base manager is a systems management cost. Installing and supporting the actual software package is an operational systems programming cost.

There is also a gray area between applications development costs and operational costs. Installed systems software packages and applications packages intend to reduce the expense and effort associated with developing applications. Some of the costs of planning for and using such packages displace program development costs. A large database manager contributes value to an installation by helping to control and protect the enterprise data resource. Such a system also contributes by providing an applications development framework within which applications may be implemented more quickly and at less expense. The costs involved in the use and support of such a package must be measured against avoided costs in programming and increased benefits in faster development of computer based function. In calculating operational costs the potential impact on programming development costs must be considered in order to arrive at a true assessment of benefits.

This chapter will primarily focus on operational costs in a broad sense with the risk that we will sometimes be approaching the fuzzy intersection of systems management costs.

The goal of this chapter is to introduce the issues which are relevant to determining whether different kinds of systems structures and physical placements impact the cost of operating a system. There are questions of systems complexity, benefits of sharing resources versus dedicating resources, the definition of roles which must be played in an organization in order to use various kinds of systems.

The criteria which will be used to represent cost is the salary paid to professional staff. As hardware costs are decreasing, salary costs are increasing and personnel costs represent a more and more significant part of a data processing budget.

This theme is frequently restated by those who survey data processing cost allocations. DATAMATION, among others, provides data on budgets and data processing salaries which lead to the inescapable conclusion that professional personnel costs represent a serious threat to the orderly growth of the industry.

Since the specific figures change from year to year we will follow our policy of not providing specific numbers. However, in general, we can observe the increasing share of the budget over time and observe that except for the largest installations, total salary costs exceed total computer hardware costs. At the time of the writing of this book (1980) roughly 50% of computer cost is attributable to personnel. In very large installations, where the percentages are somewhat lower, the absolute bill is staggering because of the size of those budgets.

Not only do personnel contribute to cost but their skills may be a limit to growth. The computer industry is beginning to become concerned about the "telephone operator" problem. The skills required to plan for, install, maintain, tune, evolve software packages are becoming rare relative to the demand. This contributes to a salary spiral, of course, but it also suggests that certain data processing plans may not be implementable because the skills are not available to bring the planned systems to fruition.

Vendors are highly motivated to address this problem for two reasons. First is that they wish to remove the limits associated with installing and using computer product. Second is that they wish to attract significant shares of the data processing budget. As hardware prices go down and as personnel prices go up, vendors receive smaller percentages of dollars expended for data processing. Some revenue can be generated by selling software function, but important cost to use will limit the salability of such product and scarce skills will limit its installability, regardless of the attractive pricing of software product.

A third reason for vendor concern about operational costs exists for those vendors who provide significant professional support to their customers. Prod-

	1965	1975	1985
Computer vendor	10	14	15
Communications costs	0	4	11
Personnel	7	21	28
System capacity in normalized transactions	1	10	34
$ per transaction to computer vendor	0.20	0.03	0.01

Figure 86.   Modified actual example of an expenditure shift (millions of dollars).

ucts which develop high installation use costs tend also to develop high systems supports costs and require high skill levels from the vendor. These costs must be represented in the price of the product, making the product less attractive in a competitive marketplace.

Figure 86 shows something of the problem. The figure speculates that over a 20 year period revenue to the hypothetical vendor has increased 50%. There is, however, a flat period within the last 10 years of the time frame. This represents the amazing price/performance improvements of the industry. Despite the enormous increase in system capacity, the vendor's hardware revenue does not increase. In fact, over the period, his share of data processing dollar has decreased seriously and his share of revenue per transaction processed has decreased by double an order of magnitude.

Figure 86 shows the magnitude of the shift of cost to personnel factors and away from hardware factors. We are particularly interested in those elements of personnel cost associated with systems programming and operational functions.

2.   COMPLEXITY

A recurring theme in the use of computer systems is the theme of complexity. Complexity seems to intrude at every point of installation and use.
Complexity seems to come from software product instability, from a multiplicity of product interfaces, from the richness of each interface and from the interactions between software products which form a complete system.

We have before mentioned that it is not clear whether distributed systems or centralized systems necessarily suggest more or less complexity. An image borrowed, inappropriately, from the world of small stand alone systems seems to associate small systems with simplicity. This association implies to some that interconnected small systems, each of which is "simple," will retain an image of simplicity.

This is not a true image of distributed systems in general. Interconnected systems may or may not imply simpler environments at each node and interconnection itself suggests enrichment of some functions, elaboration of some interfaces, exercise of control over new problems which may lead to more complexity or to a change in the details of complexity without a reduction in its level.

2.1. Operational Cost Factors

A very basic problem is that we do not know exactly what contributes to operational cost in any particular way. Consider Figure 87. It is an odd figure in that we know the name of the Y axis and the general shape of a curve. We do not know the name of the X axis. The curve represents increases in operational costs as a function of something. One possible name for the X axis is total system power. This suggests that operational costs increase as a function

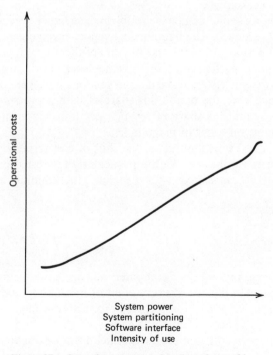

Figure 87.   Operating costs as a function of something.

of the total power of a computer system. A 300 KIPS system would cost less to operate than a 3 MIPS system. There seems to be some truth in this.

However, we can observe systems of equivalent power and almost equivalent function which do not generate the same operational expenses. They require different skills in different amounts to use. Consequently an additional component of the X axis must be some attribute or characteristic of systems software design. It is not understood how raw system power and operational interfaces relate to each other to determine operational cost.

However, we also find that identical systems may generate different operational costs as a function of the using organization's definition of success. A system which will be utilized at a 95% level requires more professional tending than a system which is utilized at a level of 50%. Those who are able to underutilize their equipment seem to be able to avoid certain operational costs.

A fourth candidate for a component of the X axis is the partitioning of power. Some feel that a collection of intermediate size units in an installation will generate less operational cost than a single very large unit. Since each unit has simpler interfaces and generates a need for fewer highly skilled professional roles, the per unit operational cost can go down if they are all within the scope of a single professional staff. It is not clear if this is so and it is not clear how system heterogeneity affects this issue.

A last mentioned (though not a last conceivable) element contributing to system cost of operation is the physical placement of the units. Nodes at distant geographical points will tend to increase operational expenses because they will require local operational support. Just how much local operational support depends upon the nature of the node and the state of the art in programmed operator or remote operator support available in system software.

We have the somewhat unhappy situation where we are aware that we are dealing with an important issue of cost, aware that it seems related to decisions about system structure and location, but not sure exactly how the cost curve behaves in general. Happily, many of us are not responsible for general understanding but for costing a particular set of alternatives whose costs may be reasonably approximated.

2.2. Operational Costs and Hardware Costs

A measure of the importance of "complexity" in operational environments is suggested by the parts of Figure 88. Assuming an annualized decrease in the price of computer hardware to be a modest 10% and starting with a system costing $5 million dollars one can project a period where operational expenses will exceed the cost of hardware. This means that the efforts invested to tune and adjust, install software, maintain software and operate the machine will be more costly than the machine itself.

The operational costs are based upon an allocation of 40% of the personnel budget for data processing as attributable to operational expense. The exact

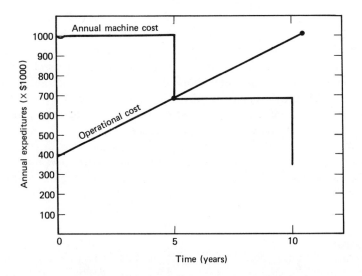

Figure 88.   Operational versus machine costs.

portion of budget attributable to operational expense depends upon the specifics of an installation and an enterprise. It is a useful figure to know; fewer
enterprises than one realizes know it.

Although it is not precisely true, a very rough measure of a personnel budget
can be approximated by setting it equal to the hardware budget. Assuming an
initial machine costing $5 million with a lifetime of five years, the annual cost
of the machine is $1 million. The annual personnel budget will also start at $1
million. Assuming no increase in staff and no need for additional skills, the
personnel budget will rise at an approximate rate of 10% a year. Thus at the
end of the productive life of the hardware the personnel budget will seriously
exceed the price of the machine. If $400,000 of the personnel budget is allocat-
able to operations and system support, then at the end of a machine life cycle
the operational budget will be close to $650,000. A new system acquired at the
end of that period will deliver the performance of the old machine for around
$3 million. This leads to an annual cost of $650,000. The suggestion is that by
the end of the useful life of a system installed "today" the costs for systems
programming and operational support of that system will exceed its annualized
cost. At the end of another five year cycle a new machine will cost around $1.8
million dollars for equivalent computational power. If there are no operational
reforms support expenses will have reached $1 million for a system whose
annualized cost is around $350,000. Notice that the total cost is relatively flat.
Around $1.4 million is being spent for a machine and its operational support
throughout the period. If it is a goal to keep systems costs flat, then any new
machine of greater capacity is acceptable only if it can demonstrate reduced
operational costs.

It is certainly naive to project costs this way. However, unless ways are found to reduce patterns of operational expense the suggestion of Figure 88 is essentially correct. The way to avoid the anomaly of spending more to operate a machine than the machine costs is to develop new operational practices and interfaces which use the machine to perform some operational tasks and which eliminate the necessity for others.

3. SOFTWARE AND OPERATIONAL COSTS

Figure 89 poses a relevant question for system designers. Is there a software knee? Is there a point at which software complexity and richness of function becomes a burden and not a tool? Are there configurations of software which, over the life of a system, actually increase rather than decrease the total cost of use of a computer system?

Software, of course, has two functions. One is to reduce programming expense; the other is to reduce operational expense. In this chapter we are interested only in the impact of software on operational expenses. The major contributions of software to operational expenses come in the area of installation, maintenance and performance prediction and tuning.

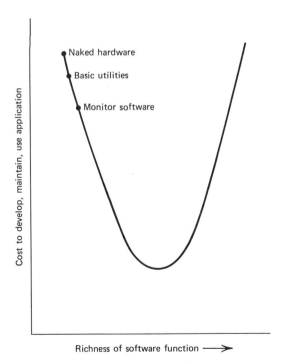

Figure 89.   Is there a software knee?

The economic requirement for good software, as for any product, is that its use add net value to an enterprise. In order for this to occur it is necessary that the cost of using it be less than the value of the function it provides and the alternative ways of getting that function. Software interfaces impose jobs and skills on using enterprises and define the difficulty associated with using a system effectively.

The earlier discussion of "degrees of distribution" addressed the impact of software structures on distribution decisions. The aspect of software which interests us here is related to notions of economy of scale. We are interested in whether there might be some basis in the claim that it is better to dedicate collections of small systems than attempt to share a large one. The central issue is whether it is worthwhile to invest enterprise resource in maintaining high utilization levels on consolidated workload machines.

It is very difficult to assess what percentage of operational costs is truly attributable to the interfaces of a software complex. The elements of cost are the effort required to install and use software, implied by the interfaces and the structure, and whether certain operational functions such as tuning and intensive performance modeling are economic.

The strong prodistributed viewpoint is that it is considerably more expensive to keep a very large, intensively shared system running well than it is to acquire and underutilize an equivalent set of smaller systems. The arguments given by the advocates of multiple small systems are:

1. The larger system must be utilized at a high rate if it is to achieve any economy of scale.

2. Larger systems are considerably more complex to use well because of their fundamental hardware complexity. More subtle resource interrelationships are involved in predicting the performance under various patterns of use and load.

3. Larger systems are fundamentally expensive to use because the software environment is so complex. This is relevant for operations because there is considerable effort and expense in tuning software, developing performance parameters, relating performance parameters in different software structures to each other and to total system operation.

4. Larger systems are more difficult to operate well because they require larger workloads to achieve high degrees of utilization. Smaller systems saturate at much lower levels of load so that the workload characterization is simpler.

There is merit in much of this argument, but it is just not clear how true the argument is when put into a broader context. It is not clear that tuning and adjusting multinode systems will not be as, or more, expensive; it is not clear just how much professional cost reduction will be achieved by permitting lower utilization levels on dedicated machines. It is not clear that operational interfaces to large processors in the future will be as functionally rich as they have been in the past. There may be some essential complexity in achieving effective performance at high levels of sharing whether the system is made of one large processor or of many interconnected smaller processors.

The benefits of distribution and increased levels of dedication are improved responsiveness and system predictability at lower cost. The methods seen as achieving these benefits are to reduce interface complexity, manage resources much more casually except when logical management is required and use stable software which will not be necessary to change over the lifetime of the application. These benefits will be achieved, of course, only when the physical mapping of the system has a good correspondence with the logical structure and when the software environment is truly stable.

4. OPERATIONAL COSTS AND DISTRIBUTION

The author has undertaken to determine, in a very rough way, whether operational costs are affected by different decisions of distribution.

The conclusions suggested by the section are to be taken with very large grains of salt. It is the approach which may be of some value. We defined four possible systems structures. After the definition of these structures we attempted to determine what reasonable operational costs might be for each structure.

4.1. Large Uniprocessor or Tightly Coupled Multiprocessor

The first system organization is a large uniprocessor at a data center operating in an environment where operations and systems management was completely centralized.

4.2. Multisystem Center

The first alternative to the large uniprocessor or multiprocessor is to define a data center which consists of a set of smaller systems which have the functional capacity of the larger unit. Six hypothetical systems, each with one-fourth the power of the large system, were used as the basis of the alternative. The smaller units differed from the large processor in the operating system which they used. The software base for the large system was an extensive heuristic, self-adjusting general purpose system with the usual nature of the largest operating systems offered by large-system vendors. The operating system base for the smaller systems was an intermediate system with considerably less ambitious resource management, considerably fewer configuration options and much reduced installation parameterization requirements. It would not attempt the same level of dynamic resource management on the smaller machines that the large system would undertake on the larger machine. By inference such a system is easier to install, maintain and extend.

Some care must be used in assessing the cost of installing and specializing operating systems of various classes since different operating systems have different system generation characteristics and different levels of preconfiguration. It is now possible, for example, to install and use some very large operating systems at reduced levels of effort by accepting preconfigured versions of the system.

It is also incorrect to assume that a large system will, per se, generate more expense to use than a small system. Associated with any operating system is a family of "utility" type programs which do various functions of data transcription, media copying, and so on. Operating systems of general equivalence in functional richness and complexity may generate different levels of support cost. This depends, in part, on the aggressiveness of a vendor or a user community in developing and making available sets of such auxiliary programs. To the extent that system programmer effort must be invested in writing such support programs a less well supported system may generate more cost to use than a better supported system.

A full investigation of the multiple machine costs must involve variations in the interconnection between the machines. There are various degrees of interconnection which will lead to different cost scenarios. The machines may be administratively interconnected. This means that there is no physical link between them. Such an environment may tend to increase operator costs if each system has its own operator staff. However, systems programming costs may be reduced if all machines have the same operating system and may share systems programming support. The sharing may be limited to installation and maintenance since each machine would have to be scheduled, tuned, and so on, independently.

The multiple machines may be interconnected by various forms of "loose" coupling. Loosely coupled systems may share disk devices or even be able to interact over I/O channels directly. Some hardware costs savings may be achieved by device and storage sharing and some economies may be achieved by providing logical capabilities to share files on shared disk devices. In addition some form of centralized scheduling for the multiple machines may be provided by a systems service which undertakes to control work assignment across multiple loosely coupled machines. The cost of such a configuration is the systems programmer effort involved in the use of the additional software package. A possible benefit of such a configuration is some reduction in operator expenses.

4.3. Distributed Peers

The third system scenario involves the physical distribution of nodes to points where it is not convenient for them to be supported by the same operational staff. Each location requires operators and some other kind of professional support. The extent of the per site costs is a function of the type of system and the type of software. Multitudinous scenarios may be created for this situation. Each distributed node may itself be a large system operating under software which provides no remote operator facility and whose interfaces are obviously intended for highly skilled staff. Although management and planning costs may not be replicated at each site, considerable site expenses are generated. In the entirely decentralized situation, of course, the local organization may also be responsible for systems design, planning, and similar activities. If the machine is large each site may truly represent a local data center with all of the staff and user costs and activities which associate with that environment.

At the other extreme the remote hardware may be an intelligent terminal with limited required support. No operator, other than application oriented users may be required, no systems programmer skills need be dispersed to a site and the per site cost will be absolutely minimum. However, various costs may be generated at the central site because of the use of intelligent terminals as opposed to unintelligent terminals. These costs may take the form of activities associated with remote software support and remote operator functions. Assessing the cost benefit of intelligent or nonintelligent terminals involves a number of cost generation issues which serve to show how complex cost analysis is even in this very basic distribution situation.

1. What does the terminal cost?
2. What productivity benefits will be achieved by its use?
3. Is it more cost effective to associate storage disks with each terminal or with some local terminal cluster controller, almost in effect using a small computer to support multiple terminal users who wish to access data files?
4. What additional costs will be generated at the central site to support remote intelligent use? Will there be a necessity to undertake some programming for the intelligent terminal and/or its associated control unit? Will there be a necessity to support software in the intelligent terminal, and what provisions does host software make for this requirement? Is there additional software fee and software support cost associated with controlling intelligent terminals?
5. Is there a net offloading of cycles in the large machine whose cost will help pay for the intelligent terminals?
6. Is there some improvement in central site responsiveness which justifies the offload of activity onto intelligent terminals?
7. What will the impact of intelligence in a local terminal be on communications costs? Will line costs change? Will the population of concentrators, front ends, multiplexors, and so on, change?

The issues involved in analyzing the benefits of using intelligent terminals are representative of the issues involved in any distribution. In order to resolve them much data must be collected and rather sophisticated analyses must be made. Data about usage patterns, machine loading, machine pricing, value of responsiveness at different levels must be collected and understood if costs are to be truly determined.

The scenario represented in this section will assume a central management function which has responsbility for systems direction and planning but with no central system software services. There is also little penalty imposed for enhanced communications professional support. In a real situation, of course, certain increased operator skills might be involved in controlling a network of systems. The dispersed systems are assumed to be identical, medium scale systems with very basic software environments.

4.4. Decentralization

The final alternative to complete single system centralization is total multisystem decentralization. Each site is completely self-managed and self-contained. It is a scenario of "cooperative" computing where systems which communicate with each other do so at the discretion of local management with no concept of central organizational or network control.

5. THE NUMBERS GAME

The reader must become very wary at this point. It is essential to remember that the intent of this section is to show the factors and elements associated with an operational cost analysis and not to demonstrate actual numbers. Organizations differ very widely in staffing practices and levels of support.

Each enterprise has an organization and staffing chart which represents the skills currently employed to support data processing and the number of employees having those skills. Care must be taken to assure that there is a proper understanding of user costs, both explicit when user units employ computer skilled people, and implicit when there are associated usage costs inherent in noncomputer job descriptions.

In addition to staffing charts each organization has a set of salary ranges associated with computer skills. It is therefore possible to determine the cost of professional skills. Using this as a starting point it is reasonable to project the operational skills costs of various systems alternatives like the ones discussed above.

There are, however, some problems.

1. Job descriptions may not be detailed enough to determine the exact costs attributable to various detailed functions. The costs attributable to the interfaces of a particular operating system or subsystem may be very difficult to determine.

2. The true change in skills required and salaries involved from one system to another may be only rather grossly quantified. Different levels of skill and different sets of specific knowledge required for the use of different systems may be difficult to determine. In some systems application programmer and system programmer functions may be combined. In others operator and systems programmer skills may be collapsed into a single job.

3. Unrealized new skills may be involved in various systems alternatives and the market value of these skills may not be well understood. In addition training and education costs involved in acquiring skills for various classes of system must be carefully assessed.

4. Entire lifetime costs must be evaluated in order to take into account costs associated with the evolution of the system over time.

With various precautions, disclaimers, caveats put into place, we can show the exercise. The first step was to undertake to determine what reasonable skills and staffing levels associated with the four system scenarios might be. Some difficult decisions are involved here because one must choose whether or not to include such functions as "corporate director of data processing" and his associated staff. We have included professionals in using departments or central staff who are responsible for systems planning and members of the operations branch of a data processing organization responsible for systems support and operations. The associated figures will indicate the job titles.

To associate numbers with functions, the author used the DATAMATION salary survey of November, 1978. The use of particular numbers in this instance of the book is a violation of fundamental policy. However, by the publication time of this book these numbers will be sufficiently obsolete that all readers will recognize that they are used only to show an idea.

The really difficult task is the determination of how many of what kinds of jobs and skills reasonably cluster around various machine system organizations and distributions. What makes this exercise most subject to question is exactly that determination. A reader undertaking the same exercise may have more guidance in this area than one undertaking to develop "general" scenarios. I have attempted to consistently err on the low side, understating the skills and costs which might be reasonably associated with various systems structures. I have used some tests of reasonableness which will be described with the figures.

5.1. The Hypothetical Large Single System

This system structure assumes completely centralized management, operations and system support functions.

Figure 90 shows a speculative cost statement for operational and management costs for such a system. The management costs include a staff which is concerned with establishing enterprise data processing direction and policy and

Director, Data Processing	40,000
Assistant to director	15,000
Technical Staff-Planners	60,000 (2 @ 30,000)
Manager, Systems Analysis	30,000
Lead Systems Analysts	88,000 (4 @ 22,000)
Senior Systems Analysts	120,000 (6 @ 20,000)
Analysts	152,000 (8 @ 19,000)
Data Base Administrator	30,000
Communications Analysts	48,000 (2 @ 24,000)
Costs attributable to management	583,000
Systems Programming Manager	30,000
Lead Systems Programmers	56,000 (2 @ 28,000)
Senior Systems Programmers	80,000 (4 @ 20,000)
Systems Programmers	90,000 (5 @ 18,000)
Data Base Specialists	126,000 (6 @ 21,000)
Services Coordinators	30,000 (2 @ 15,000)
Operations Manager	25,000
Lead Operator	30,000 (2 @ 15,000)
Senior Operator	36,000 (3 @ 12,000)
Operator	55,000 (5 @ 11,000)
Production Control Clerks	42,000 (3 @ 14,000)
Costs attributable to operations	600,000
Total costs—conjectural large uni- processor data processing center running large operating system and data base manager	$1,183,000

Figure 90.   Large uniprocessor speculative operational and management costs.

for evaluating application opportunities. The salaries associated with this staff
are at a level consistent with an enormous hardware budget of at least $1.8
million annually on a rental basis.

Of the total expenditure, $650,000 is attributable to operational and systems
support expenses. Eleven professional programmers are involved in support of
systems software. This software is assumed to include a data base manager
system as well as an advanced operating system. Some of these personnel are
involved in performance, some in version installation, others in writing various
utility functions or making local modifications to certain elements of the
systems.

The presence of the database manager implies a centralized data administration function. A data base administrator and supporting staff undertake to
coordinate data definition and design. The cost of this activity is offset by
potential savings in application development and benefits associated with data
integrity and control.

The communications analysts on the staff are responsible for planning and supporting the communications links to remote terminal users accessing function and data at the center.

The operator ,staffing is based upon a two-shift, multiconsole operation. There is always a lead operator present who acts as shift chief. Others are distributed throughout the shifts.

There can be much argument about how representative this list of personnel is. My experience has been that about half of the students I discuss it with think it is too high by a factor of 2 and half of the students think it is too low by the same margin. It represents no specific installation; it is merely intended to show the kinds of expenses associated with a large data center.

It is possible to apply a simple test of reasonableness. The $650,000 expenditure for operations represents 40% of the total personnel budget. That budget is therefore around $1.6. The figure of $1.6 million is close to the hardware budget of $1.8 million. This is reasonably consistent with the expected relationship between hardware and personnel expenditure.

5.2. The Multisystem Center

Figure 91 shows a speculative cost total for a centralized system which contains a family of smaller systems. These systems are DASD shared, they run modest operating systems and use a relatively simple data manager system that does not involve extensive data structure planning.

The ability to use such a system is constrained by the applications which operate at this data center. We are making the assumption that the work on the

Costs attributable to management (Data Base Administrator is deleted)	553,000*
Systems Programming Manager	30,000
Lead Systems Programmer	24,000
Senior Systems Programmer	54,000 (3 @ 18,000)
Programmer	90,000 (6 @ 15,000)
Services Coordinator	30,000 (2 @ 15,000)
Data Specialist	40,000 (2 @ 20,000)
Operations Manager	25,000
Lead Operator	45,000 (3 @ 15,000)
Senior Operator	50,000 (5 @ 10,000)
Operator	90,000 (10 @ 9,000)
Production Control	42,000 (3 @ 14,000)
Costs attributable to operations	470,000
Total multisystems center costs	1,023,000

Figure 91. Multisystem single site speculative operational costs.

very large processor of the previous section can be split across a family of smaller processors. This would be true only when no single application required the power of the large processor or when an application can be split across multiple processors.

The management activities for this center are not essentially different from those for the uniprocessor center. The same skills are required and will be compensated at the same level. There may be some subtle differences in the operational activities, however.

The systems programming manager is paid at the same level as his counterpart in the single system organization. The lead systems programmer, however, is not as skilled as his counterpart. The software system is simpler because of the simple datamanager and the operating system is fundamentally simpler. There is less need for the prime skills of the lead programmer. However, there may be more need for skills at the next levels because there are multiple systems which may require individual attention. As a result of this the size of the system programming staff does not decrease in any important way but there is a redistribution of expenditure across skills levels. The salary levels may be moderately lower because the software which is involved is simpler. This is reflected in Figure 91, which shows lower salaries at all systems programmer levels.

No charge is made for data base administration. This reflects the simplicity of the datamanger and implies that somewhat greater application development expenses may be associated with these systems.

It would be possible to undertake data administration functions in this environment. There are data subsystems which run on smaller machines and whose use might support a data administrative role.

An important difference between Figures 90 and 91 is shown in the operating staff numbers. The operating staff is considerably enlarged to reflect the multiple machine population, but the salaries, except at the management level, are modestly lower. This reflects that lower skill levels are required by smaller software environments but that the multiple machines require more human support.

If the systems were more closely connected it might be possible to reduce the operator burden at the cost of increasing the systems programming costs. More systems programming skills might be required to support incremental software function to provide multiple systems management from a reduced number of operators. Such a configuration might include a global scheular function on one of the interconnected system.

The details that would change the scenario dramatically are almost too numerous to mention. If there were multiple operating systems the cost picture might change. For example, if some of the systems were production systems and some were program development systems, there might be multiple software systems in the installation. This would change the pattern of systems programming costs. Differences in machine size would influence both operational and programming expenses. Different levels of coupling between systems would also influence operational costs. Channel interconnection, supported by extensions to software to support interaction across channels, shared storage devices, or interprocessor bus coupling would change expenditures for both operational and systems software types of personnel.

5.3. Geographical Distribution

Once more, as shown on Figure 92, the management costs are held steady. There is no reason to believe that the management functions would change because systems are to be placed remotely. In this scenario we maintain all the centralized systems activities associated with earlier sections.

Costs incurred at a headquarters location contain, in addition to management costs, the leadership of the communications and systems programming activities. Personnel at this center are responsible for establishing and controlling standards and activities at all remote sites. Notice that the communications analysis function has been considerably expanded. Instead of dealing with terminal interconnection this group must now contend with intersystem networking issues. The lead systems programmer is at the headquarters to offer communications software guidance and consultation.

Each site is charged with a senior systems programmer and two systems programmers. These are responsible for maintaining and installing local software, tuning and adjusting the local system and so on. Their salaries are the same as their cousins' at the multisystem center as they are dealing with the same level of software.

CENTRAL COSTS

Attributable to management	535,000
Systems Programming Manager	30,000
Communications Manager	25,000
Communications Analysts	66,000 (3*22,000)
Lead Systems Programmers	50,000 (2*25,000)
Total central costs	706,000

SITE COSTS

Senior Systems Programmers	108,000 (6*18,000)
Systems Programmers	180,000 (12*15,000)
Operations Manager	90,000 (6*15,000)
Lead Operator	84,000 (6*12,000)
Operator	120,000 (12*10,000)
Production Control	60,000 (6*10,000)
Total site costs	642,000
Total systems costs	1,348,000

Figure 92.   Distributed—six sites.

The operating staff at each site contains an operations manager, whose salary is reduced because of the small scale of the site. Each site has a lead operator and two operators. One level of operational skill is eliminated in the smaller site.

This particular scenario is attracting a good deal of interest in the industry. There is general desire to reduce the per site costs by providing programmed operator functions or by providing remote operator functions. The notion of programmed operator is to provide programs in the system which perform as many as possible of the functions which a human operator would perform. The notion of remote operator is to provide a capability at a remote site so that an operator can control a machine as if he were local to it.

In addition there is a desire to remove the local systems programmer by providing software development facilities at a center. From a single center it is desirable to provide changes and corrections to local software, remote software problem reporting and determination, remote debugging and so on. This might increase costs at the center but the total bill would probably be significantly reduced. The increased center costs might even include a dedicated machine to support remote systems programming support. It might include specialized software packages at the center and an increased center staff.

The IBM 8100 is an example of a small system which has many of the remote support features which seem desirable. There is a software feature which allows remote operation of 8100s and there are central services which can be provided to DPPX operating system 8100s from an IBM 370 package called DSX. Since the 8100 is architecturally distinct from the 370 there is a feature which provides for software development and test on an 8100 local to a 370. The 370 can be used as a pass through vehicle to remote 8100s.

5.4. Decentralization

Figure 93 shows complete decentralization. Six sites are represented, each of which is an identical small data center with its own management and opera-

Manager of Data Processing	22,000
Senior Systems Programmer	30,000 (2*15,000)
Systems Programmers	48,000 (4*12,000)
Operations Manager	15,000
Senior Operator	24,000 (2*12,000)
Operators	27,000 (3*9,000)
Total site cost	267,000
	× 6
Total cost	1,602,000

Figure 93.   Completely decentralized—six sites.

tional environment. The staffs are small, the salaries are lower, the skills levels compress. The burden of cost lies in the replicative factor.

6. COMMENTS AND CONCLUSION

What is to be made of all of this? We are warned that the numbers are very scenario specific and not to be taken seriously. We are warned that there is insufficient calibration of function to really represent differences in software interfaces which contribute to cost. The issue of complexity is not fully addressed. The expenses of installing different combinations of systems and subsystems must be better understood. The impact of software package release practices must be factored in as an element of support costs. And the list goes on.

Readers who are interested in this topic area will be able to discover in the literature published by consultant and information organizations various statistics on operational costs of various types by industry and other breakdowns. This is good information to have. But it is not as useful as a complete analysis of one's own operation.

With operational costs representing the slice of the budget that they now represent, no analysis of comparative computer systems can possibly be useful as the basis of system selection unless the support costs that systems generate are included in the analysis. It is just becoming an issue in the marketplace. It is an important one and it will become more important.

Beyond the assessment of costs there is the issue of whether certain data processing growth plans are feasible in the light of scarcity of professional talent and resource. It may be very desirable to follow a particular path but practically impossible to do so if skills are not available to implement plans.

On the particular issue of centralized versus distributed versus decentralized, it is the author's opinion that decentralization is undesirable as a mode of operation because it causes more direct costs and enlarges the risks of failure.

In general there should be strong organizational motivations for decentralization which can be shown to overcome operational and technical objections before decentralization should become a general practice within an enterprise.

Whether a centralized or distributed system will generate more operational costs depends upon:

1. Whether software packages associated with different systems structures reduce or increase aspects of operational cost because of interface complexity, sheer size and program quality.
2. Whether sufficient software system function is available in smaller systems to perform the functions necessary to perform.
3. The number of different software packages involved in a system solution.
4. The quality of documentation or training associated with a particular set of packages

5. The degree to which the software structure is in accordance with a desire to provide good performance with a minimum investment in performance analysis.

6. The extent to which increased operational and planning costs may be justified by increased efficiency in application development across different contending systems structures.

Chapter 15

Application Development Costs

1. INTRODUCTION

Application development includes activities which define a system life cycle from the inception of the concept of an application until the application is trusted as a production system. In the determination of the costs of application development a very wide range of activities must be undertaken and a very diverse set of costs is incurred.

The intent of this chapter is to introduce concepts which will be useful in trying to assess whether various system structures, various degrees of distribution will affect application development costs. It is impossible to discuss all of the aspects of application development and associated issues of software technology and project management in a detail sufficient so that a reader may consider himself expert after reading this chapter. There is a large literature in project management and software development technology which must be referenced for the achievement of expertise in this area. This chapter will introduce some basic ideas and then focus on some of the issues which enlarged choices in system structure seem to present.

The main line of discussion is whether a computer system built out of a collection of nodes is inherently more efficient a mechanism to program for than a system constructed of one large node. A closely related issue is whether there are economies of scale in programmer organization. Is it better to disperse the programmers of an organization to using departments or to centrally manage them within the structure of a data center? This issue is only peripherally addressed in this chapter. It has long been thought that there are economies of scale in centralized programming organization. Recently, however, this point of view has been brought into question for a number of reasons:

1. Organizations can grow sufficiently large and complex so that the burden of control and management overcomes efficiency of use of programmer skills.

2. Centralized programming environments are commonly associated with large systems whose software characteristics may complicate the acts of bringing an application program into production by introducing complex systems considerations.

3. The costs of application development which in any case accrue to a business department have not been counted when studying the costs of centralization or decentralization of programming talent.

In any case this is an organizational issue quite distinct from the issue of the impact of systems structure on the costs of application development. The author's opinion is that the issue is not resolvable in a general scenario but depends completely upon the specific nature of the applications and the programming skills which are relevant to application development. Small, independent operational applications will show different development cost patterns from large, functionally interdependent applications.

2. THE APPLICATION DEVELOPMENT CYCLE

Application development involves a series of reasonably well-understood stages. There is a discovery phase, a design phase, a development phase and a production/maintenance phase.

2.1. Discovery

During the discovery phase the application is conceived by recognizing the potential use of a computer device for the automation of ongoing function or new function. Resources are organized to determine what the requirements of a new application would be from the viewpoint of business needs. The feasibility of the application is determined. Initial projections of levels of effort and cost are made. An assessment is made about the practicality and benefit of the application to the business.

   Chapter 12 suggested that this activity might be undertaken by a data center staff, a business unit, or be a combined business unit and center staff effort. It is probable that opinions about whether the application should be run on a data center system, a user system, or a data center supported system at the user location will be formed even during this first phase. The dynamics of business unit/data staff relations are going to determine attitudes in this area. Those dynamics are determined by politics, dispersion of competence and skills and all of the subtleties which influence an ongoing organization.

2.2. Design

The design phase begins after the discovery efforts indicate that the application should be undertaken. During this phase alternative designs are investigated and the determination of the tendencies toward distribution of the system are made. Choices of logical applications partitionings, data partitionings, closeness of relationship between systems elements must be made to define a logical systems structure. Determination of appropriate software environments must be made. When the logical structure and software requirements are designed, then the physical design involving the nomination of specific hardware and software units and the detailed design can begin. There are expenses incurred in learning what the choices are, identifying vendors, discovering characteristics of hardware and software options. It is in this phase that the incredibly enlarged set of possible solutions is most felt and it is primarily in this phase that additional expenses should be incurred if an enterprise truly desires to explore multiple possibilities.

2.3. Development

The development phase includes more detailed design, the determination of programming methodologies to be used and the actual programming of the application. The cost of this phase is partially determined by decisions made in the design phase. The amount of programming which will be done is partially a function of how ambitious the system is to be and what kind of systems software is to support the application effort. The choice of systems software will determine what operations must be programmed into the application and what operations are available from the system. The choice of systems software will also determine what programming languages are to be used, what data structures are to be used and consequently how much effort is involved in programming the applications operations which must be programmed.

The end of the development phase is a system debugging and test stage. Program modules must be tested individually with appropriate test data (unit testing). Groups of program modules must be tested together (integration testing). After reasonable satisfaction that the application runs with test data it is necessary to demonstrate successful operation with real data before the enterprise commits itself to the system. Costs incurred involve, beyond the development and debugging of the application modules, the development of test data and standards for system acceptance.

2.4. Production

When the system enters its production/maintenance phase there are costs involved in training end users and operating the system. In addition there may be recurring costs for performance tuning, correcting additional errors found during production, and adding new functions to the system.

There is some disagreement in the industry about what the burden of maintenance truly is. Some estimate that more than 40% of the total programming costs of an application occurs as a result of maintenance. However, some claim that close scrutiny of maintenance costs will reveal that the bulk of such costs do not accrue because of finding errors but come as a result of functional extension and modification of the application. It is for this reason that there is so much interest in programming methodologies that lead to well structured, easily modifiable modular programs. Such program methodologies will also reduce the cost of debugging and testing.

3. APPLICATION DEVELOPMENT AND DISTRIBUTION

In attempting to determine how decisions about distribution affect application development costs it is necessary to identify the parameters which may apply. This is an area of high mythological content. There are those who argue strenuously that application development costs are minimized by putting applications on dedicated machines using simple software support and constraining the ambitiousness of the application. There are those who claim that application costs go up when small machines are used because they are inherently more expensive to program. There is very little knowledge about the effect on programming costs to implement applications across multiple machines, especially in heterogeneous systems.

An insight into the problem must include an appreciation for a number of issues;

1. What is the risk of avoiding a full exploration of systems structure possibilities? How quickly and cheaply can the design phase reduce the number of possibilities which must be seriously considered? How expensive, for example, will it be to determine whether an application should be placed on a large uniprocessor; a hierarchic structure of large uniprocessors and small local systems; a peer structure of intermediate systems? How many varieties of system structure must be considered? How can one determine inexpensively whether a system of a desired structure can really be assembled, installed and satisfactorily operated without exhaustive and detailed analysis? The search for an "optimum" system structure may be very difficult. The determination of the operability of candidate systems structures may also be very hard to achieve.

2. What level of application functional richness should be undertaken? To what degree should applications be integrated into larger applications and to what degree kept small? What is the value of specific application capabilities versus the cost? What is the value of integrating related applications versus separating them?

3. What cost impact will different levels of functional richness available from different systems software have?

4. Are there differences in applicable programming methodologies associated with different systems structures?

This is a formidable range of topics added to the already formidable range of issues and problems which have always been associated with managing the design and implementation of programs.

4. SYSTEM SELECTION

Figure 94 shows the range of choices which are available as possible systems hosts for an application. It is possible to actually build a system from "scratch." An organization may undertake to design the basic logic units which will form a hardware system. It can undertake to build the boards which hold the basic chips. It can undertake to design and construct the frames in which the boards will be placed. It can undertake to build a system out of a collection of frames, integrating processing units, peripherals, terminals, storage units.

At a higher system level an organization can undertake to build the basic system software at its lowest levels. This "tool" level software consists of interrupt handlers, dispatchers, I/O device managers, communication link protocol handlers, and the like. Above this level an organization may undertake to construct complete operating systems to provide application and user interfaces. The enterprise may undertake to program the application and undertake to operate and manage the environment in which the application can run.

It is not considered usual practice for an organization wishing to develop an application to start by designing a computer architecture. However, in military environments this is by no means unknown. It is almost common to start an

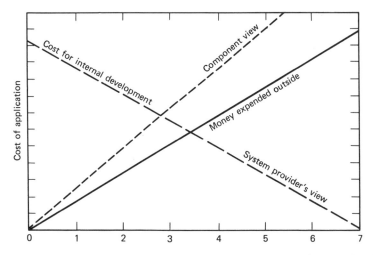

Figure 94.   Make/buy levels. 0 = design chip; 1 = build board; 2 = build box; 3 = build node; 4 = build basic software; 5 = build operating system; 6 = develop application; 7 = turnkey (facilities management).

application with a purchased microcomputer or microprocessor and to construct boards and boxes in the military application environment.

It is now not unusual for even commercial enterprises to undertake systems integration at the level of combining processors and peripherals from various vendors into systems. It is interesting to speculate if the acts of "building" a system and "configuring" a system will ever converge. A convergence would mean that an enterprise experienced no essential difference in expense between determining a system configuration to be delivered by a vendor from a configuration options list, or ordering components to be assembled into systems by the enterprise.

The message of Figure 94 is that there is now a very wide set of choices available to an enterprise investigating an application. Each of the points on the X axis of Figure 94 is a development level option. An enterprise can decide to purchase a "turnkey" system and sign a facilities management contract so that it requires no skills or internal development effort whatsoever to bring up an application. The solid line of Figure 94 shows that each potential level defines a different split of internal development funding and external product purchase. This is referred to as the make or buy decision. The dashed lines of Figure 94 suggest that there are different opinions about how one minimizes total systems development cost.

4.1. Selection and Distribution

The topics of the last section are related to distribution because the determination of the level of development effort may limit the choices of systems structure and shape.

This has been more true in the past than it is now. At the initial period of interest in distributed systems there was relatively sparse software support for interconnecting systems. Centralized systems had a long tradition of software support and had developed very high level functional software including data base managers and communications software capable of interacting with remote terminals or remote batch job entry work stations. Significant distribution usually involves some consideration of smaller systems. In the early years many such small systems had very little software support for individual processing units and there was almost none for interconnecting such systems.

It is now true that the small systems have developed operating systems, programming language support, communications support, some level of data management support and even some features for a remote operator. Small and intermediate sized systems are now more adequately supported by software so that the risk and expense of using these systems in distributed structures has been made acceptable. The distributed solution is no longer an automatic "roll your own" solution. Small systems software has moved toward the software "knee."

However, from an applications development point of view it is probably still true that the large system offers more functional richness of a kind that might reduce applications development costs. Considerably more sophisticated data management systems are available and there may yet be a richer set of available applications and application development packages for large systems than for small systems. More precisely there is a richer set of application packages for single node solutions than for multinode solutions. There are many available applications packages for small and intermediate systems used as stand-alones or packaged as "small business systems." There are also simple to use programming languages like RPG (Report Program Generator). However, there is little available application support for interconnected systems.

It is still true that some cost analysis between using single large systems and multiple small systems must be made on the basis of application development costs related to the level of effort an enterprise must expend to bring an application to fruition.

4.2. Selection Analysis

Figure 95 suggests the kind of analysis which is involved. In selecting a system one must determine exactly what functions are desired in the application. If the application is to be functionally very rich, then a very high level of systems support is probably desirable because it may reduce the application programming effort and expense in nontrivial ways.

After determining the functional richness of the application, the enterprise, in Figure 95, determines the split of program support between applications code which must be developed and code offered by the vendor. It is necessary to determine what software exists to perform desired functions and how much must be programmed into the application.

Let us assume, as an example, that for a particular application, we have been convinced that one million instructions must be created to support the function desired. The vendor of a large system offers 80% of the instructions required in his systems software.

What must now be determined is the true cost of the 80/20 split. In order to do this we must know what it will cost to create 200,000 instructions on the vendor's system.

The cost of these instructions will be determined by the quality of the compiler and debugging packages available from that vendor. However, there may be elements of cost associated with the development of an application for a system beyond writing instructions. There may be some considerable cost involved in learning the interfaces which the vendor offers applications in his software. There may be additional expense in the use of various control structures and languages which will be additive to expressing application function in code.

It is necessary to combine considerations of programming development expense with considerations of design and operational expenses. Does the large system introduce additional design expense because of its complexity? What is the true cost of installing and operating the vendor's software? What is the true

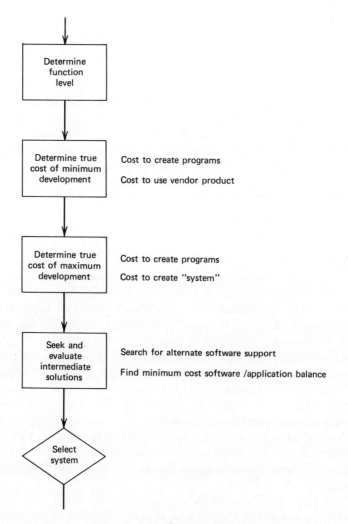

Figure 95.   True development costs.

cost, during the life of the application, of living with 800,000 lines of someone else's code? What impact will the change release and evolution policy of the vendor have on the costs of maintenance? What does the software package cost?

In order to compare an alternative it is necessary to determine how much of the vendor's code is required to support the desired functions. Software packages created by vendors tend to be large for two reasons:

1.   They must contain functional richness in order to have broad usability. Much code must be included which may not be used by a particular

application. In addition there must be code to determine which variation of a service is desired by an application.

2. They must include significant amounts of code to protect against incorrect or illegal use of systems resources. They must be sure that each request for access to a resource is well formed and legitimate for populations of applications programs they have no reason to trust. This requires space and time.

If the organization develops its own system without extensive vendor software support, it might be able to reproduce equivalent function with some seriously reduced number of instructions. This is because he need put in only the functions that he requires and because he may be able to "trust" the programs he is developing himself and eliminate some checking and protective code.

It is desirable to assess the approximate size of a pure inhouse solution. In approximating the programming cost of such a solution it is necessary to remember that instructions at different levels of a system structure cost different amounts of money to create and debug. It is possible that a purely inhouse developed solution which contained 500,000 instructions in total will be considerably more expensive than the purchase and support of the vendor code and the creation of 200,000 lines of application. It is also possible that the cost of creating an application instruction may be different from system to system.

The cost to develop an application instruction is an accounting concept which will differ from enterprise to enterprise. For discussion we will set the cost at $5.00 per application instruction. The cost to create an operative and correct instruction at a systems level will be considerably higher. A rough ratio of 3-1 is a reasonable estimate for discussion. The difference in cost comes about because instructions which have to interface to device eccentricities, which have timing dependencies, which support systems control alogorithms are just very much more expensive to develop and debug than applications instructions. However, not all "systems" instructions cost the same since there are systems support alogorithms which are not that much more complex than application operations. So there is going to be a population of $5.00, $10.00, and $15.00 instructions.

It is not necessary that the choice be between a pure inhouse solution and accepting the vendor's software at its highest functional level. The vendor may offer choices, as suggested in Figure 94. It is possible to choose the operating system and not the data manager. Other vendors may offer different splits of support software which allow one to reduce operational and installation expenses but avoid the $15.00 instructions.

One possibility is to undertake modification of the vendor supplied software. This may require a good deal of programming skill at a systems programmer level. The feasibility of this approach depends upon the structure of the vendor software, the quality of its documentation and the attitude that the software supplier has about maintaining software products that have been modified by a using organization.

4.3.   Other Factors

Another dimension to be considered is that it is possible that the cost of creating an instruction differs from one system to another in addition to a difference in cost due to the number of instructions which must be created. Because of programming language availability, compiler quality, debugging system quality, effectiveness of interactive tools, a $5.00 instruction on one system may be a $7.00 instruction on another. This may be offset somewhat, on smaller systems, by simpler interfaces and less involvement in activities other than producing code.

It is necessary to consider performance issues. Sometimes it is necessary to undertake partial inhouse solutions even with the largest software support levels. This is because using the applications interfaces normally provided introduces unacceptably long program path lengths (number of instructions necessary to perform a function) and the system cannot process the required rate of transactions. It may therefore be necessary to spend some money on $10.00 instructions in order to provide certain functions more quickly. Or it may be necessary to use a set of software provided interfaces which are more complex than the usual applications interfaces and increase the cost of applications code development.

In general it is true that the cost of buying software function is less than the cost of making it. Some estimates run as high as 4-1 for this ratio. Purchased applications packages and purchased or licensed software is currently astonishingly cheap to acquire. This may be offset by high operational support costs. From the point of view of risk, cost overruns, delays, potential failure and the like, it is difficult to determine under what circumstances risk is minimized.

It is always good practice to avoid writing programs when one can. It is particularly good practice to avoid writing systems level instructions when one can. It is nice to have a vendor providing rich software function, who is responsible and accountable. However, there are no guarantees. Putting together multiple software packages including operating systems versions, communication software versions, data management components in very large systems is also not without its costs and risks.

A last consideration involves the evolutionary cycle of an application. Figure 96 suggests two basically different concepts of the life cycle of an application or a system. Line 1 suggests an application that is constantly evolving or an underlying vendor software structure that is constantly evolving. Line 2 suggests a perfectly stable system and a perfectly stable application. These lines suggest a choice between absorbing systems and applications evolutionary changes in "small" constant chunks continuously over time or avoiding all costs until a point is reached when the entire system and application must be replaced.

There is some difference in the concept of the true life of a program. Some think of an investment in programming almost as a capital investment to be treated as a major asset. Others prefer to think of programs as throwaway

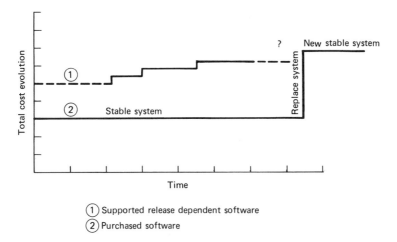

① Supported release dependent software
② Purchased software

Figure 96. Evolution and stability.

expense items. The perspective depends upon one's view of technology and enterprise business practice rates of change.

From a system selection point of view there have been complaints about the traditional way of marketing software. Vendors may release new versions of software elements constantly over time. A user is encouraged to install these new versions because they contain corrections to problems found in earlier versions, because they contain new functions along an evolutionary cycle and because the vendor withdraws support of old versions after a certain period. If a system consists of multiple software elements, each with its own release cycle, then the enterprise is constantly involved in installing new systems software components. This represents a constant resource drain and expense. Further, the development cycle for large applications may be perturbed because there is a constantly moving target. It is this kind of complaint that interests people in small software elements which do not change even if application development costs are higher because more function must be put into the application.

On the other hand the cyclic release of new versions enables the using enterprise to offload the costs of evolution somewhat onto the vendor and to spread evolutionary costs over time rather than facing dramatic terminal events.

5. PROGRAMMING

Programming costs are becoming a considerably more significant factor in total application costs as hardware costs decrease. Many people feel that programming costs already represent more than 50% of application costs and will approach 80% by the mid-1980s.

Over the years there have been serious increases in programmer productivity because of the development of higher level languages and the increase in systems support which reduces the code necessary to create. The cost per instruction, in dollars discounting inflation, is less with current languages than it was before COBOL, FORTRAN, or PL/1 usage became general. However, it is not clear that the reduction in expense has kept pace with the increasing salary levels of programmers and it is very clear that programs cannot be developed fast enough to keep up with the desired rate of application development. It is a general condition that users have a serious backlog of new applications which they just cannot undertake given the programming resource they have and the programming stylistics which are common today. It is clear that systems of the future must take on even more of the programmer's function than they now do. There is general interest in improved applications development methodologies both to reduce the cost of programming and to increase the rate at which applications can be developed.

Within this general context of discontent with programming practices and productivity there is disagreement about whether programming for "large" systems is more or less expensive than programming for "small" systems. Does the cost of an application instruction go up or down when preparing programs for a very large system as opposed to creating programs for a smaller system? From the point of view of the cost of creating code there is reason to believe that costs are lower for the larger system. This is true because:

1. The larger system is larger. The great cost in programming is writing good programs. Paying attention to minimizing the amount of space a program will occupy in memory is very expensive work. Squeezing programs to fit into small memory spaces is terribly time consuming, leads to "clever" programs which are difficult to debug and impossible to maintain and is in general a very noneconomic use of enterprise resources. The larger system will tolerate programs which are written without much regard for memory size and efficiency. It is faster so that it will execute additional instructions more quickly; it has greater configurability and therefore can grow, if necessary, to absorb populations of loosely written code.

2. Larger systems may allow simpler program structures because things can be fit into memory which would on smaller systems have to be organized into working temporary files or overlay segment structures. This is particularly true when comparing virtual memory large systems with small systems which do not have virtual memory capacity. Fewer and fewer small systems lack virtual memory support, but the ratios of virtual to real which are permissible in small systems without pathological performance may be less. In any case the virtual memory size is smaller.

3. Maintenance costs are lower because changes and modifications need not be "squeezed" into small existing spaces.

This opinion is not shared by all and there are some interesting counterarguments. One counterargument is that bad programs will cause pathological performance very quickly and will have to be tightened even on a large machine. Associated with this observation is the possibility that additional machine usage charges will occur because of increased use of the machine resource when the program is running and that this cost, over time, will be significant. But the most important set of issues is the role of good programming design methodology and discipline and whether large or small systems encourage or discourage good practices.

6. LARGE AND SMALL PROGRAMS

One of the complaints about large systems is that they lure organizations into poor design and programming practices. Applications concepts become very large, applications functions become overintegrated, and large virtual memories lead to badly structured very large programs. There is tremendous difficulty in managing large projects; they tend to be late and experience serious cost overruns and they generate large maintenance and modification expenses.

Figure 97 shows an appreciation of a programming cost concept which suggests that "large" programs are disproportionately expensive. The total cost of a program of 1 million instructions is considerably higher than the cost of 10 programs of 100,000 instructions. This is apparently inconsistent with the notion that "good" small programs are more expensive to create than large "sloppy" programs. However, the inconsistency is only apparent. If the large program and small program are of equivalent "tightness," then the large program may be more expensive than a set of smaller programs. This may be a

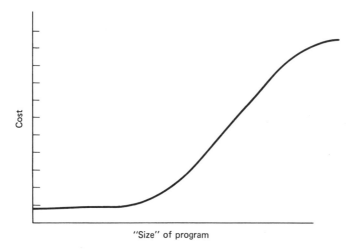

"Size" of program

Figure 97.   Programming costs.

result of the inherent complexity and lack of structure in the large program that lead to large debugging and modification costs due to difficulty in comprehending a complex logic flow.

The potential efficiency of writing large numbers of small programs is most commonly achieved when the programs are independent. When the programs are interdependent, then the benefits of modularity will be somewhat offset by expenses in integration testing and by the design effort which is involved in decomposition of function into modules. However, exponents of modular design point out, quite independently of issues in distributed processing, that over the life of an application, well structured populations of smaller programs contribute to reduced application development and maintenance expenses. An argument forwarded in favor of writing large applications in a highly modular fashion is that the application change activity becomes an activity of module replacement rather than module adjustment. The search for nondisruptive "patch space" is eliminated and the rippling error effect of changes in a program is contained.

Some people feel that the use of smaller systems will reduce programming expenses and increase program productivity in an important way. Applications concepts will tend to become smaller and more manageable. Instead of a large team working on "integrated" applications, there will be many small teams working on smaller applications. The results are shorter design and development periods and cheaper debugging and maintenance expenses for smaller programs.

The image suggested by such an argument is substantially an image of business unit application development on small machines. The underlying idea is to walk backward on the curve of Figure 97 to increase productivity and reduce cost.

There are two questions which must be brought into the discussion. Do the dynamics of writing small programs apply when the small programs are to be part of a set of cooperating programs with nontrivial interdependence? Would breaking large applications concepts into sets of small programs be economic if the target system was a large machine rather than a small one?

If the concept of an application is ambitious, there is no programming methodology which can reduce the design cost. Although it may be possible to separate and partition programs in an application structure, this activity is itself costly and the complexity or richness of the applications concept remains large even when granules of programming are properly perceived. Yet there is no question that there are important applications which are inherently large and conceptually ambitious. Reforms of the design methodologies of such applications are independent of the nature of the target systems. These reforms involve structural analysis techniques which are essentially partitioning techniques similar in nature to various concepts of structured programming.

It seems clear that what has gone wrong with programming large systems is that the programming methodologies extant are not up to the size of the applications concepts which large systems invite. A minimum programming cost approach would combine the programming disciplines of modular, well structured, layered design with the economic advantages of machines which can tolerate loose programming style. The concept of a good program has fundamentally changed. Tightness of code has been replaced by clarity of module structure and definition as the criterion for "goodness" in a program.

Some feel that the great virtue of programming small machines is that it imposes the necessity for well ordered program layering and structuring on the design. This is because any view of future changes must include the possibility that modules must be moved from one machine to another easily as more function is added to an application. But the same programming disciplines can be applied to large machines and must be applied in the interests of controlling programming costs.

A rule of thumb for determining the size of a machine which should be used in an application is that the estimated size of a program should not exceed 50% of the capacity of the memory and MIPS rate. This allows for loose programming and potential growth. In effect it provides the small machine with some of the forgiveness of a large machine. Increases in machine costs are well worthwhile. A corollary caution is to never aim an application at the largest version of an architecture so that there will always be room to grow if size and speed estimates vary in a nasty way from actuality. There is nothing more expensive than redesign because a proposed application structure won't fit on a machine node.

7. PROGRAMMING ON WHAT FOR WHAT

It is not always true that the production machine and the programming development machine are the same. Considerations in programming costs must then include the quality of debugging and language features of the system used for development and the programming stylistic which is appropriate for the machine which is to run the application. Many consider it good practice to develop programs on machines which are not production machines. This is for reasons of production data integrity and security and for reasons of systems responsiveness to the programming acitivity. Programmers' "workbench" systems which interconnect a development system with an eventual production system are part of the distributed processing arena.

8. OLD OR NEW

The thrust of the discussion so far has been on determining the nature of programming expenses for new applications. One decision which faces an enterprise is what approach to take to already running applications which might potentially profit from "modernization" which would add new function or which would make old function available on an on-line basis, perhaps in a distributed structure. There are two approaches: redesign and reprogram the entire application on a new systems structure or preserve older elements of the system and build extensions which surround and interface to the older structure. Either choice will involve some application analysis to determine what data reference and program flow patterns exist in the application in order to discover the structure and shape and degree of possible solutions.

The considerations involved in determining whether an old application should be replaced with a new distributed version or extended to contain distributed elements include:

1. Is the current programming still essentially functionally valid and does it promise to be valid for a reasonable amount of future time? How much of the current code can be preserved and how much must be replaced for reasons of business practice beyond reasons of systems structure or new interfaces?

2. Is the current structure sufficiently well understood so that its decomposition and distribution is a reasonable effort?

3. How much effort is currently being invested in maintaining the current code? Would reprogramming reduce these costs significantly over the life of the new version so that reprogramming would pay for itself over time?

4. How much hardware savings are potential in a new structure? How does the immediate replacement with new architecture compare to replacement over time with reduced price versions of the old architecture? Is the current equipment owned, leased or rented and are there expectations of reduction in price for current hardware?

5. If one attempts to preserve current programs, can software and hardware offerings be found which can interface to them on a reasonable basis with reasonable cost and effort? Will the effort to define functional interfaces between new and old components be small compared to the effort to develop a replacement system?

6. Does an extended system involve techniques of data replication and coordination which might make it more complex?

7. Are there constraints in the current application structure which make any attempt at distribution by extension clumsy and less desirable than new systems structures?

8. What is the comparative program development cost of extensions as opposed to complete programming of a replacement system?

9. Are there new applications concepts which suggest that the merger of heretofore separate systems in a new systems structure is desirable?

10. Are there definable offload points in the old application so that in-
     creased usability of the old system can be acquired by moving function
     out to smaller surrounding units?

It is the author's opinion that the burden of proof should lie with the advocates
of systems replacement. They must show that important new function can be
added to an application, that the design and programming costs are reasonable
when compared to extension costs, that the new structure has attributes which
cannot be demonstrated by surrounding an older system with satellite extensions. From "Systemantics" we learn, "If the system works, leave it alone." It is
a good principle. If on-line access is obtainable with congenial interfaces in the
context of a minimum disruption of a running system, it is a preferred approach. There is sufficent work to be done with new applications in applying
new systems concepts and structures.

9. CONCLUDING REMARKS

It seems that, theoretically, there is no clear case for a statement concerning the
impact of distributed systems on programming costs. The problems of development on large systems are addressed by the same techniques which make programming for small nodes seem an attractive undertaking: good structure,
good discipline, good documentation. A new concept of what good programming really is seems equally effective for both large and small systems. Much of
the reputation for ease of programming at low costs which is associated with
small systems comes from a scenario of developing small, stand-alone applications. This scenario need not necessarily apply to distributed systems where
interacting pieces of an application are spread across multiple nodes. Large
applications are difficult to implement whether they are on single node or
multinode systems. It is not known, in general, whether enhanced software
systems support provided by large systems currently pays for itself in total, but
the direction of such systems suggests there will be eventual payback in programming costs.

A reasonable approach seems to be to buy applications packages whenever
available, to program highly partitioned structures of large applications and to
determine, for each application, what the specific costs of using a single system
versus multiple systems will be. In many cases the programming costs may be
the same. This will tend to be true when both the single and multiple machine
solutions are supported by the same programming languages with very similar
or identical underlying software structures.

One speculation may be relevant here. It is by no means certain, but it is
possible that there will be an interval during which large machine development
costs will be seriously lower than small machine costs. This interval is suggested
by the fact that centralized database is currently much more understood than

distributed database. Much work in developing tools for programmer productivity revolves around nonprocedural programming techniques associated with database managers. For some period of time there may be very powerful process description tools linked to centralized data management before similar tools appear for distributed data management systems.

The IBM System/38 suggests that very excellent support for programming development may be offered on the base of a data manager for a small machine. However, it is not clear how quickly the same levels of programming support can be offered for multinode solutions.

Chapter 16

Concluding Observations

1. INTRODUCTORY REMARKS

We have looked at a concept that is beset by vacuous definitions, by partial views represented in a plethora of product, by high risks involved in immature software, by uncertainty about the economic goals. We are not sure whether we are seeing the birth of a new kind of system or a natural evolutionary stage coming from changes in technology and economics that we all should have expected—that we did expect—but whose implications we were a little slow in understanding.

There are two major issues in distributed processing. One is clustered around details of concept and design. The other centers around questions of economic motivation and payoff.

2. TECHNICAL ISSUES

The essential technical issues are whether possible new systems structures are as effective as more familiar structures and whether we yet know what we must know to decide.

There are severe problems for a user in the current design environment. For the most part the "systems views" of vendors are not as complete as the views developed by using enterprises. This makes it sometimes awkward to actually accomplish systems which are not so conceptually complex.

There are so many alternatives, so many vendors, so many hidden details on which a design can flounder that there is unavoidable risk in undertaking many of the systems structures we have described. However, there seem to be formidable risks in moving into new applications areas and on-line concepts with many centralized approaches as well.

There seem to be new requirements for reliability, granularity of configuration, stability of performance, ease of use. We do not yet seem to be sure to what extent these new requirements can be fulfilled only by distributed solutions and to what extent advances in large centralized systems will deliver sufficient of these attributes. If large systems become complexes of processing units in the same frame and exhibit attributes of extendability and replicatability; if large systems reform user and professional interfaces; then to what extent will distributed solutions as the literature treats them today be distinct systems?

How are the benefits of logical sharing and flexible resource allocation inherent in large uniprocessors to be achieved? How are the problems of interconnected small machines which realize economies of dedication but may suffer from resource and interconnection constraints to be overcome? How can we achieve good hardware economics, incremental growth, configurability and systems choices with various combinations of processing nodes?

When can we approach designs with certainty and assurance that they will work without hidden surprises?

Vendors must provide us with an enlarged systems concept. They must provide choices which are rationally and not arbitrarily distinct. They must provide refined interfaces, reasonable migration, fine incremental growth. They must provide mechanisms for the analysis and structuring of applications.

The key concept is "pluggability" of hardware, software and applications structures across distances of arbitrary choice, with the possibility of restructuring at low cost. When this is possible we will have a mature industry.

3. ECONOMIC ISSUES

The strong need here is to "get it all together." In the face of such diversity of equipment choices and the relationship between organizational choices and equipment choices we need a new generation of application and equipment selection and justification methodologies.

We must identify the factors which are relevant to data processing decision making and the relationships among these factors. We need refinement of techniques for value assessment and for cost assessment. We need methods for combining issues of hardware, operational and programming costs to determine the true cost of various systems solutions.

We need to understand more fully the interplay between data processing product and enterprise organization. Following is just a partial list of the things which must be considered:

1. What is the influence of trends toward centralization or decentralization on the use of data processing in an enterprise?

2. What methodologies must be available for analyzing information flow within an enterprise?

3. What skills will be required for data processing in the future?

4. How does one quantify place value of information, time value of information, productivity of end users?

5. What new kinds of cost accounting practices are needed to determine the true costs of various systems?
6. What meaning is to be given to various hardware cost trends?
7. What kinds of costs will software generate in the future? What kinds of costs will software reduce?

There is work under way in these areas. Vendors and users are beginning to cooperate in discovering the nature of enterprises and their data processing requirements. Business systems planning, structured analysis tools, organizational and systems modelling techniques are beginning to mature.

Yet we seem to be at the twentieth part of the first syllable of the beginning. We seem to be the generation which must face the problem of making the promise come true. We are assured of the technology and we have no excuse if the next 20 years of data processing are not immeasurably more satisfactory than the first 20. There will be no "40 year ripoff" if we are intelligent and careful.

Appendix A

Product Terms Used in Text

370: A generic term representing the architecture of a set of IBM processing units. The specific instruction set and logic was originally used on a line of systems called the IBM 370. Since its original use the architectural features have become "generic" and a large population of machines which are not 370s are 370-type machines.

CICS: A transaction and file management program available from IBM for use with various operating systems. It provides for on-line processing of defined transactions making relatively simple use of data file organizational concepts. CICS is an acronym for Customer Information Control System.

DOS or DOS/VS: An operating system for intermediate sized computing systems available from IBM. It is used on versions of the IBM 370 architecture including the smaller models of the 3000 series and the 4300 series of computing systems.

DPPX: The Distributed Processing Programming Executive. A full function operating system available with the IBM 8100. It provides a system framework for operations, application development and system interconnection.

DTMS: A data management and transaction handling subsystem for use with the DPPX Operating System on the IBM 8100.

IBM 3033: The top of the IBM processing system line. A 370 architecture processing unit for use with IBM software and peripheral and storage units where very fast processing capacity is required with large memory.

IBM 3790: An intelligent control unit which provides storage and program execution for a set of connected terminals. It is used as a satellite system with IBM 370 architecture systems.

IBM 4300: A line of intermediate 370 architecture processor systems including the 4331 and 4341. Compatible with 3033 systems from the viewpoint of processor architecture.

IBM 8100: A family of intermediate systems, including the 8130 and 8140, that is designed particularly for interconnection with 370 type systems and with each other to form distributed systems.

IBM Series/1: A family of small computer systems produced by the General Systems Division of IBM. There are two models, the 4933 and the 4953, with differing speed and memory size characteristics. The product is packaged to be attractive to users who wish to have maximum systems building block control over a developing application. It is used both as a small stand-alone system and as part of a distributed system.

IBM System/38: A highly packaged and integrated small business system intended primarily for stand-alone use. It provides unusually sophisticated data management and program development features for a system of its size.

IMS: A large, sophisticated data base manager offering very sophisticated data description and relationship definition, advanced recovery and integrity features. Designed to run with the MVS operating system.

MVS: The top of the line IBM operating system. It provides very advanced resource management, multiple virtual memories, and specialized interfaces for systems like IMS.

JES: Job Entry Subsystem. An IBM programming product that supports the interconnection of loosely coupled systems running different software environments. The distribution of work among machines, the transmission of data files and the return of output from machine system to machine system is permitted by use of JES.

VM: Virtual Machine. The VM/370 operating system, for example, provides an image of a machine for each user. Any of a number of operating systems may be used "on top" of VM/370 to provide an operational and development environment desired by a particular user.

VTAM: Virtual Telecommunications Access Method. In the 370-type line, including 3300s and 4300s a program designed to provide a facility for programs to send messages to each other when they are not in the same physical system.

Appendix B

For Systems Programmers

B1. BASIC IDEAS OF SYSTEMS STRUCTURE

Even the very simplified five level structure of Figure 25 carries some implications which it is worthwhile to mention. First, there is the implication that the part of the operating system which addresses the communications hardware is quite distinct from the part of the operating system which addresses storage hardware. Associated with this physical distinction is the implication that the interfaces which are used by an application program for communications services and the interfaces used for data services are unique and optimized for the special functions of the two parts. Third, there is an implication that there is no interesting or important internal structuring within the operating system layers at either side. The second point, unique interface, and the third, no further structure, are critical points for discussing and understanding software structures and their impact on distributed processing.

Notice Figure B1. This figure addresses an alternative concept of a system. The application layer sits "on top" of an operating system layer which is "vertically" decomposed into a data management part and a data communications part. This figure is a true equivalent of Figure 25 if the interfaces to each part are unique and if there is no further structuring within the operating system.

Figure B1 provides a framework for discussing some issues of interface and structure. Let us first consider the fact that CAM and DAM require some service which may be common. Dynamic allocation of memory space might be one; the ability to enqueue a particular procedure on a list of programs to run might be another. It is convenient to provide a structure in the system where these services may be made available to CAM and DAM in some shared way. This leads to Figure B2. At a layer beneath CAM and DAM, interfacing to them in the same way that they interface to the application program is a set of common operating services which provides functions of queueing, dequeueing, list management, memory allocation and so on.

The cleanliness of the figures now begins to dissolve. It may also be desirable to provide the application program with a set of services from the layer beneath

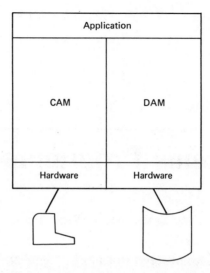

Figure B1. Alternative structural concept.

CAM and DAM. The application program may also wish to issue requests for more memory, or to enqueue procedures on a "wish to run" list processed by the system scheduler or dispatcher.

It is very difficult to draw this picture in two dimensions and as a matter of fact this difficulty rightfully suggests some problems in the structure of some current software systems. Figure B3 shows two attempts to draw a picture of

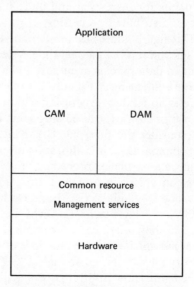

Figure B2.   Common resource services.

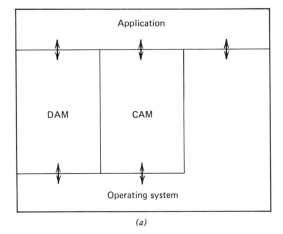

(a)

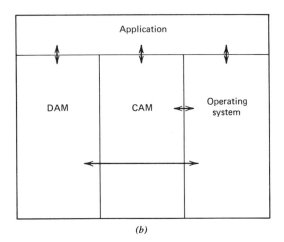

(b)

Figure B3.   Interface and structural complexity.

the idea that an application program wishes to use CAM and DAM, that CAM and DAM use another layer of resource services and that these resource services may also be used by an application program. The ambiguity of both drawings of Figure B3 lies in the fact that the common layer seems to provide a different interface to the application program than to CAM and DAM.

This property of the drawings is, in fact, a potential property of software structures. Some set of services may be made available only to authorized or specialized users like CAM and DAM, with only part of the services offered to an application program. This issue is further complicated by the possibility that an application program may be allowed, itself, to become an authorized user.

B2. DESIGN ISSUES

This kind of discussion suggests the nature of some design problems in the development of software structures. Among them, specifically, are questions which address:

1. Exactly what services which CAM and DAM use should be brought into the common layer and what should be left in CAM and DAM. For example, if CAM must enqueue requests for service to a set of terminals should it keep its own queue and apportion time within periods given to it by the lower layer, or should it enqueue on a queue managed by the lower layer which is also used by DAM and the application?

2. To what extent should CAM and DAM themselves be internally structured to define a hierarchic set of services made available to an application program? Consider Figure B4. A number of interface levels are defined which permit an application program to define what level of service it wants from CAM and DAM. An application program may wish to do some of the work CAM or DAM would do for it. This may be for some reason of the peculiarity of record structure which the application program wishes to manipulate. If the top layer of DAM, for example, offers record advance and presentation of a certain kind, it might not be convenient for the application program to use that level of DAM. It may choose to do its own record advance and talk to DAM only when it wished a new block of records. Figure B4 suggests that each layer of DAM and CAM is entered with the issue of a specific command by the application program. This is a violation of descendant hierarchic structure.

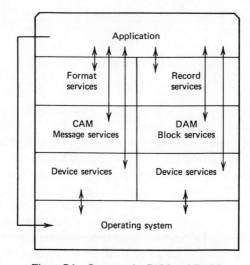

Figure B4.   Structure in CAM and DAM.

3. To what extent should the interface to the application program make its use of DAM or CAM transparent? Consider Figure B5. Here an additional layer of "operating system" has been put between CAM, DAM and the application program. This layer may be used to provide a general "message" interface to the application. The application may issue a SEND or RECEIVE whether it desires a record from a data storage device or to communicate with a terminal or another node. The intervening layer determines whether CAM or DAM is to be used on the basis of whether a storage device or a communications device will be involved. Thus it would be conceivable to allow a program to use a file on a local storage device for one run and then use a file on a remote storage device on another run.

    We have not shown enough to indicate how this would be done, but it derives from the ability for the intervening level to call DAM when a data reference is local and call CAM when a data reference is to a file at another node. CAM would talk to CAM at the other node; the remote CAM would talk to its local DAM. DAM would get a record and pass it to CAM, which would, in turn, pass it to the CAM local to the application, which would pass it through the intervening layer and onto the application. The application, logically, would not care that the record had been retrieved remotely. To accomplish this kind of thing there are elaborations yet necessary in the relationships between CAM and DAM.

    The intervening layer provides all routing through the structures so that the same SEND/RECEIVE is issued regardless of what service level entry point is desired. This provides an ability to replace layers as well as to move to different loci for layer performance. It also provides an ability not to keep all layers in the same node.

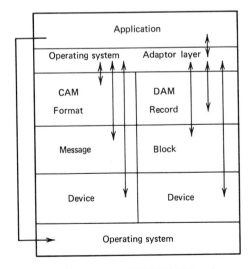

Figure B5.   Uniform CAM/DAM interface.

B3. INTERFACES

An important decision which must be made in designing an interface for application programs is which functions to make explicitly available and at what service level.

SEND and RECEIVE is common nomenclature for moving messages across the boundaries of individual running programs. In the design of a system these macrocommands may be made available to the running application program which then may issue the commands in order to talk to other applications programs which are running at other nodes.

If the decision is made to make SEND and RECEIVE avialable to an application program a further decision must be made about the nature of protection against serious error which systems software will afford an application program. This is a detail which frequently distinguishes "large" systems software designs from "small" systems software designs.

In large systems there is a tendency to protect an application program by providing for protection of the message area until the message is received or to provide synchronization algorithms between SENDING and RECEIVING programs so that synchronization errors cannot occur. In many smaller systems the application program is made responsible for protecting the message area from overwrites or for providing proper synchronization. There is an important tradeoff in design between reducing the amount of potentially complex coding which must be written in the application program and overgeneralizing systems support so that the functions which are provided have undesirable performance characteristics or interface complexity.

It is possible to decide that the function of SENDing or RECEIVing a message from another node will not be made explicitly available to an application program. The motive for doing this is to provide a level of transparency so that the application program need not be aware of when it is talking to another node. The application program issues commands for data or services as if everything was in the same node. Some element of systems software discovers that a data element, queue or procedure is at a remote node and issues appropriate SENDs, RECEIVEs, requests for remote execution or enqueueing as it perceinves the need. The element of systems software which accomplishes the determination of a need for an off-node reference must have some table of element locations which it may inspect to determine where a data or procedure structure is located in the system.

There is a conceptual structure which is available and may be used in designs constrained by former history. If DAM is a database manager of the IMS type it is possible to place node to node communications capability within the DAM structure. An application program would issue the usual data calls to DAM and DAM would determine whether a local or remote data reference was involved. When DAM determined that a remote reference was involved it would exercise its own CAM-like coding to effect a cross-box data movement.

It would do this by using its private specialized CAM to talk to a private specialized CAM in a copy of DAM at the other node. Then that other node would exercise the data management portions of DAM to retrieve the record and send it to the CAM-like code of the requesting node. Figure B6 indicates this structure. IMS multisystem coupling has overtones of this design.

This arrangement of software function suggests that certain cross-node references, those related to the issuing of GETs and PUTs, for example, would go through DAM and DAM's private communication code. Other off-box references would still be available to an application program by direct use of CAM. Thus requests for remote operator functions or program start would be submitted by issuing SENDs and RECEIVEs to CAM and only data locus transparency would be provided by DAM and its private CAM-like code.

Alternatively, DAM itself might be a user of CAM to accomplish remote data requests and transmission. There are a tremendous number of factors to be considered in deciding the tripartite relationships here. If DAM to DAM communication is to be rather rich in implementation so that any DAM may talk to any DAM in a large and complex interconnection structure, then it is probably preferable for DAM to be a CAM user rather than rely on its own private communication code. The CAM functions of routing control and specialized recoverability and synchronization services would not profitably be duplicated in DAM coding. However, if DAM to DAM communication is to be restricted to two communicating DAMs it might be more efficient for DAM to conduct this communication privately.

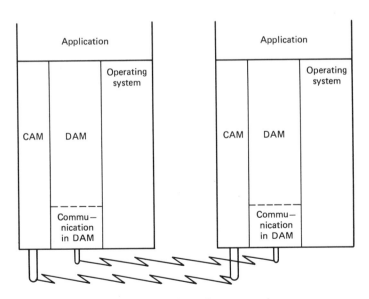

Figure B6.   Communication: subsystem to subsystem.

B4. FUNCTION DISTRIBUTION IN LAYERS

There are two related issues which must now be considered. First is the nature of the communication mechanism. The CAM provided with the system may or may not control all off-box references whether they are across teleprocessing lines or across channels or other kinds of interbox connections. If the DAM to DAM references are across channels in a system whose CAMs only control teleprocessing interconnect, then it is necessary for DAM to provide its own cross-box communications or to use some other service of the operating system. Figure B7 indicates that DAM will either call CAM or channel services in the operating system once it determines where it wishes to make an off-node reference.

The second relevant issue concerns the specific structure of the software elements involved. Chapter 7 suggested an internal structure for DAM and CAM. In defining an internal structure a set of decisions must be made about what specific activities will be performed in each layer. Any software structure is composed of a large number of fundamental activities or operations. When defining the structure of a software component there are always a large number of ways of dispersing specific operations across layers. For example, there is a

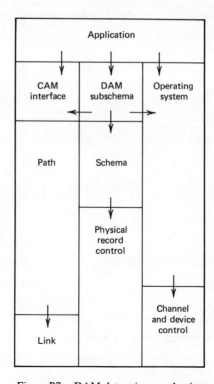

Figure B7. DAM determines mechanism.

set of things which obviously must be done in the link control layer. There is a set of things which must be done in the path control layer. However, there will be a certain number of operations which could be optionally placed in either link control or path control. In addition to deciding what the responsibilities for certain operations will be at the application/system interface, designers must decide identical issues in the layer to layer interfaces within the system.

An example of a functional decision between layers is shown as Figure B8. The upper layer starts an activity with the symbolic name of a data set it wishes to reference. Before this data set can be referenced it is necessary to associate a device name representing the physical residence of that data set. The upper layer has been asked by an application program to provide a record but has discovered that no record is available and more records must be read from the device. The lower layer is responsible for issuing I/O commands to the device.

The two layers may be designed so that it is the responsibility of the upper layer to make the association between the symbolic file name and the device

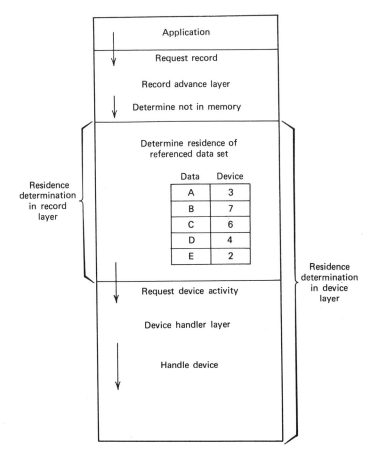

Figure B8.   Possible function allocation.

name and pass the device name to the lower layer. Alternatively it is possible to design so that the lower layer does the association, receiving from the upper layer only the symbolic data set name. The association of data set name and device name is truly a function which may go from one layer of the system or another.

If the only point of entry into the layers is from another layer in the same structure, there is little system-wide implication for how the "layer portable functions" are allocated. However, if another software structure can call for services from a given structure, then the functional allocation assumes more global importance.

Consider DAM as a user of CAM. It is possible to allow DAM entry to CAM layers directly or to allow DAM to call CAM interfacing layer for routing through CAM layers. In either case the exact relationship between CAM and DAM will be influenced by CAM decisions about how it has placed functions in various layers. The amount of work which DAM has to do to prepare for a CAM call, the degree to which there may be duplicated function in CAM and DAM is a function of the consistency of the layering decisions between the two software structures.

So far we have discussed a number of software structure issues in the relationship of CAM, DAM and application programs. These topics are interesting to distributed systems designers for a number of reasons. Decisions which software designers have made represent a set of possibilities and a set of constraints for distributed designs. Part of the development of a distributed system is the search for suitable underlying software to support desirable distribution options. The design of underlying software structures will make some distributions more effective or more profitable depending upon interface definition, layering definitions and functional dispersion among the layers. The fact is that in the current software world some product is just not suitable for certain kinds of distribution.

Bibliography

Adiba, M. and D. Porter, A Co-operation System for Heterogeneous Database Management Systems, *Information Systems,* Vol 3, No 3, 1978.

Ahituv, N., and M. Hadass, Organizational Structure of a Complex Data Processing Department, *Information & Management,* Vol 1, No 2, February 1978.

Ahuja, V., Routing and Flow Control in Systems Network Architecture, *IBM Systems Journal,* Vol 18, No 2, 1979.

Albrecht, H.R. and L.C. Thomason, I/O Facilities of the Distributed Processing Programming Executive, *IBM Systems Journal,* Vol 18, No 4, 1979.

Alsberg, P.A., Data Distribution Strategies, *Proc Berkeley Workshop on Distributed Data Management and Computer Networks,* 1976, p 127.

Alsberg, P.A. and J.D. Day, A Principle for Resilient Sharing of Distributed Resources, *Proc 2nd Int Conf of Software Engineering,* October 1976.

Anderson, G.A. and E.D. Jensen, *Computer Interconnection Structures,* Distributed Processing Tutorial, IEEE, New York, 1978.

Anderson, H., IBM versus Bell in Telecommunications, *DATAMATION,* May 1977.

Anthony, J.M., Jr., Decentralization Can Be Good Medicine, *Computer Decisions,* December 1969.

Ashenhurst, R.L. and R.H. Vonderohe, A Hierarchical Network, *DATAMATION,* February 1975.

Becker, H., Preparing for Distributed Data Processing, *DataComm User,* January 1977.

Becker, H., Luxury of DDP Requires Slowed Down Entry, *Data Management,* Vol 17, No 8, August 1979.

Belady, L.A. and M.M. Lehman, A Model of Large Program Development, *IBM Systems Journal,* Vol 15, No 3, 1976.

Bergland, R.G., *Comparing Network Architectures,* Distributed Processing Tutorial, IEEE, New York, 1978.

Bernard, D., Management Issues in Cooperative Computing, *ACM Computing Surveys,* Vol 11, No 1, March 1979.

Black, D.R., Connecting a Mini, *DATAMATION,* October 1976.

Booth, G., Distributed Information System, *National Computer Conference AFIPS,* 1976, Vol 45.

Bradford, E., Evolution of a Corporate Distributed Processing Network, *IEEE Trends and Applications,* 1978.

Branscomb, L.M., Computing and Communications—A Perspective of the Evolving Environment, *IBM Systems Journal,* Vol 18, No 2, 1979.

Bray, O.H., Distributed Data Base Design Considerations, *IEEE Trends and Applications: Computer Networks,* 1976.

Brenner, V.B., How to keep Control of a Distributed Processing System, *Data Systems,* February 1979.

Brinch-Hansen, P., The Programming Language Concurrent PASCAL, *IEEE Transactions on Software Engineering,* June 1975.

Brown, F., Distributed Processing: There Ain't No Free Lunch, *Computer Decisions,* April 1977.

Bucci, G. and D.N. Streeter, A Methodology for the Design of Distributed Information Systems, *Communications of the ACM,* April 1979.

Burnett, D.J. and H.R. Sethi, Packet Switching at Phillips Research Laboratories, *Computer Networks,* Vol 1, No 6, November 1979.

Carlson, E.D. and M.C. Smyly, Practical Problems in a Distributed Application, National Computer Conference, *AFIPS Conference Proc,* 1978.

Carren, D., Multiple Minis for Information Management, *DATAMATION,* September 1975.

Caswell, S.A., Word Processing Meets D.P., *Computer Decisions,* February 1977.

Cerf, V.G. and A. Curran, The Future of Computer Communication, *DATAMATION,* May 1977.

Champine, G.A., Six Approaches to Distributed Data Bases, *DATAMATION,* May 1977.

Champine, G.A., Current Trends in Database Systems, *Computer,* May 1979.

Chandy, K.M., Models of Distributed Systems, *Proc 3rd Int Conf Very Large Data Bases,* 1977.

Chang, E.J.H, A Distributed Medical Data Base, *Computer Networks,* 1976.

Chu, W.W. and G. Almacher, Avoiding Deadlock in Distributed Data Base, *ACM National Conference,* 1974.

Clark, D.D., An Introduction to Local Area Networks, *Proc IEEE,* Vol 66, No 11, November 1978.

Colon, F.C., Coupling Small Computers for Performance Enchancement, *National Computer Conference AFIPS,* Vol 45, 1976.

Computerworld, Special Report: Distributed Processing, a Concept in Search of a Definition, *Computerworld,* March 28, 1977.

Corr, F.P. and D.H. Neal, SNA and Emerging International Standards, *IBM Systems Journal,* Vol 18, No 2, 1979.

Cotton, I.W., Networks, *Bulletin of American Society for Info Science,* February 1976.

Couger, J.D., Evolution of Business System Analysis Techniques, *ACM Computing Surveys,* Vol 5, No 3, September 1973.

Crabtree, R.P., Job Networking, *IBM Systems Journal,* Vol 17, No 3, 1978.

Cullum, P.G., The Transmission Subsytem in Systems Network Architecture, *IBM Systems Journal,* Vol 15, No 1, 1976.

Curtice, R.M., The Outlook for Data Base Management, DATAMATION, *April 1976.*

Davenport, R.A., Distributed or Centralized Data Base, *The Computer Journal,* Vol 21, No 1, February 1978.

Davenport, R.A., Distributed Database Technology—A Survey, *Computer Networks,* Vol 2, No 3, July 1978.

Davies, C.T., Jr., Data Processing Spheres of Control, *IBM Systems Journal,* Vol 17, No 2, 1978.

Dawes, N.W., A Simple Network Interacting Program's Executive (SNIPE), *Software Practice and Experience,* June 1977.

Denning, P., Operating Systems Principles for Data Flow Networks, *Computer,* Vol 11, No 7, July 1978.

Deppe, M.E. and J.P. Fry, Distributed Data Bases—A Summary of Research, *Computer Networks,* Vol 1, No 2, September 1976.

Dijkstra, E.W., *A Discipline of Programming,* Prentice-Hall, Englewood Cliffs, N.J., 1976.

Dooley, C.R., Get Prepared for the Next Step in Distributed Data Processing, *Data Communications,* April 1979.

Down, P.J. and F. E. Taylor, *Why Distributed Computing,* Hayden Books, New York, 1977.

Eade, D.J., P. Homan and J. Jones, CICS/VS and Its Role in Systems Network Architecture, *IBM Systems Journal,* Vol 16, No 3, 1977.

Ellis, C.A., Consistancy and Correctness of Duplicate Database Systems, *Proc 6th ACM Symposium on Operating Systems,* November 1977.

Ellis, C.A., A Robust Algorithm for Updating Duplicate Data Bases, Proc 2nd Berkeley Workshop on Distributed Data Management and Computer Networks, 1977.

Elovitz, H.S. and C. L. Heitmeyer, *What Is a Computer Network,* Distributed Processing Tutorial, IEEE, New York, 1978.

Elstein, A.D., Distributed Data Processing in A Manufacturing Environment, *Data Management,* August 1979.

Emery, J.C., Managerial and Economic Issues in Distributed Computing, *IFIP Proceedings,* 1977.

Enslow, P.H., Jr., What Does Distributed Processing Mean?, *Distributed Systems, Infotech State of the Art Report,* 1976.

Enslow, P.H.,Jr., What Is a Distributed Data Processing System?, *Computer,* January 1978.

Falor, K., Distributed Doesn't Mean Random, *DATAMATION,* September 1979.

Farber, D.J., Networks: An Introduction, *DATAMATION,* April 1972.

Farber, D.J., A Ring Network, *DATAMATION,* February 1975.

Feidelman, L., The New Look of Data Entry, *Infosystems,* December 1977.

Fitzgerald, A.K. and B.F. Goodrich, Data Management for the Distributed Processing Programming Executive, *IBM Systems Journal,* Vol 18, No 4, 1979.

Ford, J.B., Enhanced Problem Determination Capability for Teleprocessing, *IBM Systems Journal,* Vol 17, No 3, 1978.

Forsdick, H.C. et al., *Operating Systems for Computer Networks,* Distributed Processing Tutorial, IEEE, New York, 1978.

FORTUNE, Distributed Data Processing/Data Communications, Inserted Advertising Section by International Data Corp, 1977.

Foster, J.D., Distributed Processing for Banking, *DATAMATION,* July 1976.

Frazer, W.D., Potential Technology Implications for Computers and Telecommunications in the 1980s, *IBM Systems Journal,* Vol 18, No 2, 1979.

Fried, L., Centralization: To Be or Not to Be, *Infosystems,* January 1976.

Frederickson, D.H., Describing Data in Computer Networks, *IBM Systems Journal,* Vol 12, No 3, 1973.

Fusco, G.P., SNA and Distributed Systems, *Data Management,* Vol 16, No 1, January 1978.

Gale, E.G., L.L. Gremillion, and J. L. McKenney, Price Performance Patterns of U.S. Computer Systems, *Communications of ACM,* April 1979.

Gibson, R. and P. Anderson, Technical Overview of the Renaissance Octubus System, *Computer Architecture News,* June 15, 1979.

Gray, J.P. and T.B. McNeil, SNA Multiple-System Networking, *IBM Systems Journal,* Vol 18, No 2, 1979.

Green, P.E., An Introduction to Network Architectures and Protocols, *IBM Systems Journal,* Vol 18, No 2, 1979.

Halsey, J.R., L.E. Hardy, and L.F. Powning, Public Data Networks: Their Evolution, Interfaces and Status, *IBM Systems Journal,* Vol 18, No 2, 1979.

Hannon, J. and L. Fried, Should You Decentralize?, *Computer Decisions,* Vol 9, No 2, February 1977.

Hardgrave, W.T., Distributed Database Technology, *Information and Managment,* Vol 1, No 4, August 1978.

Hawkins, C., Multi-Minicomputer Systems, *Minicomputer Forum,* 1975.

Hayashi, T and C. Takai, Considerations on the Design of a Network Oriented Operating System, *Proc 4th Int Conf on Computer Communications,* September 1978.

Healy, M., Will the Mini Kill Off the Mainframe?, *Data Processing,* September 1976.

Hebalkar, P.G. and C. Tung, Logical Design Considerations for Distributed Data Base Systems, *Proc IEEE 1st Int Computer Systems and Appl Conf,* November 1977.

Hedeen, A.J., Networking: Building a Software Bridge Between Multiple Hosts, *Data Communications,* March 1979.

Hofri, M. and Jenny, C.J., *On the Allocation of Processes in Distributed Computing Systems,* IBM Zurich Research Laboratory, 1978.

Holt, R.C., et al., Structured Concurrent Programming with Operating Systems Applications, Addison-Wesley, Reading, Mass., 1978.

Horning, J.J. and B. Randell, Process Structuring, *ACM Computing Surveys,* Vol 5, No 1, March 1973.

Hunter, J.J., Distributing a Database, *Computer Decisions,* June 1976.

Infotech, Intercommunication within Distributed Systems, *Distributed Systems: Infotech State of the Art Report,* Infotech International, 1976.

James, C., Evolution Not Revolution, *Data Processing,* November 1976.

Jensen, E.D., The Honeywell Experimental Distributed Processor—An Overview, *Computer,* January 1978.

Johnson, J.R., The Changing D.P. Organization, *DATAMATION,* January 1975.

Jones, J.R., Distributed Processing—Age of the Application Analyst, *Infosystems,* June 1977.

Jordan, J., Fiber Optic Links for Data Communications, *Telecommunications,* Vol 13, No 9, September 1979.

Joyce, J., Principles of Database Management in a Distributed System, *Computer Communications,* Vol 1, October 1978.

Keet, E.E., Distributed Data Processing—The Key Is Software, *Data Communications,* October 1977.

Kelley, N.D., Saving 20 Percent of Mainframe Capacity, *Infosystems,* December 1977.

Kiely, S.C., An Operating System for Distributed Processing, *IBM Systems Journal,* Vol 18, No 4, 1979.

Knotlek, N., Selecting a Distributed Processing System, *Computer Decisions,* June 1976.

Kunii, T. and H. Kunii, Design Criteria for Distributed Database System, *Proc 3rd Int Conf Very Large Data Bases,* 1977.

Labetoulle, J., E.G. Manning, and R.W. Pebbles, A Homogeneous Computer Network: Analysis and Simulation, *Computer Networks,* Vol 1, 1977.

LaVoie, P., Distributing Computing Systematically, *Computer Decisions,* Vol 9, March 1977.

LeLann, G., Pseudo-Dynamic Resource Allocation in Distributed Data Base, *Proc 4th Int Conf on Computer Communications,* September 1978.

Lorin, H., Distributed Processing: An Assessment, *IBM Systems Journal,* Vol 18, No 4, 1979.

Lowenthal, E.I., *A Survey—The Application of Data Base Management Computers in Distributed Systems*, Distributed Processing Tutorial, IEEE, New York, 1978.

Luke, J.W., Unravelling the Confusion of Distributed DP, *Infosystems,* December 1976.

Manning, E.G. et al., A UNIX-based Local Processor a Network Access Machine, *Computer Networks,* Vol 1, No 2, September 1976.

Mardell, M., DP Strategy—Distributed Data Processing, *Computer Decisions,* 1978.

Marill, T. and D. Stern, The Datacomputer—A Network Data Utility, *Proc AFIPS National Conf,* 1975.

Maryanski, F.J., A Survey of Developments in Distributed Data Base Systems, *Computer,* February 1978.

Mathison, S.L., A New Alternative for Corporate Data Networks, *Data Communications,* April 1979.

McCartney, L., Project Paradise Comes Down to Earth, *DATAMATION,* September 1978.

McClellan, S.T., Distributed and Small Business Computers—A Fast Track, *DATAMATION,* May 1979

McDonald, A.R., Minicomputers—Their Place in the Sun, *Data Management,* Vol 14, No 2, February 1976.

McFayden, J.H., Systems Network Architecture: An Overview, *IBM Systems Journal,* Vol 15, No 1, 1976.

McGee, W.C., The Information Management System IMS/VS, *IBM Systems Journal,* Vol 16, No 2, 1977.

Metcalfe, R.M. and Boyer, D.R., Ethernet: Distributed Packet Switching for Local Computer Networks, *Communications of the ACM,* Vol 19, No 7, 1976.

Miller, M., A Survey of Distributed Database Management, *Information and Management,* Vol 1, No 6, 1978.

Mills, D.L., Dynamic File Access in a Distributed Computer Network, University of Maryland, College Park, Maryland, TR-415, October 1975.

Myers, G.J., Composite Design Facilities of Six Programming Languages, *IBM Systems Journal,* Vol 15, No 3, 1976.

Patrick, R.L., Decentralizing Hardware and Dispersing Responsibility, *DATAMATION,* May 1976.

Person, R., How TI Distributes Its Processing, DATAMATION, April 1979.

Peterson, J.L., Notes on a Workshop on Distributed Processing, *Operating Systems Review,* Vol 13, No 3, July 1979.

Ramamoorthy, C.V., et al., Architectural Issues in Distributed Database Systems, *Proc 3rd Int Conf Very Large Data Bases,* 1977.

Reynolds. C.H., Issues in Centralization, DATAMATION, March 1977.

Rockart, J.F. and J. S. Leventer, Centralization versus Decentralization of Information Systems: An Annotated Bibliography, CISR Report 22, Center for Information Systems Research, Sloan School, MIT.

Rockart, J.F., et al, Centralization Vs. Decentralization of Information Systems: A Preliminary Model For Decision Making, Center for Information Systems Research, Sloan School, MIT.

Sarch, R., Communications Processors—Trends and Trade Offs, *Data Communications,* January 1979.

Scherr, A., Distributed Data Processing, *IBM Systems Journal,* Vol 17, No. 4, 1978.

Scrupski, S.E., *Distributed Processing Grows as Its Hardware and Software Develop,* Distributed Processing Tutorial, IEEE, New York, 1978.

Seigle, D., DDP—Door to Office of the Future, *Telecommunications,* Vol 13, No 9, September 1979.

Severino, E.S., Databases and Distributed Processing, *Computer Decisions,* Vol 9, No 3, March 1977.

Severino, E.S., Using Distributed Computing, *Computer Decisions,* Vol 9, No 5, May 1977.

Shapiro, H.M. and P. Stein, Catching Up with the Big Ones, *Computer Decisions,* November 1977.

Sherman, K., Going the Distributed Processing Route, *Small Systems World,* October 1979.

Shneiderman, B., Information Policy Issues: Selecting a Policy Framework and Defining Schema Horizontally, *Information and Management,* Vol 5, No 1, October 1978.

Simonette, I., Rings in Distributed Computing, *Computer Decisions,* January 1976.

Slonin, J., D. Schmidt, and P. Fisher, Considerations for Determining the Degrees of Centralization or Decentralization in the Computing Environment, *Information and Management,* Vol 2, No 1, February 1979.

Spangle, C.W., The Impact of Distributed Systems, *Computers and People,* December 1977.

Stanford Research Institute, The Promise of Distributed Processing, *SRI Business Intelligence Program Guidelines,* No 10, December 1976.

Statland, N., Impending Impact Of Distributed Information Systems, *Installation Management Review,* Vol 7, No 1-4, 1978.

Steinwedel, J., Personal Computing in a Distributed Communications Network, *Byte,* February 1978.

Stevens, W.P., G.J. Myers, and L. L. Constantine, Structured Design, *IBM Systems Journal,* Vol 13, No 2, 1974.

Stewart, H.M., Performance Analysis of Complex Communications Systems, *IBM Systems Journal,* Vol 18, No 3, 1979.

Stone, H.S. and S.H. Bokari, Control Of Distributed Processes, *Computer,* Vol 11, No 7, July 1978

Streeter, D.N., Centralization or Dispersion of Computing Facilities, *IBM Systems Journal,* Vol 12, No 1, 1973.

Streeter, D.N., Productivity of Computer-Dependent Workers, *IBM Systems Journal,* Vol 14, No 3, 1975.

Sunshine,C.A., Intercommunication of Computer Networks, *Computer Networks,* 1977.

Surden, E., Support Problems Exist, Vendors Admit, *Computerworld,* January 9, 1978.

Thomas, R.H., A Solution to the Update Problem for Multiple Copy Databases, *COMPCON 78,* February 1978.

Tibbals, H.F. and P. Curran, Optimizing Function Distribution in a Terminal Network, *Microprocessors,* Vol 1, No 6, August 1977.

Trumpey, L., Implementing a Distributed Processing System, *Infosystems,* January 1977.

Van Rensselaer, C., Centralize? Decentralize? Distribute?, *DATAMATION,* April 1977.

Wagner, F.V., Is Decentralization Inevitable?, *DATAMATION,* November 1976.

Waters, F.C.H., Design of the IBM 8100 Data Base and Transaction Management System, *IBM Systems Journal,* Vol 18, No 4, 1979.

Wecker, S., Computer Network Architectures, *Computer,* Vol 12, No 9, September 1979.

Weingarten, R.A., An Integrated Approach to Centralized Communications Network Management, *IBM Systems Journal,* Vol 18, No 4, 1979.

Weissenberger, A.J., Analysis of Multiple Microprocessor System Architectures, *Computer Design,* June 1977.

Wenig, R.P., Prepare for the Switch to Distributed Processing, *Data Communications,* July 1979.

Williams, G. and P. Nesdore, Shooting for the Most Efficient DDP Architecture, *Data Communications,* September 1979.

Willoughby, T.C., Staffing the MIS Function, *ACM Computing Surveys,* Vol 4, No 4, December 1972.

Wirth, N., MODULA: A Language for Modular Programming, *Software Practice and Experience,* Vol 7, No 1, January 1977.

Woods, L., Distributed Processing in Manufacturing, *DATAMATION,* Vol 23, October 1977.

Woods, L., IBM 8100: First Impressions, *DATAMATION,* Vol 25, March 1979.

Wulf, W. and R. Levin, A Local Network, *DATAMATION,* February 1975.

Yasaki, E.K., It's a Question of Experience, *DATAMATION,* September 1976.

Yasaki, E.K., Evaluating and Selecting Hardware for Remote Sites, *DATAMATION,* October 1976.

Yeh, R.T. and K.M. Chandy, On the Design of Elementary Distributed Systems, *Computer Networks,* Vol 3, No 1, February 1979.

Zelkowitz, M.V., Perspectives on Software Engineering, *ACM Computing Surveys,* Vol 10, No 2, June 1978.

Ziegler, K., Jr.., A Distributed Information Systems Study, *IBM Systems Journal,* Vol 18, No 3, November 1979.

INDEX